NEGATIVE GEOGRAPHIES

**Cultural Geographies
+ Rewriting the Earth**

Series Editors
Paul Kingsbury, Simon Fraser University
Arun Saldanha, University of Minnesota

NEGATIVE GEOGRAPHIES

Exploring the
Politics of Limits

Edited by David Bissell,

Mitch Rose, and Paul Harrison

University of Nebraska Press | Lincoln

An earlier version of chapter 7 first appeared in *In Exile: Geography, Philosophy and Judaic Thought*, by Jessica Dubow (New York: Bloomsbury, 2020).

Library of Congress Cataloging-in-Publication Data
Names: Bissell, David, 1982– editor. | Rose, Mitch, editor. | Harrison, Paul (Geographer) editor.
Title: Negative geographies: exploring the politics of limits / edited by David Bissell, Mitch Rose, and Paul Harrison.
Description: Lincoln: University of Nebraska Press, [2021] | Series: Cultural geographies + rewriting the earth | Includes bibliographical references and index.
Identifiers: LCCN 2021009795
ISBN 9781496226785 (hardback)
ISBN 9781496227829 (paperback)
ISBN 9781496228246 (epub)
ISBN 9781496228253 (pdf)
Subjects: LCSH: Cultural geography. | Political geography. | Negation (Logic) | BISAC: SOCIAL SCIENCE / Human Geography | SOCIAL SCIENCE / Media Studies
Classification: LCC GF50 .N39 2021 | DDC 304.2—dc23
LC record available at
https://lccn.loc.gov/2021009795

Set in Minion Pro by Laura Buis.

DB: For Hannah

MR: For Mom, Dad, and the ocean crossers before them

PH: For Charlotte and Sadie

Contents

Illustrations

Preface

On the second floor of the National Gallery in Washington DC there is what looks at first like a large white box. Its dimensions fill the gallery, a cube of roughly three by three by three meters made of heavy plaster with a concrete texture. When you walk closer, you realize it is an inverted cast of what seems like a Victorian living room. There is an inside-out fireplace and depressions along the bottom that are clearly skirting boards. Other small details can be gleaned around the cast, but not many; no photographs, carpets, wallpaper, furnishings. Rather it sits like a fossil, a remnant of a life (many lives perhaps) whose stories, dramas, successes, and failures are signaled by a stone cube but not actually revealed. While it appears to us in monumental dimensions, it does not speak. It invites us in but simultaneously blocks us out. Its allusion to domestic stories, family dramas, and period history in solid monumental form captures our attention. But the sculpture itself withholds these narratives, hides them beneath its impenetrable surface. This makes one's engagement with *Ghost* frustratingly one-sided.

As cultural geographers, we are inclined to read Rachel Whiteread's sculpture in terms of its positive dimensions, that is, in terms of the objects we can see and the activities, practices, rhythms, and atmospheres of daily life to which they allude. Yet Whiteread's sculpture is obdurate. Rather than objects and activities we are confronted with a silent surface. Even as we might try and glean evidence of what the room looked or felt like—the laminar indentations, the inverted fireplace—we are simultaneously confronted by the fact that we simply cannot enter. All we can do is circle, listening for the calls of those that once lived here even as there is nothing to hear. In not disclosing, in not being relatable, in not being available, the room shuts down—utterly and thoroughly—our attempts to know it. However proximate we might get, the room withdraws, stretching out the distance between it and us. And so, we walk away, attracted to other works of art clamoring for our attention, reconciling ourselves to the fact that there is nothing to see here.

One of the qualities we admire about Whiteread's work is it confronts us with a situation we rarely consider in academia: the possibility of not knowing. Surely one of our most sacred beliefs is that human beings have the capacity—if not the responsibility—to know. The sciences and the institutions built to serve it are constructed on this foundation: a faith that the universe is knowable and that humanity has the capacity to reveal its secrets. If we have the right method, technique, or approach then every obstacle can be cracked and the mysteries residing therein will be laid before our eyes, available for our wonder. Despite the numerous critiques that have been laid at the door of the Enlightenment, we often take for granted the extent to which this faith structures the work we do. The belief that human beings have the power to know—and thus change—the world. Are not the philosophies of Descartes, Kant, Hegel, Marx, Heidegger, and Deleuze an exhortation to realize this power? To unleash humanity's untapped potential by shining a light on the previously unthought, unrecognized, and unrealized? While there is a long tradition of being cynical about the place and possibilities of the human in the universe, even the most misanthropic approximations are built on a presumption of human ability: a faith in humanity's capacity to rule (or destroy) the world.

The underlying purpose of this book is to question this faith. Without wanting to undermine the political potential of the human or denigrate the human desire to pursue and create change, we want to recognize how all such efforts are necessarily limited, bounded by certain existential conditions of being a living being. As Whiteread's sculpture willfully, playfully, and frustratingly demonstrates, there are limits to what we can know and what we can do. Thus while there are a number of agendas and ambitions being pursued in this collection, it is driven by this distinctive disposition: a desire for academic work to be not simply more humble but (perhaps more subversively) more feeble. In recognizing limits—in making plain the impenetrable boundaries to human contemplation, consideration, and change—our aim is to check our inclination to invest so powerfully in our own freedom, knowing, and power. It is to delay our tendency to overestimate not only our own capacities, but the capacities of others or indeed the capacity of capacity itself. It is, in short, motivated by a desire to see weakness and fragility not as temporary states but as underlying conditions. While such a statement is anathema to the Enlightenment tradition—where we are regularly urged to be more free in our thinking and doing—perhaps less investment in the human and human capacity is precisely what the world needs.

Like so many edited books in geography, the ideas for this collection began at the American Association of Geographers annual meeting in Tampa in 2014 where some of the contributors presented their initial ideas in a session on "The Politics of the Negative." It was followed by another AAG session on "Negative Geographies" in Washington DC in 2019. Both sessions benefited from engaging and encouraging feedback, which confirmed that a book on this topic would make an important contribution and have a ready audience. Generous funding from the ESRC-funded Aberystwyth University Transformative Research program enabled us to convene a workshop in July 2017, which brought many of our contributing authors together in Aberystwyth to present draft chapters and collectively explore the book's theme. In terms of individual acknowledgements, we want to give sincere thanks to Bridget Barry at the University of Nebraska Press for her enthusiasm for our project and her ongoing support as we developed the manuscript. We are also grateful to Paul Kingsbury and Arun Saldanha, editors for the Cultural Geographies + Rewriting the Earth series, for their support and critical feedback. Most importantly we want to give a heartfelt thanks to Paul Simpson who provided generous (and repeated) feedback on earlier versions of this collection and to Thomas Dekeyser for his astute suggestions on reading and ideas while we were developing the introduction. We would also like to thank Vickie Zhang for compiling the index. We are obviously most grateful to our contributing authors for their insightful chapters, thoughtful discussion, and friendship. Thank you for staying with us over this eight-year journey.

NEGATIVE GEOGRAPHIES

1 Negative Geographies

Mitch Rose, David Bissell, and Paul Harrison

Negativus (adj.) That which refuses/denies
—*Oxford Latin Dictionary*, 1982

A Question of Limits

This book emerges from a growing sense that we are living in negative times. We submit that this is hardly a contentious diagnosis. Over the last eight years, since we first initiated this collection, we have watched with despair as a series of catastrophic, once-in-a-generation world events piled up. We have witnessed the rise of right-wing nationalism, events of ecological destruction that are too many to count, severe racial injustices and horrific violence, the intensified policing of borders: long-standing problems that are the consequence of long-standing inequalities. Our despondency arises from the brute and incontestable reality of the problems themselves, their wickedness, persistence, and perpetual irresolution. But it also stems from a sense of futility, from the fact that the issues we now face are ones we have known about all our lives and that many of us have dedicated ourselves to researching and writing about. The world now knows a lot about neoliberalism, global inequality, systematic racism and sexism, and climate change. As geographers we have no doubt played a part in pushing this knowledge into everyday public discourse and political consciousness. And yet the problems not only persist but grow more monstrous. In spite of the small victories we cling to, the idea that a deeper, more comprehensive grasp of the issues will lead to fundamental change feels ever more remote. As Berardi (2017) suggests, it is as if subjectivity itself has become disaffected and impotent.

Such sentiments of pessimism and futility are at odds with the positivity and zeal that characterizes our contemporary theoretical milieu. With cultural geography's emphasis on becoming, potential, and possibility, we may indeed be accused of what Doel (2009) terms "miserly thinking." If only we cast the net wider to deepen our appreciation of the agencies and processes at play in the world, then perhaps we would have more cause for optimism and joy? For almost two decades now, cultural geographers have been arguing that tracing the connective relations that engender our social and cultural world allows us to better grasp its more-than-human constitution and recognize that it is not reducible to human agencies and, by extension, heroic social actions that mark the better and the just through a reductively human frame. The emphasis has been on mapping the entanglements between earth processes and cultural practices, speculating on how relays and feedback loops are co-implicated, pluralizing the operations of power and pointing to multiple sites of intervention. The message here is not one of impotence but one of teeming potentiality, and the imperative is to be moved by joy, to let go of poorly posed problems and become active through creative experimental practices. In contrast to a previous obsession with individuated subjects and embedded structural forces, this is a cultural geography of apprehending the agency of relations where the task is to recognize their autonomous reality independent of their terms (Roberts 2019).

We appreciate this optimism and have contributed to this body of work ourselves (Bissell 2015, 2016; Dewsbury et al. 2002; Harrison 2002; M. Rose 2006, 2010). We have been entranced by its didacticism and seduced by its romantic inflection. Yet while our contemporary theoretical landscape is full of discussion about the possible, the potential, and the infinite nature of human (and nonhuman) capacity, such optimism seems curiously disconnected from the reality of our time. Our central contention is that the relational thinking that has come to characterize cultural geography *does not sufficiently consider the question of limits: the limits of capacities, powers,*

ROSE, BISSELL, AND HARRISON

and relations. We are not against relational thinking. But we do contend that relational ontologies leave little space to admit finitude and the problems that the nonrelational poses. This collection is motivated by a belief that, without admitting such finitude, we have an inadequate understanding of contemporary power. And that the brute reality of finitude has been overlooked in much contemporary cultural geography.

The aim of this book is to ask what it means to struggle with limits. We are not seeking to undermine hope or take away the capacity for social change, but we are asking our readers to consider more closely the limits of existence within which all such claims about hope, power, and capacity are made. Negative geographies should not be understood as a geography of pessimism and inadequacy, though both sentiments are inflected in the work we present. Rather, it is a geographical perspective that endeavors to step back from the question of doing—from the business of practical, relational *activity*—to bring into focus the question of what can be done. The passive voice is key here. How is the very question of doing situated within a context of the doable, and how do we widen our scope to see how the context of doability resides within a negative space, a dark and obscure situation, that provides no light, no guidance, but whose obdurate inscrutability is precisely what precipitates all action? This introduction will lay out how we conceptualize this negative space, the nature of the question it situates and, perhaps most significantly, the stakes involved in posing it. It situates our perspective on the negative by illustrating how it runs through a distinctive trajectory of questioning, a trajectory our contributors demonstrate in their chapters and that indeed is already running through the discipline more broadly. We do this through five sections.

The next section, "Negative Definitions," introduces the question of negativity by elaborating the unique set of problems the term poses. The second section, "Negative Traditions," explores how the question of the negative has traditionally resided in geographical thought, and the third section, "The Negative Now," examines contemporary trends in the geographical literature exploring the limits of affirmation. In the fourth section, "The Politics of the Negative," we lay out the key contribution of this book to geographical thought and its contemporary modes of political analysis. Finally the fifth section introduces the chapters themselves and how they each, in their own way, endeavor to elaborate how limits impose themselves on many of our key geographical terms—place, bodies, landscape, memorials, intention, governance, democracy, agency—and in doing so change the way we see those terms and their political potential.

Negative Definitions

We confess that there is a problem with posing the question, "What is the negative?" The problem itself is straightforward: how to define that which is, by definition, not some*thing*? How to give a straight description of that which has no content, no "as" this or that, no nounal or prepositional properties that give it clear delineation or form. Indeed the very grammatical functionality of "is" (the negative *is* this) is paradoxical (see Harrison this volume and Wylie this volume). The closest we can get to answering this question is to say the negative is negation, the non, the not. It is not the anti or the opposite, it is the vanishing point, the empty cave echoing into nowhere, the bottomless pit where you drop the flashlight or toss the stone but hear no sound and see no light. And yet to say the negative has no content is not to say that it does not exist. To take an example, we can say that the future exists. It is not material and cannot be touched, but it can be perceived. Its existence is akin to the existence of a secret, something real and known, but only in terms of its mystery. The future is there, in front of us, but its content is the blindness in the middle of our vision. We worry about the future, plan for the future, and care for the future, but all such engagements are defined by the future's utter obscurity, experienced as an existential structure of our delimited nonclairvoyant lives. To push this example further we can look at Anderson's (2010) work on state emergency planning. Here Anderson highlights how the state summons a wide range of powers to prepare for future events; events that are perceived as genuine and real but by no means present or material. While Anderson's main concern is the extensive range of resources brought to bear on the future (planning systems, emergency procedures, etc.), what remains in the background are their utter futility; the fact that no preparations have any bearing on the future itself and what the future brings. It is in this sense that the future is a limit (total and nontranscendable). It stands outside us, untouched and unaffected by our various plannings, creatings, and doings. As living beings we are exposed, utterly and inescapably, to the future and its various boons and burdens (see Dubow this volume). These are the kind of limits this book endeavors to illuminate. And they are all around us. We are limited by our ability to know other people, their nature and needs, which we strive to understand and yet so often fail (see Rose this volume); we are limited by the susceptibility of our own bodies, which we protect and keep safe but whose longevity we cannot ensure; and we are limited by the precarity of our love, predicated as it is on the capricious destinies of others. These negativities reside at the edge of our vision, inscrutabilities we encounter *as inscrutabilities*, irresolvable mysteries whose nature and content cannot be divined but whose impact is real, cutting through us with depth and certainty, collapsing our intentions and eviscerating our will.

So what does this have to do with geography, a discipline usually concerned with positive expressions of place, regions, landscapes, and other spatial formations that can be mapped, circumscribed, or traced? It is true that the negative, as far as we conceive it, has no geography in the traditional sense. On the contrary the negative cuts through and breaks apart the positive world we inhabit. But this is not to say that the negative cannot be thought of spatially. The purpose of this book is to illuminate a dimension that is essentially outside the world but whose entropic power nonetheless haunts the world, impinging upon its various activities and forms of willing, even as it never effectively touches them. In this rendering the negative is spatial because it is separate—it stands apart from the world of creating and doing. Indeed it is the separation, the fissure between positive space and negative space that ensures the negative's unalienable difference; that negative geographies remain a site of radical alterity, an absolute outside, forever removed from that which could touch, relate, and thus potentially transform, colonize, or otherwise transfigure. This is a space that is not only underrecognized in contemporary geographical thought, it is utterly ignored and, in the case of some of geography's most influential theorists, actively denied. Take for example the following statement by Deleuze (1983) in his commentary on Nietzsche: "there is no other power than affirmation, no other quality, no other element: the whole of negation is converted in its substance, transmuted in its quality, *nothing remains of its own power or autonomy*" (176, original emphasis). Denials to the contrary, this is a profoundly metaphysical avowal. The point is not simply that the priority of affirmation is ontological, it is that the negative is politically and morally dubious. While this transmutation of the negative into affirmation is necessary for Deleuze to open the way for ceaseless becoming, its consequence is to strip away any space that could potentially be outside being; a space for something utterly unknown and unforeseen, not simply a new composition but something whose disruptive power resides precisely in the fact that it was not part of the relations that preceded it. It is this negative space that our book seeks to reinsert; a dimension outside being, where something radically different and unforeseen can remain apart.

Again our argument is not against relationality or relational thinking. Nor is it even against affirmation per se. Our aim is to give space for the negative, to insert the negative back into our theoretical landscape. In doing so we offer a different perspective that not only reorients our conception of politics but also (paradoxically) of relationality itself. Indeed illuminating a space for the negative potentially brings us back to thinking relationality anew, that is, in terms of the figures that stand apart, beckoning from afar, never connecting, never touching, never knowing, but calling upon one another nonetheless. As already suggested the negative impinges and haunts the world even as it does not touch it. While such a conception of relations no doubt bends our current thinking, we can see such relations all around us. Is it not the unsayability of our feelings that compels us to speak them? Is it not the needs of our body that beckon us to self-care? While words will never be sufficient and hunger will inevitably return, the space of the negative—the unbridgeable divide that keeps terms apart—summons us to respond, draws us toward it, even as it provides no means for connection. In this sense, we agree with Deleuze (1994) that "something in the world

ROSE, BISSELL, AND HARRISON

forces us to think" (139). The distinction we make is that such somethings are not always *things* and not always *in the world*. Our hunger forces us to think; other people force us to think. Here we draw attention to problems that we cannot resolve but must consider nonetheless; the nonfigural opaque problems that demand response, even as no response will be sufficient.

Thus we arrive at the essential circularity of the negative. The difficulty we have shown in trying to define its arcane phenomenality is the fundamental problem. As Derrida (1976) suggests, the strange essence of the negative is that "it has never taken place: it is never present, here and now. If it were, it would not be what it is" (314; also see Harrison this volume). Thus we circle around it: the negative is mystery, displacement, a black hole, a vacuum, a "there" whose thereness is defined by its withdrawal. None of these answers are sufficient, and it is the insufficiency that prompts further answers, further turning: the problem never goes away. This is not a dialectic where synthesis, resolution, and settlement transfigure the problem through time. On the contrary, the negative is the same problem in different guises demanding redress but allowing no settlement. Yet the circle keeps the negative—and the various modalities of willing it summons—alive, not as a force, but as a problem. At the heart of every theory, every story, every desire to be sovereign, is the problem of the negative; modes of willing borne from emptiness and the summon to close the void. Thus, while we may travel many roads, cross infinite thresholds, and transcend endless obstacles, there is no resolution or satisfaction. There are simply turnings: turnings toward and turnings away from the problem of the negative.

Negative Traditions

Our framing of the negative is indebted to but also contrasts with how the relationship between negativity and limits has conventionally functioned in much social thought. In metaphysics (Aristotle, Parmenides, Hegel), psychology (Freud, Lacan), philosophy of mind (Russell, Grice), and linguistics (Wittgenstein), negativity is often posed as a productive means to counter some limit so that thought, subject, mind, ego, or language can be advanced (Horn 1989). In all cases thought reaches some end point until negativity arrives to instigate some advance. By contrast our collection frames the problem of the negative in terms of the limits to what can be thought, touched, or brought into relation. Negativity for us does not facilitate transaction but breaks it with uncompromising finality. To draw out this distinction, this section outlines how the negative has historically operated in cultural geographical thought by unpacking its presence in two intellectual traditions—the critical and existentialist traditions—both of which have served as key intellectual repositories for the discipline. By exploring areas of convergence and divergence between these traditions we situate the perspective we are developing in this project.

THE CRITICAL TRADITION

Perhaps the most obvious example of the discipline's interest in the negative can be seen in its use of dialectics. While dialectics is often associated with Marx, it is through Hegel that the negative is given its powerful redemptive function. For Hegel (1991), dialectics is not simply a method (as it was for Plato) but a process imminent to the world that pushes various positions, moments, or points of understanding toward a broader holistic truth. Understanding this truth means attuning to the world's dialectical mechanism, that is, seeing how long-held ideas or concepts are challenged by the world itself and, in the process, forced to adapt. Logical concepts, for example, as well as historical truths, are revealed and refined as they encounter incompatible sensory experiences and information. The point, for Hegel, is that truth is derived from negation. In a dialectical world, understanding evolves toward truth as it is incrementally negated. It is the process of failure, contradiction, and breakdown, and its ultimate overcoming or sublation, which leads to expanded and higher knowledge.

Marx (2000) appropriates Hegel's ideas about the operative role of negation in a more politically charged manner by moving its target from the thinking subject to the laboring one. Where, for Hegel, transformation comes from contradictory ideas, for Marx this formulation overlooks how it is the laboring body that makes reality. Because laboring bodies are essentially enslaved to one manner of production, Marx argues they are unable to

ROSE, BISSELL, AND HARRISON

receive new bodily experiences that shift (and thus evolve) thought. Under such conditions the negative power of the dialectic becomes curtailed, stymying the potential for transformation (Dunayevskaya 2002). The negative power of dialectics is similarly curtailed in the work of Adorno and Horkheimer (2016) through their analysis of the rational state. The horrors of the Second World War revealed what they term the state's sacrificial character. In their framing, reason and rationalist science are akin to the mimetic sacrifices of ancient peoples where sacrifice was a way of exerting control over that which transcended them to ensure the social-spiritual order. They argue that a similar structure resides in modern forms of citizenry where a subject's capacity to transform their ideas through negation is sacrificed to a belief in the state's rational order—a structure that finds its horrific apogee in Fascism, where mass extermination appears perfectly reasonable to a depoliticized national citizenry (see Carter-White this volume).

Adorno's (1990) idea that citizens relinquish critical capacities in the service of an ordered state system is arguably a bedrock presumption of the critical tradition, as is the ambition to free the power of negation through critical intervention. Such approaches have had long-standing influence in geography. Just as Adorno attempts to supersede state rationality by restoring a concept of reason that is open to negation, geographers seek to crack open the corrosive orthodoxies that circulate in our society creating uneven social hierarchies. This perspective is especially evident in key cultural geographical work that explores how dominant meanings are contested and negotiated (Cosgrove and Jackson 1987; Duncan 1990; G. Rose 1993; Gregory 2004), as well as work that charts the tactics of counter-hegemonic political movements (Mitchell 2003; Sparke 2007; Purcell 2013). Critical human geography seeks to *negate* these unquestioned hegemonic ideas about who we are, how we act, and what is normal, by exposing various counter empirics that destabilize seemingly entrenched powers.

THE EXISTENTIALIST TRADITION

The second tradition of the negative influencing cultural geography emerges from the work of Heidegger and Lacan, for whom negation is not precipitated by contradictory experience but by an encounter with an open-ended and contingent world. Each author figures this encounter differently, but its effect is to force a reckoning or unveiling that creates new potentialities of consciousness in the subject. In Heidegger (1996) this existential dimension takes the shape of angst—a primordial despair arising from the recognition that the world one is in is not a necessary world but a contingent one, defined by events that have no intrinsic purpose and over which one had no hand in creating. Angst thus constitutes a moment of negation whereby *Dasein* is faced with an existential situation it must address either by fleeing from this recognition (and embedding itself in the world more purposefully) or reconciling itself to its lack of ownership over its being. Crucially, this negation is a moment of illumination which Heidegger terms the *Augenblick*—a fleeting view that reveals to *Dasein* its world *not* as a set of preestablished projects but as an arbitrary, and thus changeable, situation. This negative moment delivers *Dasein* to "an event of freedom," whereby *Dasein* is given the opportunity to accept its world in a manner that is self-conscious and chosen (McNeill 2006; M. Rose 2012).

The event of negation holds similar potential for Lacan (2002). While Heidegger understands unalienated existence as a matter of being-in-the-world, Lacan frames it through the infant-mother relation, where the infant understands itself as part of a presubjective primordial unity. Negation here arrives through the interruption of the other through various levels of socialization (Fink 1995). At one level the other is represented by the father, who stands for all that pulls the mother away from the infant—other children, work, the mother's own physical and emotional needs. These others impose upon the infant a recognition that it and the mother are separate beings, meaning its needs must be mediated through relation rather than directly and immediately met. A more significant level is that represented by language, which allows the infant to identify and speak its needs but also alienates the infant by giving it a language that is never its own and so can never express its desires. In both cases the intrusion of the other is both the advent of subjectivity and its loss. Negation allows the infant to emerge into a social world as an individual expressive being, but it is also a partial freedom compromised by the very language that gives that freedom definition.

The role of the negative in Heidegger and Lacan is similar to that of the critical tradition since it is predicated upon an event of reckoning; an encounter that moves the subject to a moment of self-consciousness or awakening. However, the distinctiveness of the existentialist tradition resides in how negativity inheres in the structures of existence itself. We can see the influence of this tradition most clearly in work that is avowedly poststructural, such as in the deconstructive work of Dixon and Jones (1996, 1998), the genealogical work of Hannah (2017) and Legg (2008), and the psychoanalytic work of Nast (2000), Kingsbury (2005, 2016), and Blum and Secor (2011) to name just a few (also see Byrne and Healy 2006). In this work the emphasis is on the political significance of appreciating the existential contingencies embedded within certain framings of existence. Negation transposes subjects from a condition of ontological harmony to one of alienation, which gives perspective on the ontological situation framing its subjectivity.[1]

IRRESOLVABLE NEGATION

The critical and existentialist traditions are two dominant ways that the negative functions in cultural geographical thought. Whether operationalized through Hegelian dialectics or Foucauldian genealogy, the negative's functionality involves common characteristics. While our perspective of the negative retains some of these characteristics, it is also distinct for three main reasons.

First, in the critical and existentialist traditions, the negative *engenders and transacts*. While the traditions above differ in how they do this, the role of the negative in both instances is to move thought, consciousness, and self-recognition from one position to the next. In contrast, we do not see the negative as a modality of passage. On the contrary we see it as something that inhibits passage, obstructs relations, or cuts them short. The negative in our view is not an antagonistic friend, a cheeky challenger that through tough love provides its service to enlightenment. On the contrary it is what weakens our confidence and undermines our reasoning; it illuminates not what is possible but what is impossible; it does not shine a light in the darkness but blows out the match.

Second, in the critical and existentialist traditions the negative creates a *division* between obscurity and knowledge. The negative arrives as an obstruction, obstacle, or crisis that ultimately works to bring certain revelations (about society, consciousness, our existential situation) to light. Our conception of the negative, however, is not defined by what is unknown but by what is unknowable. Rather than approaching limits to knowledge as a horizon to be surpassed, we understand the negative as a limit on *what can be known*. Such unknowabilities do not sit at the margins of what we study but reveal themselves again and again at the heart of our scholarly endeavors. Thus while every theory, concept, or model addresses something unknown, we emphasize the dimension that remains unknowable, forcing the problem to return in a new guise.

Third, and most significantly, in the critical and existentialist traditions the negative works by being *resolved*. Negation poses a problem or obstruction which knowledge, understanding, or consciousness transcends, overcomes, or otherwise defuses. However, our conception of the negative *is not* resolvable. Death is not resolvable, the unknowability of the other is not resolvable, the needs of the body are not resolvable. While reckoning with these limits may instigate various kinds of practices, such practices do not solve the problem. They are simply responses, not heroic actions that work to instigate knowledge, enlightenment, or change, but feeble answers, whispered in the dark, barely audible. In short we are making a distinction between a conception of the negative as transaction—as passage—and a conception of the negative as limits—as that which breaks passage. In making this distinction, we acknowledge continuities. Marx, for example, traces all human society, culture, and meaning back to the basic fact that human beings have a *natural* body that must be fed, sheltered, and satisfied (see Bates 2015). And Lacan argues that language can never provide a safe haven for the subject, haunted as it is by the inadequacy of language and the desires of the other (Žižek 1993). In this sense our contribution is complementary rather than supplementary. It is distinct even as it resides within a tradition. And as we explore in the next section, we are not alone in rethinking the question of the negative and considering the various ways it might be brought back into the conversation.

The Negative Now

Thus, if the negative has always been with us, residing in various ways within the geographical tradition, then why make an issue of it now? What is it about this moment in the discipline (and in the world) that makes the question of the negative urgent or necessary? Partially, as already suggested, the answer lies in our current historical moment. But we would also suggest that there is a broader trend in the humanities and social sciences questioning affirmationist thinking. The Afro-pessimist work of Wilderson (2010), Warren (2018), and Hartman (1997), the nihilist philosophies of Brassier (2007) and Thacker (2015), the accelerationist philosophies of Land (1992) (who openly advocates for human extinction), and the apocalyptic literatures on the Anthropocene (Danowski and Viveiros de Castro 2017; Moten 2017) all (in very different ways) swing an axe to the positive, modernist faith in improvement and the hope that knowledge and ingenuity can march humanity toward brighter horizons. Geography has not been immune to these developments and, while it is too early to identify a movement, there have been a range of emergent responses that have challenged geography's faith in affirmationism and its overreliance on concepts, terminologies, and other ideas associated with potentiality by posing questions about the limits of the body (Harrison 2008; Abrahamsson and Simpson 2011), the nonrelational (Harrison 2007), and what comes after affirmation (Harrison 2015). These interventions represent the spearhead of a trend querying the limits of relationality and the subtractive power of the negative.

The aim of this section is to bring some of this work into relief and illustrate how it provides the operative groundwork for the collection. While the work discussed below only occasionally invokes negativity, or indeed the politics of limits, it nonetheless represents a similar gesture to what we are attempting to achieve in this book—it attempts to create space for the negative. By drawing attention to the gaps, aporias, and limits that cannot be incorporated into and subsumed by relational activity or positively recalibrated into transformative trajectories, this work draws attention to the dark, broken corners of geographical thought where failure, exhaustion, and frailty are real (see Philo this volume). To be clear this work is not necessarily guided by our own theoretical stars but taps into a similar sentiment in its attempt to foster more aporetic understandings of relationality, an understanding that admits the role of the nonrelational and the impossibilities immanent to relational ontologies. The following discussion highlights three overlapping yet distinctive bodies of contemporary cultural geographical work, each of which illuminates a site where limits are playing a significant role in the analysis.

INCAPACITY

The body has been a topic of geographical interest since the 1980s, though it intensified significantly as nonrepresentational theorists opened our understanding of what the body is and what bodies can do. Rather than approaching bodies as limited self-contained systems that can be manipulated, represented, contorted, or structured through various forms of power, contemporary cultural geographers seek to illustrate the plasticity of the body and the various vectors of sensation that they compose through their encounter with other agencies and fields. Our aim here is not to critique this concept of the body or to argue that the body does not have these various capacities, but we would argue that not enough attention has been paid to bodily attrition, depletion, exhaustion, and subtraction. As Philo (2017) suggests, in addition to exploring "what enhances the human, distributes it [and] grows its capacities," the field needs to be "alert to what diminishes the human, cribs and confines it . . . silencing its affective grip, banishing its involvements" (257–58). There are many ways to think about these curtailments, but one way is to consider the limits of the body itself. Indeed, while nonrepresentational theory has seized upon Deleuze's (2005) Spinozist statement that "we do not even know what a body can do" (255), it has been less inclined to recognize that which a body cannot do or, in Harrison's (2009) terms, "its impossibilities and its 'not-being-able-to'" (432) (see also Sharpe 2014). Complementing cultural geographical writing on disability (e.g., Butler and Parr 2005; Macpherson 2009), Bissell's (2009) work on the body in pain, for example, illustrates how the body can be defined by incapacity. As Bissell suggests, pain offers no handholds for relation. It cannot be reasoned with, acted upon, or creatively transformed. One cannot touch one's pain or wrestle with its power. On the contrary pain grabs hold of us, crushing our resistance and highlighting our impotence.

This conception of the body as a composition diminished rather than afforded by life is also present in contemporary work on economic austerity. For example, Hitchen and Shaw (2019) bring to light the "shrinking worlds" brought about by the dismantling of the welfare state and a regulated job market. Through the elimination of social protections, deep cuts to public services, stagnating wages, and precarious working conditions, citizens at the sharp end of austerity experience what they term "a grinding loss of world" where "life is dampened and slowed" and becomes "numbing and oppressive" (n.p.). Disintegration and contraction are similarly foregrounded in Hitchen's (2019) research on public library closures, which focuses on the feelings of paranoia and entropy that perpetually hang over staff. As Wilkinson and Ortega-Alcázar (2019) argue, austerity draws attention to the unrelenting weariness associated with waiting for government support, assessing new government rules, and the ongoing need to demonstrate eligibility. Such affective contours are not "passionate or intense, but instead are listless and still . . . moments of inertia, flatness, impasse" (163).

The emphasis on bodily attrition, weakness, passivity, and vulnerability not only rebuts nonrepresentational theory's emphasis on bodily capacity but also the consequence of disassociating those capacities with something that could be distinguished as human. As Harrison (2011) suggests, in the ambition to reduce the subject to a distributed swarm of impersonal forces, the subject is flattened to the point that it lacks anything that could be identified as distinctive or unique. In contrast, these authors offer "a humanist politics for the posthuman age" (Dawney 2013, 633). This is a humanism that acknowledges how subjects emerge from vital impersonal forces, but also recognizes the specificity of the one, the hurting singularity of a unique *you* that *I* care about. Thus what emerges from the ashes of the Cartesian subject (so lampooned by poststructural thought) is perhaps a more humble humanism, and with it, a different sort of phenomenology that is attentive to the fragility and vulnerability of the human.

INACCESSIBILITY

Nonrepresentational theory has vastly expanded cultural geography's objects of analysis, opening out from a narrow preoccupation with rarefied cultural representations to an appreciation of a world overbrimming with things taking place. Signification and sense-making emerge through all manner of performative practices, and because all things happen in concert with the vibrant matter of nonhuman objects, there is a renewed sense of power as distributed and dispersed, rather than centralized and top down. But what is often overlooked in this work are the gaps and blind spots that are also a constituent aspect of the world. For example, what about the autonomous realities of technical objects and the nonrelational dimension of our interaction with them? For Ash (2013) the thick information circuits between a mobile phone and a mobile phone mast operate not only outside the human but outside relation. Drawing inspiration from object-oriented ontologies (Harman 2002), Ash draws attention to the hidden atmospheres of unrealized information potential always imminent to every human engagement with technology. In this rendering it is the withdrawn, nonrelational qualities of objects that become key to their political possibilities which, as Shaw and Meehan (2013) write, may be found in "the space of objects-in-themselves, the unlockable forces that are never fully revealed" (220; also see Dekeyser 2018).

This emphasis on the unseen, hidden, and withdrawn is also a feature of contemporary work on absence. Edensor's (2008) work on regeneration, for example, explores the ghostly reminders found in the crevices and forgotten pockets of Manchester's gentrified suburbs. The landscape,

ROSE, BISSELL, AND HARRISON

he argues, holds within it the resonances of things gone, reminders of material structures no longer present but still echoing as things removed, omitted, or erased, absences, he suggests, that are "folded into the fabric of the city" (325). Frers (2013) similarly argues that absence is felt precisely because it is part of our corporeal experience. When something is part of our bodies or our everyday life experience, its withdrawal can feel like a desertion. As Frers would put it, I miss *you* because you were once part of me. For bodies to experience something as absent it "needs to already be part of their corporality, of memorized bodily practices" (438). Taken together we can see how this work conceptualizes absences as a strange form of relationality. Absence is felt. But it is felt as something gone or missing. It impinges upon us as a loss, an aching for something that was once part of us and is no longer there, a feeling of no longer feeling (also see Hetherington 2004).

For Wylie (2009), in contrast, absence is not "behind-the-curtain" potential but a fundamental silence or what he terms an invisibility "at the heart of a point of view" (278). In his meditation on landscape memorial benches, he argues that the benches reference something singular and distinctive and simultaneously something irretrievably gone. Similarly Colls (2012) draws attention to the enigmatic nature of our bodies and how often we confuse and misread the corporeal signals they send to us and others. Absence, in this work, cannot be thought as a blind spot waiting to be revealed. On the contrary, it marks the ineliminable hollows that shadow all relational activity. Absence is not simply what is not seen, it is what is utterly inaccessible—silent, enigmatic, and impervious to empirical investigation. Inaccessibility points to a negative space, a dimension that is not only outside our jurisdiction, but beyond all sense and thus immune to all knowledge and comprehension.

FINITUDE

The final domain of work we wish to highlight questions what is lost when we focus on the world's ceaseless becoming. What happens when every object or being appears only as a process, as an unfolding, a situation that ceaselessly morphs, turning like a kaleidoscope that has limitless permutations? Here we draw attention to work that deals with endings; that is, with events predicated on the simple truth that things do end. Dying and death is perhaps the most explicit expression of finitude (see Maddrell this volume). There is a politics of death, as Joronen's (2016, and this volume) work on the military strategies of the Israel Defense Forces in Palestine explains, and there is a politics of the mourning that happens in death's wake, as Hodge (2015) details in relation to asylum-seeker bodies. Death can provoke all manner of adjustments, and we recognize the various processes underway in its wake (Stevenson et al. 2016). But death also rips through us, tearing the very fabric of our world, pulling the rug from beneath our feet. The consolation that "in affect we are never alone" (Massumi 2015, 6) is not only unconvincing, it misses something crucial about what death is: a fundamental cutting off from the world (Carter-White 2012). To not acknowledge the finality of death, to see it only in terms of the processes it instigates or triggers, is to ignore the singularity of what is gone. It frees us from reckoning with a world transformed. Thus, while we do not deny that life always proceeds (despite our despair and desperation), the literature we are highlighting lingers over the "nonexchangeable singularity of what has been lost" (Pratt 2012, 108).

Recent work on trauma has also been instrumental in encouraging us to pause over what is gone. For Pratt (2012) the experience of migration and mobility—while engendering a range of global connective forces—also tears families apart, cutting through the connective relations that orient us (see also Bissell and Gorman-Murray 2019). Similar work on traumatic memory highlights how individuals might attempt to obscure or obliterate injurious memories in an attempt to cut the emotional resonances connected to particular events (Muzaini 2015). Similarly Schwanen et al. (2012) illustrate the frustration when memory fails, when, regardless of how much we want to remember, we cannot summon the past. Such limits illuminate a domain of life that does not become. Trauma by definition is a dead end, an obstacle we ceaselessly return to, rehearse, and replay without transformation or resolution. Try as we might to leave trauma behind, it exists because it cannot be resolved.

ROSE, BISSELL, AND HARRISON

These diverse bodies of cultural geographical work certainly insist that vitality and vulnerability are not mutually exclusive. It is experiences of finitude that propel us into speaking and listening in the first place. Countdown clocks of all kinds force questions that provoke our stuttering responses. That we share this exposure to finitude with each other and with other living things (Greenhough and Roe 2010) invites an ethics of hospitality to others (Dikeç et al. 2009), gathering us into wider communities of difference. Yet while Adams-Hutcheson's (2017) work on lives in the aftermath of the Christchurch earthquakes of 2010 and 2011 shows how trauma can connect, her work also shows the holes at the heart of trauma, that there remains a "shattered sense of loss when places are gone" (111). Thus, rather than emphasizing the connective aspects of such collectives, reckoning with finitude impels us to "write the world differently" (Romanillos 2011, 2550) such that broken threads are not knotted back together, where gaps persist rather than being sutured up, where we make space for the negative.

In sum, the ambition of this section has been to illustrate that alongside cultural geography's interest in the creative, vital, transformative forces that shape our world, there has also been a growing interest in the gaps, fissures, and tears that cut through these forces and sever their various connections. Incapacity, inaccessibility, and finitude are conditions of corporeal existence. They are conditions that cannot be negotiated, faced down, or willed away. On the contrary, they are conditions to which all living beings must submit. Seen from the perspective of relational ontologies, living beings seem infinitely creative and capable, and perhaps they are. But if so, we also have to acknowledge how they are infinitely vulnerable. Bodies fail because they are exposed to a world that affects them in a manner where they cannot affect back. Our relations are not always relations of exchange. On the contrary, they are often relations of servitude—relations of beings subservient to that over which we have no power.

The Politics of the Negative

At this point it may seem that the ambition of this book is simply to accentuate the frailties and incapacities of the human condition: to shout "NO" to geography's current obsession with "yes." While it would be disingenuous to suggest that such sentiments play no part in this project, we have ambitions beyond simply emphasizing the withering, the desperate, and the powerless. As we suggest in the subtitle, this book is about the *politics of limits*, which is to propose that there is a politics to be gleaned from our perspective on the negative and the conceptual problems it exposes. While we will leave it to our various authors to think through this question in detail, we would initially suggest four guiding propositions which, while necessarily broad-brush, we think summarize what we might call a "politics of the negative."

Do not become enamored of power.
It is an irony that Foucault (2000, xiv) used this phrase to capture the key points of Deleuze and Guattari's revolutionary *Anti-Oedipus*, a text that argued for a rethinking of our conscious and unconscious desires as a product of historically contingent free-flowing forces, rather than unified in an "ego," as prevailing Freudian psychoanalysis would have it. But whereas Foucault's aim was to reveal the distributed fluidity and liminality of power machines, our aim is somewhat different. Our suggestion here is to view politics not through the light of its accomplishments but through the darkness of its futility. From the perspective of the negative, power looks less like an ebullient force shining against the various obstacles it finds and more like a desperate echo, a cry in the dark, seeking to lay hold of something that always escapes. This is not to say that politics is necessarily ineffective. But it is to suggest that things do not work as well or as often as cultural geographers are often willing to believe.

Presumptions about power's efficacy are not unreasonable at a time where insidious developments in securitization, especially through the development of new digital technologies, have compelled cultural geographers to trace the increasingly diffuse nature of mechanisms of power that reveal forces of domination. As Bissell et al. (2012) write: "It is, no doubt, appealing *to suspect*: to imagine a hidden logic, a structure of control underpinning diverse collective arrangements that *can* be 'exposed,' a

ROSE, BISSELL, AND HARRISON

riddle that can be deciphered, a thread that can be traced, or a conspiracy that can be unmasked beneath totalising environments of control" (705). Echoing Foucault's invitation to identify and trace new techniques of power, Deleuze's (1992) uncharacteristically bleak observations in his late essay on the rise of the control society have prompted considerable attention to how modulating forms of "free-floating" distributed control have replaced previously disciplinary powers that were wielded within specific institutions. While we do not refute such observations, we are wary about how they can be marshaled to exaggerate power's efficacy, such that even the accident or the disruption becomes interpreted as a strategic, operative dimension of power, rather than evidence of power's futility (Dillon and Reid 2000). The same can be said of bodily powers. Even the redemptive faith Foucault (1988) finds in "technologies of the self" are utterly contingent on the experiential expertise accrued by capacious bodies, leaving little room for admitting bodily impotence in its myriad incarnations. The key point here is that power is seductive. Its positive presence outshines the limitless problems that gave them cause. Politics in these chapters is not conceived in terms of what it achieves, but in terms of its precarity; small gestures striving to respond to that over which nothing can be done.

Power is a marker of our subjection, not our freedom.
One of the lasting insights to emerge from the conceptual earthquakes precipitated by Foucault (1995) and Deleuze (1987) was the idea that power produces (also see Butler 1993, 1997). In their wake a generation of cultural geographical work has grappled with power in terms of its performativity. Rather than conceptualizing power in terms of revolutionary contests between oppositional forces, power has come to be understood as a multidimensional field of agencies vying and contesting in search of diverse incremental shifts and adjustments. While this model extended our understanding of the forces themselves, it somewhat mischaracterized the field in which they parlayed. In Deleuze (1994) and Latour (1993) in particular, forces have no source; they are singular and originary, characterized in terms of their degree and configuration rather than their nature or essence.

Power, in such framings, emerges from relations and relations only. It represents modalities of willing whose form and structure is determined purely by other forms of willing.

One of the consequences of this perspective is that it presents forces as agencies whose nature it is to be free: free to roam, seek, create, and transform until they meet other agencies, other forces, also seeking their freedom. The dynamic of power and resistance in Foucault is predicated on an image of interacting forces, seeking their freedom at the expense of others; pushing and twisting each other as they seek the horizon of their various desires. From the perspective of the negative, however, power is not indicative of freedom but precisely the opposite. It is indicative of our utter beholdeness. As Rose (2014) has argued elsewhere, the will is not only *not* free, but on the contrary, "is always already exposed, already situated in a set of demands that it cannot be independent from" (219). From this perspective it is precisely our lack of power—over our bodies, our neighbors, and our futures—that engenders various modalities of desire, willing, and governance (see Joronen this volume). Is it not the silence that inclines us to speak? Is it not the mystery that incites our inquisition? The negative stands as a primordial provocation. It is the negative's impenetrability, its irresolvability, that demands action (see Maddrell this volume). Power seen from this perspective is not the free striving of a will but a haunted, futile attempt to mitigate vulnerability. While it is no doubt a striving, it is a striving determined by a primary incapacity rather than the free pursuit of desire.

Admit the nonrelational.
Ignorance, hesitation, and inaction have always been anathema to modernity, a tradition that has consistently celebrated vital, active capacities over passive submissions (see Zhang this volume). There are likely many everyday and exceptional situations that are demanding of action. As we acknowledged earlier, recent cultural geographical work has been exercised by the generative possibilities of the "encounter" (Wilson 2017), some of which is inspired by Deleuze's (2005) reading of Spinoza. Here there is celebration of the surprises that can be found out through our engagements with

ROSE, BISSELL, AND HARRISON

others, of the differences we can find out about others and how, through encounters where we learn to be affected, we develop shared affinities and understandings of each other and the world. Yet the focus on contact and exchange that is foregrounded in work on encounter comes at the expense of admitting those aspects of situations that are nonrelational in the sense that they are not about connection or communication. We are arguing that there is a place in cultural geography for reckoning with the limits of activity and engagement (see Bissell this volume). Nonrelations draw attention to aspects of experience that are radically incommunicable, such as the singular pain or suffering of an other which can never emphatically be known and only hesitantly acknowledged. The politics of nonrelations is also about admitting the significance of impassable gaps, tears, and fissures that shoot through our ordinary attempts to relate to others, manifesting perhaps in experiences of incomprehension and confusion (Bissell and Gorman-Murray 2019).

Our aim here is to suggest that there is a politics to letting otherness be other, rather than seeking to enroll this otherness into our own schemas of comprehension. To be clear, we are not promoting fatalism, resignation, or disengagement. Rather, following Spivak (1999), if we reckon with a topology of thought involving interruptions, fractures, and breaks, while the other might prompt our interest and cue our questions, the other simultaneously and incessantly withdraws from our attempts at grasping (see Zhang this volume). Indeed, it is precisely the pursuit of knowing the other on our terms that has perpetuated the wicked problem of colonial violence in its different manifestations. In letting otherness be other, there are clear parallels to work being undertaken in the discipline that seeks to decolonize geographical knowledges by challenging such practices that sustain colonial modernity (e.g., Noxolo 2017; Jazeel 2017). Our wager is that admitting the nonrelational is to accept that there are things that we cannot know of the other. And it is this situation of not knowing, of our distance from others, that invites us into the labor of creating relations. We want to engage with and encounter others not so much in spite of, but *because* of, such limits.

Every force embeds an ethical demand.
Ethics has played a powerful role in relational ontologies, particularly when it comes to acknowledging and honoring our imbrication with others. Whatmore (2002) in particular emphasizes that acknowledging our intimate relations with a range of human and nonhuman others situates an ethics of care, a situation where we as subjects are forced to acknowledge and nurture the connections that engender our existence (also see McCormack 2014). We are skeptical of this conception of ethics for two reasons. First, while relational ontologies emphasize how bodies are dependent on other bodies, they are not beholden to any *particular* body. Thus, even as numerous bodies are ontologically necessary for my existence, they are simultaneously faceless, they have no name or character. There is no singular "you" that engenders "me." There are only disaggregated composites, conglomerations of affects that foster my capacity, here and there, to enact myself as a subject. While our aim is not to lay claim to an essentialist humanism, we propose that if the "I" and "you" are wholly relational, that is, if the subject is only ever an expression of its relations, then there is nothing singular or distinctive about *a* subject, nothing that makes the death of one or the disappearance of another tragic, nothing specific to be mourned, nothing unique that is lost. Indeed, loss itself is simply a reconfiguration of relations, mourning a new composition of affects.

The second reason we are skeptical is that there is no conceptual mechanism by which the recognition of relational imbrication leads to its care. The world is full of examples of living beings cutting themselves away from that which nurtures them, of hurting that which they are reliant on. As Dreyfus (1990) suggests, in his critique of Heidegger's notion of authenticity, recognizing one's situatedness in a world does not automatically lead to one's caring for it. While Heidegger presumes care arises from a sense of ownership, that is, from a sense of investment in the relations that we engender with the world we are in, there is nothing about those relations themselves that demand such attention. Relational ontologies seem to imply the same presumption, that is, that simply seeing or acknowledging our imbrication engenders our care. But there is nothing about relationality

ROSE, BISSELL, AND HARRISON

itself that demands concern. To reiterate the point above, relationality has no face. It does not summon or need and thus embeds no ethical demand.

The conception of the negative we are proposing, however, does embed an ethical demand. While subjects are compositions, and those compositions no doubt emerge through affecting encounters, they are also more than this. Subjects are also modalities of willing and existing that emerge in relation to the negative. As such, they embed a demand to take care of and nurture that which is their origin. There is a demand to take care of the future because the future is what gives rise to me as subject, that is, it gives rise to a will that seeks to face what comes. While such activities of course have no bearing on the negative, there is a demand to try—a demand to do our best. While Whatmore's relational ethics embeds a similar logic—that we must take care of that which allows us to exist—the problem is that nothing *in particular* allows us to exist. There are no specific relations that implore us to care for the Asian elephant or even the climate. Can we not build new relations with artificial climate domes or even depose others so we can build relations with foreign climates? The negative, however, poses a clear demand. We must take of that which allows me, in my uniqueness, to exist. While such a demand can be ignored, and no doubt is, it is immanent to every form of willing. Ultimately, then, we suggest that there is an *ethics* to be found in silence, withdrawal, ineffectiveness, and ignorance (see Rose this volume).

In sum, the politics of the negative we present is one that seeks to acknowledge and reckon with how people, actions, and events are necessarily beyond our grasp. In illuminating a limit, we mean shining a light on that which cannot be properly seen, how we are always already exposed to a radically unassimilable outside, a negative space that is beyond conscription. The negative as limit, then, is not the same as diagnosing a diminishment in powers of acting and feeling. As some of the chapters suggest, admitting the negative as limit might actually be much more about affirming the unimaginable richness and complexity of a world that overwhelms our capacities even as it undermines our illusions of mastery. This is a negative that impels us to accept, with greater sincerity, our corporeal vulnerabilities, our weaknesses, and our incapacities in the face of a world that is perhaps more mysterious, unknowable, and unpossessable than we might previously have been comfortable in admitting. It might well be this very exposure that actually gives rise to so much of who we are: our beliefs, our desires, our tendencies, and ultimately, our relations.

Chapter Summaries

We have given a broad-brush introduction to the perspective that has driven the development of this text. But as an introduction it represents a jumping-in point, a first turn around a circle that we and the other contributors will continue to sketch, elaborating and developing the perspective in different ways even as we and they circulate around the same problem. The chapters in this book each have their own perspective on the problem of the negative. While there are numerous zones of correspondence, they nonetheless reflect the distinctive preoccupations of the authors. For Carter-White and Joronen the problem is inflected through the problem of violence and killing, for Wylie and Zhang it arises through the problem of memory and trauma, and for Rose and Dubow it is the problem of other people and their relation to sovereignty. Below we provide summaries not simply to give a sense of what's to come but to give a heads-up on how they circle around the problem we have struggled to illuminate, how they each cut through the problem of the negative in a distinctive and singular manner.

Chris Philo reckons with the limits of an affirmationist geography. Beginning with a confession of some personal experiences of bleakness, Philo is concerned with the dissonant movement between the lightness of affirmation and darkness of disenchantment that link these reflections on his own sensibilities with recent developments in human geography. To explore this movement more fully, Philo enlists the analytical lens of Simone Weil's writings on the ontology of creation. What he finds particularly instructive in Weil is how her account of creation oscillates between the lightness and joy she finds in all manner of small things and a contrasting dark void where evils and injustices happen. Drawing out Weil's Janus-faced "spiritual geometry," which is on the one hand enchanted, meaningful, and good, and on the other, indifferent, cold, and contingent, Philo identifies parallels in contemporary human geography. What emerges here is a questioning of what he calls the "new positivism" within the discipline, the current zeitgeist for conceptualizing relatedness, abundance, and enchantment. Resonating with Weil's dissonance, this new positivism is brought into sharp relief through a negative geography that admits isolation, broken relations, and being cut off.

Paul Harrison poses the question of limits in terms of the persistent obduracy of the nonrelational for conceptual thought and personal life. Harrison reckons with the challenges of relating to nonrelations marked by withdrawal, dissolution, and nondisclosure which elide the thematizing tendencies of naming, discourse, and epistemology. The tensions of relating the nonrelational are presented through two accounts. The first is a more institutional account that describes the emergence of the "non-" in the context of the development of nonrepresentational theory. Here, Harrison speculates on how different cultural geographers have grappled with the challenge of relating what the *non-* prefix actually refers to. In the face of the futility of attempting to name and describe a kind of nonrelation that elides and sidesteps epistemological demands, Harrison provides a rawer, more confessional account that folds the institutional with the intimate to evidence the incessance of the non-. In this account, in the face of institutional demands for positions and declarations, he intimates a shifting personal relation to the non- in terms of withdrawal marked by suffering and reduction, rather than presence marked by joy and plenitude. In providing these accounts, which themselves must inevitably struggle with the challenges of discourse, this chapter invites consideration about the fragility of all claims, dispositions, and convictions.

Vickie Zhang explores the question of limits in terms of affirmation in critical academic practice. In the context of cross-cultural fieldwork in geography, Zhang enrolls postcolonial and feminist theories to speculate on what might be required, practically and conceptually, to do the important work of cross-cultural translation. Through bringing Sedgwick's and Spivak's accounts of love into conversation, translation in both the narrow linguistic sense and the wider sense of relaying between cultural worlds emerges as a commitment that involves both submission and labor. Zhang proceeds to describe an uncomfortable period of overseas fieldwork in China as an Australian of diasporic Chinese descent, the child of immigrants, raised in Australia, and working at a western institution. Working with intransigent experiences of doubt in the field, folded through a series of resonating autobiographical vignettes, Zhang describes a situation that cannot be easily resolved through the idealized activities of affirmation or critique. As a response to the question of what it might take to turn love into a political principle, Zhang introduces hesitancy as an alternative disposition for surviving the impasse.

Avril Maddrell explores how we go on after limit experiences associated with the death of others and considers the implications for political action. Reflecting on how grief is often characterized by pervasive disempowerment, Maddrell argues that the death of others can induce a disabling sense of impotence owing to an inability to articulate, act, or change a monumental loss. However, in addition to this weighted passivity, she shows how this vulnerability can also give rise to and necessitate new forms of agency. Maddrell's argument responds to an intimate, autobiographical account of her experience of losing her stillborn child. Through this account, she reflects on how her grief gave rise to oscillations of passivity and, importantly, activity. In terms of the latter, she describes how her volunteer work for a stillbirth charitable organization helped her to go on. Through this work, Maddrell describes how a personal and family grief can be part of a collective community of experience, where one's own singular loss is felt in relation with other people, places, and practices. Framed through a feminist analysis that highlights the significance of acts of citizenship in everyday life, Maddrell demonstrates some of the ways in which volunteering can be understood as an everyday embodied politics of gifting, collectivity, advocacy, and activism, whereby grief, with its oscillations between passivity and action, might become a catalyst for democratic politics.

David Bissell explores limits in terms of the bodily vulnerabilities associated with exhaustion. Responding to the relative absence of work on exhaustion in geography, as well as the way that the concept has traditionally been treated in an individualized biomedical sense, Bissell seeks to open up more geographical ways of thinking about exhaustion that are better attuned to its spatialities. Acknowledging that exhaustion is a multivalent concept that has a changing history, he draws out the concept of exhaustion in three ways. First, a focus on exhausting bodies foregrounds how bodies can be pushed to their limits through the laboring activities that they undertake. Second, a focus on exhausting places (informed by Simmel and Perec) highlights the capacities of places to exhaust bodies. Third, a focus on exhausting possibilities (informed by Deleuze) considers exhaustion more affirmatively as a necessary threshold for a transforming present. These understandings move exhaustion beyond a problem of bodily fatigue toward a more ontological problem concerning relations of exposure and enclosure and the transformation of the present. Each understanding of exhaustion oscillates between thinking of exhaustion in terms of the negation of vitality and as a condition of vitality, highlighting the vulnerabilities that are immanent to the vital.

Jessica Dubow explores limits in terms of temporality. Her context is Žižek's suggestion that the refusal by Israel Defense Forces soldiers to serve in the occupied Palestinian territories in early 2002 represented a "miraculous moment" of political dissent, an instance where the derailing of secular defenses reached toward the theological. Dubow argues the ways in which Žižek's invocation of this as an extraordinary act overturns the analogy that Carl Schmitt locates at the core of his state of exception; namely, that the sovereign suspension of the law corresponds to the miracle's suspension of the rules of nature. For, rather than evaluating this act of refusal in Schmitt's juridical terms, Dubow suggests that the powerlessness of this act requires an alternative way of thinking about the miracle that is not analogous to juridical order. She explains how Franz Rosenzweig's Judaic account of the miracle offers a way of thinking about refusal that demotes sovereignty and recognizes the excesses and obliquities of an ethical act. To do this, she elaborates on Rosenzweig's conception of time to develop the idea of "negative temporality." This is not the theological negation or transcendence of predictive, historical time. Rather, it is a time whereby another "concealed" time makes itself present in *this* time. Dubow argues that this negative temporality deserves to be called "miraculous" since it intervenes on behalf of the incomplete, the unexceptional, and the unpreserved.

John Wylie explores limits from the perspective of cultural geographical terms that question settled notions of order, settlement, and identity. Describing a diverse set of experiences that mesh palpably felt vulnerabilities with engagements with literature, Wylie's chapter focuses on encounters with a family of words associated with the prefix *dis-*. Taking dislocation, disorientation, disappearance, and distance in turn, he offers some provisional suggestions for questioning the status of words that have traditionally been considered as secondary or derivative from supposedly primary states. Yet echoing Derrida's haunted logics, rather than being understood in this pejorative sense, Wylie invites consideration of dislocation, disorientation, disappearance, and distance as primary negative preconditions of their ostensibly positive prefixless formulations. Through highly personal reflections that thread the dislocation of his daughter's elbow, the disorientations of Brexit, and the impossibility of disappearance, Wylie shows how each of these terms can assist in querying the complacent and erroneous geographies of order and stability.

Mikko Joronen explores how vulnerability has an operative role in practices of governing. By analyzing the various techniques Israel uses to target and regulate civilian life and maintain its control of Gaza, Joronen considers how the nature and origin of power—sovereign, bio-, and thanatopower—might be located in the very vulnerability of life itself and in the mobilization of

ROSE, BISSELL, AND HARRISON

precarious, fragile, and finite bodies. During military campaigns, he shows how there are dualistic logics embedded in preemptive warning techniques deployed by the Israel Defense Forces in advance of air strikes in Gaza. While warning techniques on the one hand suggest care, on the other hand they move responsibility for civilian deaths to the civilians themselves. These dualistic logics are also present outside of military assaults through the way that food supplies entering Gaza are finely calculated, such that minimal necessary calories are provided to maintain life while also ensuring precarity. Joronen explains how these techniques constitute an ambivalent form of government premised on the ability *to wound* life without killing it and so to care for it without letting *it recover*. Here a precarious population is maintained by keeping death, and vulnerability to it, at a proper distance. Crucially, it is not that the power of vulnerability resides with the sovereign power, but rather the state makes use of the finitude and vulnerability of life itself.

Richard Carter-White explores limits in terms of intersubjective relations in the context of atrocities committed by the Nazi *Einsatzgruppen*, mobile close-range killers enlisted to exterminate Jews. Through devastating perpetrator testimony and historiographical accounting, he outlines two principle intersubjective relationships that developed based on witnessing and negation. First, responding to psychological disturbances experienced by reluctant perpetrators, he describes how strategies that negated witnessing were incorporated into the killing operations. Second, he describes how more enthusiastic killers intensified witnessing through degrading and thus negating their victims, which had the effect of solidifying a killing community. While different, Carter-White explains how in both cases the responsibility of the singular perpetrator is effectively deposed to others. In analyzing the complex relationship between reluctant and enthusiastic killers, he draws on Esposito's writings on immunity to argue that the negativity of reluctant perpetrators became a weakness to be perpetually negated and overcome by a group ethos of violence. Carter-White demonstrates the power of the different perpetrators' belief in the negative which ultimately negated itself. The psychological fallout experienced by perpetrators in response to their task ultimately expedited the development of concentration camps for mass murder.

Mitch Rose explores limits in terms of the unknowability of others and how this unknowability inheres as a key but underacknowledged dimension of political life. In the context of the rise and fall of the January revolution in Egypt, Rose describes how the potentials of democracy were ultimately destroyed because the multiple infinite differences of the population were reduced to simplistic divisions based on political polarities. He reflects on this situation to argue that politics is necessarily tragic because it always involves our submission to the otherness of others. Rose's argument brings Cavell's writing on difference and tragedy into conversation with Mouffe's writing on democracy. Where Cavell emphasizes how other people always resist our understanding and elide comprehension in spite of our beliefs and projections, Mouffe's response to this problem is that rather than attempting to rectify this unknowability, we should acknowledge and accept this unknowability as a limit. It is the ultimate unknowability of people's interests, desires, and needs and the way that we are beholden to others whose interests, desires, and needs we do not know that makes democracy inherently tragic. Yet far from a futile or hopeless situation, Rose argues that acknowledging these limits is a vital but overlooked dimension of politics, concerned with how we come to terms with our submission to others and recognize the responsibilities of being beholden.

Notes

Thanks to Paul Simpson for his helpful comments on the initial draft (and for reading it a second time).

1. While we use the word "transpose" above, we acknowledge that the negative does not transact or effect subjectivity in Heidegger and Lacan in the same way it does in the critical tradition. Indeed, it would be misleading to characterize the encounter with the negative as transactional. A more accurate description would be that angst and the other reveal or illuminate a condition, a situation, which may (or in Heidegger's case may not) engender a transformed perspective.

ROSE, BISSELL, AND HARRISON

References

Abrahamsson, Sebastian, and Paul Simpson. 2011. "The Limits of the Body: Boundaries, Capacities, Thresholds." *Social & Cultural Geography* 12 (4): 331–38.

Adams-Hutcheson, Gail. 2017. "Spatialising Skin: Pushing the Boundaries of Trauma Geographies." *Emotion, Space and Society* 24 (August): 105–12.

Adorno, Theodor W. 1990. *Negative Dialectics*. London: Routledge.

Adorno, Theodor, and Max Horkheimer. 2016. *Dialectic of Enlightenment*. New York: Verso.

Anderson, B. 2010. "Preemption, Precaution, Preparedness: Anticipatory Action and Future Geographies." *Progress in Human Geography* 34 (6): 777–98.

Ash, James. 2013. "Rethinking Affective Atmospheres: Technology, Perturbation and Space Times of the Non-Human." *Geoforum* 49 (October): 20–28.

Bates, Stephen R. 2015. "The Emergent Body: Marxism, Critical Realism and the Corporeal in Contemporary Capitalist Society." *Global Society* 29 (1): 128–47.

Berardi, Franco. 2017. *Futurability: The Age of Impotence and the Horizon of Possibility*. London: Verso.

Bissell, David. 2009. "Obdurate Pains, Transient Intensities: Affect and the Chronically Pained Body." *Environment and Planning A* 41 (4): 911–28.

———. 2015. "How Environments Speak: Everyday Mobilities, Impersonal Speech and the Geographies of Commentary." *Social & Cultural Geography* 16 (2): 146–64.

———. 2016. "Micropolitics of Mobility: Public Transport Commuting and Everyday Encounters with Forces of Enablement and Constraint." *Annals of the American Association of Geographers* 106 (2): 394–403.

Bissell, David, and Andrew Gorman-Murray. 2019. "Disoriented Geographies: Undoing Relations, Encountering Limits." *Transactions of the Institute of British Geographers* 44 (4): 707–20.

Bissell, David, Maria Hynes, and Scott Sharpe. 2012. "Unveiling Seductions beyond Societies of Control: Affect, Security, and Humour in Spaces of Aeromobility." *Environment and Planning D: Society and Space* 30 (4): 694–710.

Blum, Virginia, and Anna Secor. 2011. "Psychotopologies: Closing the Circuit between Psychic and Material Space." *Environment and Planning D: Society and Space* 29 (6): 1030–47.

Brassier, Ray. 2007. *Nihil Unbound: Enlightenment and Extinction*. Basingstoke: Palgrave Macmillan.

Butler, Judith. 1993. *Bodies That Matter: On the Discursive Limits of "Sex."* New York: Routledge.

———. 1997. *The Psychic Life of Power: Theories in Subjection*. Stanford CA: Stanford University Press.

Butler, Ruth, and Hester Parr, eds. 2005. *Mind and Body Spaces: Geographies of Illness, Impairment and Disability.* London: Routledge.

Byrne, Ken, and Stephen Healy. 2006. "Cooperative Subjects: Toward a Post-Fantasmatic Enjoyment of the Economy." *Rethinking Marxism* 18 (2): 241–58.

Carter-White, Richard. 2012. "Primo Levi and the Genre of Testimony." *Transactions of the Institute of British Geographers* 37 (2): 287–300.

Colls, Rachel. 2012. "Feminism, Bodily Difference and Non-Representational Geographies." *Transactions of the Institute of British Geographers* 37 (3): 430–45.

Cosgrove, Denis, and Peter Jackson. 1987. "New Directions in Cultural Geography." *Area* 19, no. 2 (June): 95–101.

Danowski, Déborah, and Eduardo Viveiros de Castro. 2017. *The Ends of the World.* Cambridge UK: Polity.

Dawney, Leila. 2013. "The Interruption: Investigating Subjectivation and Affect." *Environment and Planning D: Society and Space* 31 (4): 628–44.

Dekeyser, Thomas. 2018. "The Material Geographies of Advertising: Concrete Objects, Affective Affordance and Urban Space." *Environment and Planning A* 50 (7): 1425–42.

Deleuze, Gilles. 1983. *Nietzsche and Philosophy.* New York: Columbia University Press.

———. 1992. "Postscript on the Societies of Control." *October* 59 (January): 3–7.

———. 1994. *Difference and Repetition.* New York: Columbia University Press.

———. 2005. *Expressionism in Philosophy: Spinoza.* New York: Zone.

Deleuze, Gilles, and Félix Guattari. 1983. *Anti-Oedipus: Capitalism and Schizophrenia.* Minneapolis: University of Minnesota Press.

———. 1987. *A Thousand Plateaus: Capitalism and Schizophrenia.* London: Athlone.

———. 1994. *What Is Philosophy?* New York: Columbia University Press.

Derrida, Jacques. 1976. *Of Grammatology.* Baltimore MD: Johns Hopkins University Press.

Dewsbury, John David, Paul Harrison, Mitch Rose, and John Wylie. 2002. "Enacting Geographies: Editorial Introduction." *Geoforum* 33 (4): 437–40.

Dikeç, Mustafa, Nigel Clark, and Clive Barnett. 2009. "Extending Hospitality: Giving Space, Taking Time." *Paragraph* 32 (1): 1–14.

Dillon, Michael, and Julian Reid. 2000. "Global Governance, Liberal Peace, and Complex Emergency." *Alternatives* 25 (1): 117–43.

Dixon, Deborah, and John Paul Jones. 1996. "For a *Supercalifragilisticexpialidocious* Scientific Geography." *Annals of the Association of American Geographers* 86 (4): 767–79.

———. 1998. "My Dinner with Derrida, or Spatial Analysis and Poststructuralism Do Lunch." *Environment and Planning A* 30 (2): 247–60.

Doel, Marcus. 2009. "Miserly Thinking / Excessful Geography: From Restricted Economy to Global Financial Crisis." *Environment and Planning D: Society and Space* 27 (6): 1054–73.

Dreyfus, Hubert L. 1990. *Being-in-the-World: A Commentary on Heidegger's "Being and Time," Division I.* Cambridge MA: MIT Press.

Dunayevskaya, Raya. 2002. *The Power of Negativity: Selected Writings on the Dialectic in Hegel and Marx.* Edited by Peter Hudis and Kevin Anderson. Lanham MD: Lexington Books.

Duncan, James. 1990. *The City as Text: The Politics of Landscape Interpretation in the Kandyan Kingdom.* Cambridge UK: Cambridge University Press.

Edensor, Tim. 2008. "Mundane Hauntings: Commuting through the Phantasmagoric Working-Class Spaces of Manchester, England." *cultural geographies* 15 (3): 313–33.

Fink, Bruce. 1995. *The Lacanian Subject: Between Language and Jouissance.* Princeton NJ: Princeton University Press.

Foucault, Michel. 1988. "Technologies of the Self." In *Technologies of the Self: A Seminar with Michel Foucault,* edited by Luther Martin, Huck Gutman, and Patrick Hutton, 16–49. London: Tavistock.

———. 1995. *Discipline and Punish: The Birth of the Prison.* New York: Vintage.

———. 2000. Preface to *Anti-Oedipus: Capitalism and Schizophrenia,* by Gilles Deleuze and Félix Guattari, xi–xiv. Minneapolis: University of Minnesota Press.

Frers, Lars. 2013. "The Matter of Absence." *cultural geographies* 20 (4): 431–45.

Greenhough, Beth, and Emma Roe. 2010. "From Ethical Principles to Response-Able Practice." *Environment and Planning D: Society and Space* 28 (1): 43–45.

Gregory, Derek. 2004. *The Colonial Present: Afghanistan, Palestine, Iraq.* Oxford: Blackwell.

Hannah, Matthew G. 2017. *Dark Territory in The Information Age: Learning from the West German Census Controversies of the 1980s.* Aldershot UK: Ashgate.

Harman, Graham. 2002. *Tool-Being: Heidegger and the Metaphysics of Objects.* Chicago: Open Court.

Harrison, Paul. 2002. "The Caesura: Remarks on Wittgenstein's Interruption of Theory, or, Why Practices Elude Explanation." *Geoforum* 33 (4): 487–503.

———. 2007. "How Shall I Say It . . . ? Relating the Non-Relational." *Environment and Planning A* 39 (3): 590–608.

———. 2008. "Corporeal Remains: Vulnerability, Proximity, and Living on after the End of the World." *Environment and Planning A* 40 (2): 423–45.

———. 2009. "In the Absence of Practice." *Environment and Planning D: Society and Space* 27 (6): 987–1009.

———. 2011. "Flētum: A Prayer for X." *Area* 43 (2): 158–61.

———. 2015. "After Affirmation, or, Being a Loser: On Vitalism, Sacrifice, and Cinders." *GeoHumanities* 1 (2): 285–306.

Hartman, Saidiya V. 1997. *Scenes of Subjection: Terror, Slavery, and Self-Making in Nineteenth-Century America.* New York: Oxford University Press.

Hegel, Georg Wilhelm Friedrich. 1991. *The Encyclopaedia Logic, with the Zusätze: Part I of the Encyclopaedia of Philosophical Sciences with the Zusätze.* Indianapolis: Hackett.

Heidegger, Martin. 1996. *Being and Time: A Translation of Sein und Zeit.* Albany: State University of New York Press.

Hetherington, Kevin. 2004. "Secondhandedness: Consumption, Disposal, and Absent Presence." *Environment and Planning D: Society and Space* 22 (1): 157–73.

Hitchen, Esther. 2019. "The Affective Life of Austerity: Uncanny Atmospheres and Paranoid Temporalities." *Social & Cultural Geography.* https://doi.org/10.1080/14649365.2019.1574884.

Hitchen, Esther, and Ian Shaw. 2019. "Intervention—'Shrinking Worlds: Austerity and Depression.'" AntipodeFoundation.org, March 7, 2019. https://antipodefoundation.org/2019/03/07/shrinking-worlds-austerity-and-depression/.

Hodge, Paul. 2015. "A Grievable Life? The Criminalisation and Securing of Asylum Seeker Bodies in the 'Violent Frames' of Australia's Operation Sovereign Borders." *Geoforum* 58 (January): 122–31.

Horn, Laurence. 1989. *A Natural History of Negation.* Chicago: University of Chicago Press.

Jazeel, Tariq. "Mainstreaming Geography's Decolonial Imperative." *Transactions of the Institute of British Geographers* 42 (3): 334–37.

Joronen, Mikko. 2016. "'Death Comes Knocking on the Roof': Thanatopolitics of Ethical Killing during Operation Protective Edge in Gaza." *Antipode* 48 (2): 336–54.

Kingsbury, Paul. 2005. "Jamaican Tourism and the Politics of Enjoyment." *Geoforum* 36 (1): 113–32.

Kingsbury, Paul, and Steve Pile. 2016. *Psychoanalytic Geographies.* London: Routledge.

Lacan, Jacques. 2002. *Ecrits: A Selection.* New York: W. W. Norton.

Land, Nick. 1992. *The Thirst for Annihilation: Georges Bataille and Virulent Nihilism; An Essay in Atheistic Religion.* London: Routledge.

Latour, Bruno. 1993. *We Have Never Been Modern.* Cambridge MA: Harvard University Press.

Legg, Stephen. 2008. *Spaces of Colonialism: Delhi's Urban Governmentalities.* Oxford: Blackwell.

Macpherson, Hannah. 2009. "The Intercorporeal Emergence of Landscape: Negotiating Sight, Blindness, and Ideas of Landscape in the British Countryside." *Environment and Planning A* 41 (5): 1042–54.

Marx, Karl, and David McLellan. 2000. *Karl Marx: Selected Writings.* Oxford: Oxford University Press.

Massumi, Brian. 2015. *Politics of Affect.* Cambridge UK: Polity.

McCormack, Derek P. 2014. *Refrains for Moving Bodies: Experience and Experiment in Affective Spaces.* Durham NC: Duke University Press.

McNeill, William. 2006. *The Time of Life: Heidegger and Ethos.* Albany: State University of New York Press.

Mitchell, Don. 2003. *The Right to the City: Social Justice and the Fight for Public Space.* New York: Guilford.

Moten, Fred. 2017. *The Universal Machine: Consent Not to Be a Single Being.* Durham NC: Duke University Press.

Muzaini, Hamzah. 2015. "On the Matter of Forgetting and 'Memory Returns.'" *Transactions of the Institute of British Geographers* 40 (1): 102–12.

Nast, Heidi J. 2000. "Mapping the 'Unconscious': Racism and the Oedipal Family." *Annals of the Association of American Geographers* 90 (2): 215–55.

Noxolo, Pat. 2017. "Decolonial Theory in a Time of the Re-colonisation of UK Research." *Transactions of the Institute of British Geographers* 42 (3): 342–44.

Philo, Chris. 2017. "Less-Than-Human Geographies." *Political Geography* 60: 256–58.

Pratt, Geraldine. 2012. *Families Apart: Migrant Mothers and the Conflicts of Labor and Love.* Minneapolis: University of Minnesota Press.

Purcell, Mark Hamilton. 2013. *The Down-Deep Delight of Democracy.* Oxford: Wiley.

Roberts, Tom. 2019. "Resituating Post-Phenomenological Geographies: Deleuze, Relations and the Limits of Objects." *Transactions of the Institute of British Geographers* 44 (3): 542–54.

Romanillos, José Luis. 2011. "Geography, Death, and Finitude." *Environment and Planning A* 43 (11): 2533–53.

Rose, Gillian. 1993. *Feminism and Geography: The Limits of Geographical Knowledge.* Minneapolis: University of Minnesota Press.

Rose, Mitch. 2006. "Gathering Dreams of Presence: A Project for the Cultural Landscape." *Environment and Planning D: Society and Space* 24 (4): 537–54.

———. 2010. "Envisioning the Future: Ontology, Time and the Politics of Non-Representation." In *Taking-Place: Non-Representational Theories and Geography*, edited by Ben Anderson and Paul Harrison, 341–61. London: Ashgate.

———. 2012. "Dwelling as Marking and Claiming." *Environment and Planning D: Society and Space* 30 (5): 757–71.

———. 2014. "Negative Governance: Vulnerability, Biopolitics and the Origins of Government." *Transactions of the Institute of British Geographers* 39 (2): 209–23.

Schwanen, Tim, Irene Hardill, and Susan Lucas. 2012. "Spatialities of Ageing: The Co-construction and Co-evolution of Old Age and Space." *Geoforum* 43 (6): 1291–95.

Sharpe, Scott. 2014. "Potentiality and Impotentiality in JK Gibson-Graham." *Rethinking Marxism* 26 (1): 27–43.

Shaw, Ian, and Katie Meehan. 2013. "Force-Full: Power, Politics and Object-Oriented Philosophy." *Area* 45 (2): 216–22.

Sparke, Matthew. 2007. "Geopolitical Fears, Geoeconomic Hopes, and the Responsibilities of Geography." *Annals of the Association of American Geographers* 97 (2): 338–49.

Spivak, Gayatri Chakravorty. 1999. *A Critique of Postcolonial Reason: Toward a History of the Vanishing Present.* Cambridge MA: Harvard University Press.

Stevenson, Olivia, Charlotte Kenten, and Avril Maddrell. 2016. "And Now the End Is Near: Enlivening and Politizising the Geographies of Dying, Death and Mourning." *Social & Cultural Geography* 17 (2): 153–65.

Thacker, Eugene. 2015. *Cosmic Pessimism.* Minneapolis: University of Minnesota Press.

Warren, Calvin L. 2018. *Ontological Terror: Blackness, Nihilism, and Emancipation*. Durham NC: Duke University Press.

Whatmore, Sarah. 2002. *Hybrid Geographies: Natures Cultures Spaces*. London: Sage.

Wilderson, Frank B. 2010. *Red, White & Black: Cinema and the Structure of U.S. Antagonisms*. Durham NC: Duke University Press.

Wilkinson, Eleanor, and Iliana Ortega-Alcázar. 2019. "The Right to Be Weary? Endurance and Exhaustion in Austere Times." *Transactions of the Institute of British Geographers* 44 (1): 155–67.

Wilson, Helen. 2017. "On Geography and Encounter: Bodies, Borders, and Difference." *Progress in Human Geography* 41 (4): 451–71.

Wylie, John. 2009. "Landscape, Absence and the Geographies of Love." *Transactions of the Institute of British Geographers* 34 (3): 275–89.

Žižek, Slavoj. 1993. *Tarrying with the Negative: Kant, Hegel, and the Critique of Ideology*. Durham NC: Duke University Press.

2 Negativism Again
"Everything . . . Less Than the Universe Is Subject to Suffering"

Chris Philo

Opening

It has been a bleak year so far, 2018, or at least I have felt it as such. A bleak or "negative geography" has become apparent to me, experienced as an attunement to the worlds in which I live and move marked by isolation, disconnection, and darkness. It approaches a sensibility of cut-off-ness, of relations nonexistent or broken, in sharp contrast to that of thoroughgoing relatedness, of everything—human and otherwise—delicately, "tentacularly," interacting and mutually shaping (Haraway 2016a, 2016b), as so celebrated in the zeitgeist of my academic mooring in human geography. The contributions of Paul Harrison (2007, 2008, 2009, 2010, 2011a, 2011b, 2015) are an exception, given his lonely struggle against the hegemony of the relationalist paradigm washing across so many different theoretical shores of our discipline (Marxist, feminist, poststructuralist, psychoanalytical, and more). I find myself taking pleasure or at least sanctuary in small things—a bee buzzing around parched garden flowers; talking with the cat about mice in the kitchen; kicking a ball with my son beside our local nature-walk; recollecting summer holidays past with my elderly father; a gentle run along the canal; a coffee and kind words with a colleague; an emailed note of thanks from a student for dissertation advice proffered—at the same time as the broader relations or "patterns" of my current world (particularly my working world) either elude or oppress me. These remarks teeter on queasy self-referentiality, I admit, but they serve an intellectual purpose with respect to what I claim in this chapter.

I have therefore decided to craft an argument geared to my current intimations of negative geography, engaging with what I describe as a "new positivism" abroad in vast swathes of current human geography energized by the various turns known as nonrepresentational, more-than-human, object-orientated, practice-based, experimental, and affective. My specific muse for this argument is a reading of works by and about the French intellectual Simone Weil (1909–43), a compound of "philosopher," "theologist," and "political theorist" (all in scare quotes because none properly captures what or why she wrote) who was almost never published in her short lifetime. There is no unanswerable logic for why Weil should now play the central role in this chapter; and, in truth, stumbling across one of her texts in a secondhand bookshop in late summer of 2018, when I was conceiving this piece, was the catalyst for settling my narrative around her writings. Flicking through this text, *The Need for Roots* (Weil 2002a), reminded me that years previously I had read more of her work, drafted notes, and even penned a short, unpublished paper borrowing lightly from her. At the same time, though, an awareness grew of how her picturing of creation—oscillating between the lightness (or enchantment) of small things and the darkness (or disenchantment) of large patterns—comprised a resource to think about both my unquiet current self and the broader intellectual project for this chapter of engaging with the negative.

Initially I supposed that, barring a brief discussion by Lorna Gold (2000, 113–14; 2004, note 11, 107–8) when considering parallels between Weil and Chiara Lubich (1920–2008), an Italian Catholic activist and founder of the Focolare Movement for an "Economy of Sharing," I would be alone in bringing Weil to the table of contemporary geographical theorizing.[1] After completing the first draft of this chapter, however, I encountered writing by Angela Last (2017a, esp. 151–55) that introduces Weil's "geopoetics" as an imaginative conjuring of "material existence and its connection with large cosmic processes," central to which is Weil centering "humanity's vulnerability to geophysical phenomena" (152).[2] Using as a scene-setting device the same Weil quote that I had already chosen for my title, Last explains how Weil "regards the universe as a divine (but abandoned) creation and studies natural processes as the seat of a deeper truth and beauty" (152), albeit a terrible "truth and beauty." Such a picturing of dark, often empty cosmic nature cannot afford a model for a more "moral order" on earth, thus countering any call on (a supposedly good, benign) nature made by many ideologies and philosophies: "nature cannot serve as a model for new socialities, but merely as a reminder of human vulnerability" (161). Echoing with her wider rethinking of the relationships between materialism and humanism, or perhaps better "materialism and individualism" (Last 2017b, 83), Last advances arguments about "rematerializing" the human as individual (material) body *contra* a materialism that demands a potentially "totalitarian" collectivization of massed (or, more subtly perhaps, assembled) human *with* nonhuman entities.[3] I believe that Last's contribution and my own offering below are complementary, meeting at various points if diverging at others.

What Last does not explicitly address is Weil's concern for geometry: an understanding of how geometry grasps the timing-spacing of objects and movements in the universe, in which case Weil even called it "une sorte de danse" ("a sort of dance") (in Winch 1989, 41),[4] anticipating Törsten Hägerstrand on "the choreography of existence" (Pred 1977). Weil's geometric focus suggests another way of chiming across into human geography, but for me the particular provocation lies in how her geometry—it might be called a "spiritual geometry" or "supernatural geometry"—is, by some reckoning, Janus-faced: on the one hand, apparently signaling an enchanted universe with every smallest particle bathed in a positive light of value, meaning, and goodness; but, on the other, emphasizing a wholly indifferent universe ruled by the darkness of cold contingency, negativity, and, as in my chapter's title, a recognition that "everything . . . less than the universe is subject to suffering" (in Winch 1989, 134). This latter recognition sits at the heart of what has been termed Weil's "negative theology," and it informs my meditations on a negative geography. Informed too by recent rehabilitations of "darkness" as itself potentially an occasion of lively-ness (e.g., Edensor 2013, 2015, 2017; Edensor and Lorimer 2015; also Orange 2018), a refrain echoing below is of movements *between* light and dark: in recent versions of my own self, in how certain developments in contemporary human geography might be couched and then critiqued, and in how Weil's ontology of creation pivots from the illuminations of each smallest thing to the darkest voids of indifference.

In Search of Negativism? And Then Some Enchantment

Writing in 1977 on the relations between phenomenology and historical geography, Mark Billinge gave his paper the main title "In Search of Negativism." Curiously, the construct of *negativism* remained uninspected here, simply being a jokey allusion to how Anglophone geography's explicit engagements with phenomenology comprised one of several intellectual maneuvers then being initiated—during the 1970s—as assaults on the hegemony of *positivism* across the discipline. The extent to which positivism was really hegemonic at this time is debatable, not least because it was so rarely even named by many who might otherwise be labeled quantitative geographers, locational analysts, or spatial scientists (Hill 1981; also D. Bennett 2008). Nonetheless, insofar that positivism, in its Comtean, Vienna Circle, or other forms, loosely conformed with many presumptions of the conventional scientific method parachuted down into the (Western) geographical academy from the late 1950s onward (Barnes 2002; Gregory 1978), then Billinge's musings about a countermove—toward negativism—do make sense.

That said, Billinge's paper might retrospectively be critiqued for implying that phenomenology is a "negative" philosophy, characterized by a wish to negate the more "positive" proposals of other intellectual positions, and perhaps itself permeated by a certain negativity of style and address. Billinge (1977, 56) couches his account as drawing upon "the intellectual history of phenomenology as a radical alternative to positivism in the natural and social sciences" and teases out a handful of basic principles from Edmund Husserl (1859–1938) to underscore their inherent negating of the so-called natural attitude of the conventional sciences. Objections can also be raised to how Billinge (and other geographers who early engaged with phenomenology-as-philosophy) understood what Husserl meant by concepts such as "experience," "perception," and (especially) "intentionality," failing to grasp just how removed were such concepts from any notion of the autonomous, self-reflexive, meaning-generating, individual human subject (cf. Pickles 1985). Such a failing allowed easy ripostes from other geographers ("scientific," Marxist, structuralist) along the lines that phenomenological (and hence the broader span of humanistic) geography lodged itself too firmly in the subjectively capricious whims of endlessly inconsistent individual human beings (researchers included). For Billinge, however, the chief lesson to be derived from phenomenology—"that there are non-quantifiable sources which deserve and demand our attention, and that a subjective viewpoint is not necessarily illegitimate" (Billinge 1977, 66)—was actually a positive one, resonating with other currents of cultural, perception, and landscape research in the saggy orbit of historical geography. It is unclear whether Billinge believed this lesson to be an entirely good thing or whether he supposed that more rigorous analysis was still required about "the origins of . . . subjectivity" (66): in fact, he seemed oddly displeased in almost all directions, possibly the most obvious source of negativism in his piece as a whole.

Writing over three decades later, Tara Woodyer and Hilary Geoghegan published a paper with the captivating title of "(Re)enchanting Geography," their aim being to chart a gathering stream of work within and beyond human geography concerned to "enchant" the focus and practice of inquiry:

> There is, however, a spectre of hope in our midst. It appears in the form of a different way of being, working and writing that enables the application of geographical innovation, transforming dulling and deadening apprehension and paralysis into an affirmative, "reparative" attitude. . . . For geographers, this hope comes in the form of "enchantment"—an open, ready-to-be surprised "disposition" before, in, with the world. In this article, we make sense of, and space for, the unintelligibility of enchantment in order to encourage a less repressed, more cheerful way of engaging with the geographies of the world. (Woodyer and Geoghegan 2012, 195–96)

Through both critiquing "disenchantment" narratives as these have played out in contemporary human geography, with Foucauldians and the Frankfurt School among others in their sights, and carefully revisiting various moves made by older (pre-2000s) versions of geographical humanism, Woodyer and Geoghegan appraise this "spectre of hope" shimmering through the discipline's current intellectual mists. The trajectory of their account could not be more explicit, tacking toward these "less repressed, more cheerful" and, as I will say shortly, resolutely "positive geographies."

In part, these authors derive inspiration from the many species of phenomenological-geographical inquiry arising since Billinge wrote in 1977, not just breaking with Husserl's "transcendentalism" by speaking about the phenomenological constitution of everyday life-worlds—taking seriously lived, felt, shared, and situated meaning-making, as in the constitutive phenomenology of Alfred Schütz (1899–1959) (e.g., Ley 1977)—but, more significantly, latching on to the intimately sensed corporealities of lively encounter between people and things, beings and forms, agencies and materials (e.g., Lea 2008). Under diverse rubrics—postphenomenological geographies, nonrepresentational geographies, more-than-human geographies, object-orientated geographies, geographies of practice, affectual geographies, and more—such encounters have become the stuff of countless studies since the early 2000s, continuing to proliferate far beyond their founding statements (e.g., Anderson and Harrison 2010; Thrift 1996, 2007a; Whatmore 2002; and many others). Retaining faith with the Husserlian injunction "to the things themselves" (in Billinge 1977, 58), this orientation toward "enchanting geographies" is indeed an enchanting of things—very much in the curve of philosopher and political theorist Jane Bennett's two books on *The Enchantment of Modern Life* (2001) and *Vibrant Matter: A Political Ecology of Things* (2010a)—wherein living in among the vibrating strands of matter, organic and inorganic, releases a sense and sensibility of "wonder" for human and perhaps other co-dwellers, registered grandly (in deep feelings and thoughts) or embedded more prosaically in finding small ways to survive and thrive, to go on, to feel well and do good. Tellingly, Last (2017b, 73) refers to such an orientation as "feel-good materialisms." When debating her wish to intervene in "the micro-politics of sensibility-formation," Bennett herself echoes, if more hesitantly, Woodyer and Geoghegan's enthusiastic embrace: "the story of vibrant matter I tell seeks to induce a greater attentiveness to the active power of things. . . . Perhaps this new attentiveness will translate into more thoughtful and sustainable public policies. I am not sure that it will, but it is, I think, a possibility worth pursuing for a while" (Bennett 2010b, n.p.).

Woodyer and Geoghegan offer a persuasive way of illuminating a current moment in human geography, one that I would suggest is *still* very much current. A proper, fuller evidencing of that headline claim is beyond the scope of the present chapter, but I wager that a routine trawl of many geographical journals since the mid-2000s would reveal any number of papers that could be framed as looking to enchant, or to reenchant, a particular subject-matter through delving deeply into the intimate people-thing relations—embodied, sensed, felt, maybe spoken, if haltingly—supposedly integral to that subject-matter. Millions of tiny energies are apparently being spied on the loose, circulating around congeries of humans, animals, landforms, buildings, and more, entangling them together into fragile but generative ecologies of co-being, inducing intimations in the more sentient of the co-participants about "what matters" (about what matters matter) that can, on occasion, translate into more programmatic agendas for "what might be done," here and now, for the best, in this constellation of often odd assortments. The watchwords become vitality and liveliness, with everything glistening with the exuberance of buzzing, teaming, swarming, cavorting, darting, and dancing, spun into motion by the sheer "push" of the world, and with the scholars in attendance seduced by the more-and-more—the sheer moreish-ness—of the scenes before them (Philo 2017b). Rocks and frocks, waters and porters, rains and trains, glens and pens, caves and raves, clifftops and laptops, and so on and on: a profusion of exciting—and sometimes excitable—studies has arisen around such multiplicities, collectively amounting to a more far-reaching transformation of the discipline than perhaps effected by any of its previous brushes with "isms" and "ologies" (feminism and Marxism excepted). Moreover, much work retaining explicit allegiances to given "isms" and "ologies"—think of the "emotional geographies" scholarship of many feminist geographers (showcased in the journal *Emotion, Space and Society*) or of "magical Marxism" (Woodyer and Geoghegan 2012, 202–3)—has readily, if not uncritically, engaged with some version or other of these enchantments. Insofar as a lineage can be followed back to phenomenology, then, what has resulted since 1977 has hardly been the negativism anticipated by Billinge, but rather something much more positive: an alertness to what may be positive, affirmative, constructive, and generative, even generous, disclosed within the materials under scrutiny. To play on words, what has ensued might be caricatured as this "new positivism": not a return to positivism as a philosophy buttressing the conventional scientific method, to be sure, but a pervasive stance of positivity before the world being studied.

A New Positivism? And Its Critique

"In Foucault country, it always seems to be raining" (Thrift 2000, 269). This quote has always puzzled me. Its target is Michel Foucault (1926–84) as a critical socio-spatial theorist and investigator of unjust social conjunctures, constituting one of a few sporadic broadsides directed by Nigel Thrift (e.g., 2007b) against what he sees as Foucault's retreat from an early engagement with phenomenology—notably in the latter's reading of existential versions of psychology (e.g., Foucault 1987, esp. chap. 4)—into a form of inquiry that, certain tendencies to the contrary, can be read as prioritizing structure and discourse over the disruptive potentialities of life and play. I would dispute or at least qualify this reading of Foucault (e.g., Philo 2012, 2013), while grasping why, in terms of both ontology (on what tracts of "the real" Foucault alights) and epistemology (on what forms of knowledge he finds there), an intellectual case can be made for supposing that there *is* more to be told than a solely Foucauldian story. That said, the Thrift quote strikes me as offering a slippery shift in the terms of intellectual engagement, in that at root he is simply questioning Foucault for being gloomy, pessimistic, and negative, forever raining negative thoughts about power and its discontents upon the empirical landscapes at hand. He prefaces the "Foucault country" remark with the objection that, "though [Foucault] embraced a positive notion of power, the fact is that his world view is not very positive" (Thrift 2000, 269). This move turns critique into an appraisal of how cheerful, optimistic, and positive one can be *in* the world, almost irrespective of the theoretical merits or substantive acuteness of the work one does *on* the world, with the latter placed in a strangely secondary bracket compared to the former. In certain respects, it is actually a renouncing of critique, a proposal that the practice of critique—as in the careful critical-scholarly appraisal of an academic work from the inside out, scrupulously deconstructing it by exposing its own logical disjunctures or patiently disclosing its weaknesses with reference to alternative intellectual oeuvres—should be replaced by a more blunt assessment of where it sits on a positivity-negativity spectrum. The usual standards of critique are substituted for reflections on what positively can be deduced, what optimistic findings and recommendations advanced, in order (at one level) to cheer the scholar-reader and/or (at another level) to enable positive social change for peoples and places "under" study. The happy canons of a new positivism should prevail.

There are already signs, though, of this new positivism fraying at the edges or darkening at its heart. The aforementioned work of Harrison has always confronted what might be less pleasant, more exhausted, dissipated, decaying, immobile, or otherwise f(l)ailing about the world, yet still open to deploying the conceptual tools of postphenomenological or nonrepresentational geographies. A similar emphasis has surfaced in disquisitions from a handful of geographers focusing on subject-matters such as pain (Bissell 2009, 2010), Holocaust testimonies (Carter-White 2009, 2012), and even death (Romanillos 2011, 2014). Mitch Rose, meanwhile, draws away from his deep concerns for "dwelling" as human practice to develop insights into what he terms "negative governance," entailing the withdrawal of the state from any "positive" act of shielding citizens from the vulnerabilities of chaotic life (Rose 2012, 2013).

Particularly instructive for my purposes are shifts in the thinking of Ben Anderson, someone in the engine room of the (chiefly but not exclusively)

UK-based nonrepresentational and, as he might prefer to call it, "affective" turns. His 2014 book *Encountering Affect* is a major accomplishment, replete with statements about the affirmative dimensions of his inquiries, a commitment to a certain positivity, even hopefulness, about what might be possible if the generative immanence of life in its many manifestations—human, nonhuman, organic, inorganic, machinic, even textual—is carefully discerned from the multiple spacings of the world. "In learning to attend to the vagaries of affective life," he writes, "the techniques and sensibilities that compose human geography and the types of politics that animate the discipline might change" (Anderson 2014, 7). His affirmative preferences are not unqualified, though, and to some extent his book might be read as fissured by a tension between such a will to affirm and a darker, more troubled ambition of reconstructing "the organisation of affective life," asking how its insurgent, excessive energies can still, on occasion and in place, be dragooned, on purpose or more "circumstantially" (McCormack 2017), into holding-back-and-down situations where "life is calculated, specified, assessed, managed and otherwise intervened in" (Anderson 2014, 14, 16; also Anderson 2017). He diagnoses "the risk . . . that the escape of affect over existing determination [somehow evading all 'organisation'] is invoked in catch-all terms, given a positive value and becomes nothing but the latest iteration of a search to find and found hope in the living of everyday life" (Anderson 2014, 99). In another formulation, he strives to avoid "giving life's productivity a positive value or finding in life a guarantee that things might be different and better or necessarily oppositional to modes of power" (168). Borrowing and learning from Foucauldian notions of "biopower," Anderson reflects:

> Countering the reduction of life in certain accounts of biopower, theorists have argued that this affirmative vision of life requires a practice of research that is vital and creative. This approach has generated many insights, but my starting-point has been different. I have tried to avoid starting from "affect itself" or affect "as such." Which is another way of trying not to give a positive value to life's generativity. (Anderson 2014, 165)

Extending Foucault's concept of "apparatus" (or *dispositif*: Anderson 2014, chap. 2), Anderson reaches a perspective on how different practices of power can both generate liveliness and press upon it, maybe boxing it in organizationally, institutionally, and physically.[5] Additionally, he explicitly positions this perspective as approaching one of critique, and I take a subtext of his book to be rescuing critique from its somewhat maligned position in the new positivism, recasting it as "an atmospherics, based on an attempt to bring a seemingly settled apparatus to crisis" (Anderson 2014, 74; also 19, 71–76). His quest is thus for a species of affirmative critique, where the positivity of affirmation and equally expected negativity of critique can fold together.[6]

Simone Weil

For the remainder of this chapter, I consider a complex body of writing wherein a toing-and-froing of sorts can be discerned between a vision loosely akin to a positive geography (or an enchanted "geometry" full of light, love, and well-being) and one more aligned with a negative geography (or a disenchanted "void" weighed down with dark, evil, and suffering). Such a contrasting of visions, while perhaps implying more dissonance than actually existed in the mind's eye of the author concerned, nonetheless can serve to enlarge—and to throw a different relief on to—the lines of debate already specified during the first half of my chapter. The author here is the French intellectual and religious guide Simone Weil, and a secondary purpose of what follows is merely to offer a thumbnail recounting of her life and work to an audience of geographers and cognate scholars.[7]

Weil's life was short and, in many respects, difficult. Prefacing a translation of her last manuscript, titled in English *The Need for Roots*, T. S. Eliot states that "the reader of her work finds himself confronted by a difficult, violent and complex personality," someone who nonetheless could be judged "a great soul" and who "was three things in the highest degree: French, Jewish and Christian" (Eliot 2002, vii, viii, x).[8] Consistent with her focus on "activity" as the key mode to thought and spiritual life, Weil labored hard, sometimes in factories or fields and often to the detriment of her health,[9] and hence was no armchair thinker, notwithstanding the volume of words issuing into her notebooks and manuscripts (the latter mostly only published posthumously). She loved equality, opposed slavery, was especially critical of defective conceptions "belonging to the white race" (Weil, 2002a, 217), denounced Hitler and his delusions of "greatness," knew if quarreled with "her" Marx, engaged with anarchist activities in 1930s Spain, and was "more truly a lover of the people than most of those who call themselves socialists" (Eliot 2002, x). She was also in many respects conservative, a believer "in a well-ordered social life" (Weil 2002a, 298), an unforgiving critic of the weakness displayed by the Vichy regime in the face of German aggression, a spiritual puritan who unrelentingly assailed the established Church for its compromises, and, by all accounts, a far from easy person to have around (although see Thibon 2002, x).

There is no need to offer biographical detail, for which see Abosch (1994, esp. chaps. 1–7), except to underline that Weil's initial education and academic work, for a dissertation and then when lecturing, was primarily "philosophical." As Peter Winch explains, her student dissertation on *Science et perception in Descartes* (Science and perception in Descartes) was a platform for everything that followed, since it entailed a radical revisioning of Descartes's famous aphorism "Je pense, donc je suis" (I think, therefore I am) whereby—through various moves across a number of years—Weil replaced Descartes's first-person "I" perspective with what she called "'the materialist point of view,' the point of view of the third-person observer of . . . activity" (Winch 1989, 33).[10] On this token, it was no longer an "I" that thinks, but rather an imagined observer able to see the unfolding "geometry" of the universe: an imagined observer who could be taken as God, the ultimate source of everything (in which regard Weil's alternative to Descartes is to say that it is pure, godly "thought" that thinks as the guarantor of existence, not any singular "I" and certainly not any individual human being).

Her philosophical mindset never deserted her but became mixed with reflections that might be cast as contributions to "political theory," deploying extensive historical and cross-cultural comparative knowledge to fashion arguments about "oppression" and "liberty." Her manuscript for *The Need for Roots* (Weil 2002a) was authored when she was based in England, at Ashford in Kent, working for the Free French government in exile and specifically on plans for renewing Europe once Hitler's Germany had been vanquished. Unsurprisingly, references to Hitler, as well as about how the devastation of European civics and institutions might be repaired, peppered her writings. *The Need for Roots* is arguably a geographical text in the most traditional senses of "geography," since the long part 2, titled "Uprooted-ness," provides dense reflections on, in turn, "uprootedness in the towns," "uprootedness in the countryside," and "uprootedness and nationhood." At one point Weil ventures the following claims about uprootedness and the loss of roots in nameable places:

> It [uprootedness] is the kind one might call geographical, that is to say, concerned with human collectivities occupying clearly defined territorial limits. The actual significance of these collectivities has wellnigh disap-peared, except in one case only—that of the nation. But there are, and have been, very many other examples; some on a smaller, sometimes quite a small, scale, in the shape of a town, collection of villages, province or region; others comprising many different nations; and yet others comprising bits of many different nations. (Weil 2002a, 98–99)

It could be instructive to run Weil's thoughts in this respect alongside those of the early humanistic geographers, notably Ted Relph and his claims about "place and placelessness" (Relph 1976). Similarly, her notes about the relations between nation and state—contrasting the unlovable "cold, metallic surface of the State" with "the hunger for something to love which is made of flesh and blood" (Weil 2002a, 114), meaning peopled places such as the nation in its ancient boundaries—could interest the (geo)political geographer, particularly given the context of a Europe where such an appeal to "flesh, blood and soil" had taken such a sinister turn (one that Weil despised, even as she understood its dismal logic).[11]

What strikes most about Weil's later writings, though, including *The Need for Roots*, is the eruption of a fierce religious dimension, an uncom-promisingly spiritual web of arguments, such that ultimately the roots required lie in the realm of a pure love for God—for the truth that the Godhead produces and sometimes reveals—and in an ascetic, self-denying conduct directed by that love and truth. These considerations are the ones of most relevance to my own account below, and it is instructive that part 3 of *The Need for Roots*, almost as long as part 2 and titled "The Growing of Roots," is principally an investigation into how God's universe may—or should—figure in the "education" of people about the deeper wellsprings of rootedness to be found "among the truths eternally inscribed in the nature of things" (Weil 2002a, 216). Weil's reasoning is labyrinthine, including her distinctive take on the work of science, arithmetic, and indeed geometry, notably in forms practiced by the ancient Greeks, but at one level it distills to the formula that, "instead of talking about love of truth," it would be better "to know the truth about what we love" (Weil 2002a, 251). The admonition is that we must learn to love the world/universe in all of its faces, however unpleasant, and from that love discern, if in a limited fashion, the truth implanted within these multiple "things" by God: truth at once physical-mechanical (like the laws of gravity) and more symbolic (revealing aspects of God's mystery, although Weil appears to mean this symbolism quite abstractly, opening on to what she repeatedly calls "supernatural truths," rather than the anthropocentricism of telling quaint parables). Weil asserts that "the beauty of the world" (2002a, 258) is what should attract our love, even or especially as "scientists," but that—as intimated earlier and to be revisited shortly—this beauty may be terrible, *in*different to the trifles of human existence, saturated with evil and suffering. Even so, for Weil, it is in this terrible beauty that we should be rooted, loving it and its tests, even as we personally suffer, necessarily effacing our own selfhood, which precisely does not matter and must not comprise *the* (debased) root of our love and truth-seeking.

Positive Geography/Geometry/Theology?

To advance such remarks is to run ahead of ourselves, and I must backtrack to explain what might appear, superficially, to be the resemblance between, say, Woodyer and Geoghegan's enchanted geographies and Weil's spiritual geometry. It is worth pausing to hear Weil's remarks about her sense of geometry: "Geometry . . . becomes a double language," she asserts, "which at the same time provides information concerning the forces that are in action in matter and talks about the supernatural relations between God and his creatures" (Weil 2002a, 288–89). Such a doubling is apparent above, in my description of Weil's dual physical-mechanical and spiritual-supernatural understandings of forces like gravity, and such is the doubled reading of geometric—spatially textured—resonances between materialities and spiritualities conjured throughout the collected essays of *Gravity and Grace* (Weil 2002b).[12] Moreover, there is perhaps a triple language here, since for Weil geometry also becomes the key to decoding human relations located, as it were, between matter and God or between "nature" and "super-nature": "When Weil speaks of a geometry of human relations, she has in mind more than just an *analogy* with geometry as applied to [physical] space" (Winch 1989, 136, original emphasis). The parallel here with Hägerstrand's time-geography, already flagged, can also be noticed, perhaps too with reference to the ingenious writings of Martin Gren (1994), who seeks to slip between the "visible geographies" of Hägerstrand (the spiky geometries of his time-space "web model") and the "invisible geographies" of Gunnar Olsson (the deceptive lines of power that are at once the delimitations of culture, myth, and taboo: see endnote 12). Weil slips similarly to Gren, then, always alighting at once on the visible and the invisible, the surficial and the hidden, the superficial and the beyond.

To return to the resemblance with Woodyer and Geoghegan's enchanted geographies, at first blush Weil's immediate concern for geometry is allied with a celebration of "beauty," since for her "the 'order' of the world (in which consists its beauty) is expressed in geometry," which also means that "to recognise order and beauty in the world, . . . one must . . . transcend the perspective of one's own projects and see things from a centre which is not a particular place in the space of facts" (Winch 1989, 136).[13] On one reading, Weil adopts what could be framed as a more-than-human openness to the multiple "things" of the universe, subverting an anthropocentric stance on these things by coming to refuse (as already implied) the human "I" of Descartes's foundation stone, and instead experimenting with an abstracted—third-person, pure-thought or even godly—picturing of all things. In such a picturing everything—indeed, every single thing, large or small—seems to matter as disclosing order and beauty, demanding our attention and indeed love.

Weil proposes that we, humans, must nurture the capacity for paying attention to the multiple objects of the universe, positioning it as a mental exercise akin to prayer, and she characterizes it as comprised not solely by the "muscular effort" of contracting brows or withholding breath, but rather by achieving a genuine openness to the objects under consideration: "Attention consists of suspending our thought, leaving it detached, empty and ready to be penetrated by the object. . . . Above all our thought should be empty, waiting, not seeking anything, but ready to receive in its naked truth the object which is to penetrate it" (Weil 1951, 56). Winch confirms that "paying attention, a notion central to the thought of Simone Weil, is of the essence here. It involves letting the individual case speak for itself and not imposing one's own favourite preconceptions on it" (Winch 1987, 290; also Winch 1989, 11–12).[14] Parallels might be drawn with the "reduction" characteristic of the Husserlian phenomenology debated by Billinge, supposedly suspending both common-sense and academic-intellectual judgments when comported before the objects of the world, and yet paying attention for Weil becomes a device for ascertaining certain godly truths otherwise undetected. Weil herself adds that "all faulty connection of ideas in compositions and essays" result from the "fact that thought has seized upon some idea too hastily, and being thus prematurely blocked is not open to the truth" (Weil 1951, 56). "We must submit to the demands of the subject-matter which is the object of attention," insists Winch (1989, 12), "rather than attempt to dominate it." Revealingly, Winch deploys Weil's stipulations regarding objects, paying attention and not jumping to hasty theorizations in the context of a book review tackling an edited collection on the anthropology of violence, taking to task the editor's introduction—with its essentialist reading of violence as "strategically, consciously employed resource"—for displaying a "penchant for *a priori* theorising [that] seems to stand between him and not merely the phenomena under discussion[,] but the contributions to his own book" (Winch 1987, 290).

It is instructive to follow Weil's injunction, faced with the "domain" of "all the accomplished facts in the whole universe," that it is vital "to love everything as a whole and in each detail" (Weil 1951, 1). She speaks of wanting to love so much: "so many things that I love and do not want to give up; so many things, which God loves because otherwise they would not exist," while she also speaks of the universe as "the home which lays claim on our love" (in Abosch 1994, 89, 91). She clarifies that these things include much that the traditional Catholic Church would have her forsake, not least "all countries inhabited by coloured races; the entire secular life of the countries of the white race; everyone there guilty of heresy against the traditions" (Abosch 1994, 89). Elaborating, Heinz Abosch accepts that "this philosopher declares her allegiance to an entire universe of indiscriminately encompassing love: 'Our love must fill the collective space to the same extent, with the same intensity, as sunlight'" (Abosch 1994, 91). It is a matter, then, of love diffusing, proliferating, and illuminating in two different directions: from the Godhead out into every corner and sinew of creation, whose very being is only made possible by such godly love, *and* from all of us as we attend lovingly to everything filling this "collective space."

In her spiritual geometry, the sense is palpable of even the smallest thing—object, event, word, image—mattering, "dancing" in the overall "spatio-temporal pattern," as when Weil writes that "all parts of the world are equally centres" (in Winch 1989, 122, 123). Everywhere is a "centre," everywhere touched by a godly sheen, enchanted. Winch explores such ideas using the example of a woman walking through fields on a fine day, navigating by reference to distant mountains or obstacles such as rivers or fences, but also being distracted by—or, better, attracted to—brightly colored, perfumed flowers, crinkled bark, or singing birds. There is the movement, the dance, the geometrical orientations of our bodies-in-motion with little cognitive input; and then there is also the immersion in the world, the letting-of-the-world come to her, as she is "taking notice, with varying degrees of attention, of different features of her surroundings" (42). Intriguingly, Gustave Thibon, friend, confidante, and editor of her manuscripts, likens Weil to "a guide" rather than "a geographer": not so much describing—or even concerned with how we might describe—"the countryside," but evoking how we might be guided as travelers by the objects, places, and spaces among which we move (123). This dispersed geometry of things imparts a kind of "energy," for Weil a spiritually charged energy, a vision that Winch (1989, 121–22) suggests may owe something to the Jewish-Dutch philosopher Baruch Spinoza (1632–77) and his determinist energetics (which have themselves influenced certain currents in contemporary human geography leading toward the likes of more-than-human geographies: e.g., Ruddick 2010). There are links to be spied between Weil and Spinoza, albeit ones that, as I will show below, question the extent to which Weil's universe—complete with its many (ostensibly) happy details, points, and geometric relations—can be regarded as conformable with any new positivism.

Negative Geography/Geometry/Theology

Seeds of Weil's negativism have already been sprinkled through the preceding text, but I need to press further. It is clear that Weil looked critically upon many worldly "geographical" phenomena of her vexed age—notably its geographical rootlessness, as explained, and all the abuses then resulting—even as her critical responses comprised not so much overtly political but instead spiritually charged (attentive, loving, and truth-seeking) resistance to these secular assaults on the integrities of people-place relations. The core issue for present purposes, however, is that Weil's spiritual geometry, far from being adequately captured as a sunlit enchanting of the proliferating things of the world/universe, is actually much bleaker, negative, pooled in shadows and proceeding from—what Thibon acknowledges as most "shocking" about her writings—"a transcendent God who has tied his own hands in the presence of evil and who abandons the universe to the sport of chance and absurdity" (Thibon 2002, xxxiii). To oversimplify, for Weil the universe has of course been created by God—the divine power has created *every*thing, and so *every*thing cannot but be beautiful, perfect, and truth-full—but this God is not an everyday interventionist God, but rather one who has become "absent," leaving all of the things of nature, humans included, to the "natural laws" of "determination" or "necessity" as always mediated by the unavoidable happenstances of "contingency."[15] This God is not directing the show, not meddling, remedying, or answering prayers, but simply letting things be, quite possibly being or becoming "evil" in how humans interpret what comes to pass. The picture is akin to Spinoza's God-forsaken materialist-determinist universe, but on Weil's watch "God remains mysteriously present in creation" (Thibon 2002, xxxv), still there "outside the universe, [but] at the same time the centre" (in Winch 1989, 120), still loving, still caring.[16]

Tellingly, Weil's thinking here returns to matters of geometry:

> On the plane of events as such, whether one considers the universe as a whole, or as any one of its parts, carved out as seems suitable in space, in time and under whatever classification; or as another part, or yet another, or a collection of parts, in short, making use of the notions of whole or part as seems to one to be suitable, conformity to the will of God remains invariable. There is as much conformity to the will of God in a leaf which falls unnoticed as in the Flood. On the plane of events, the action of conformity to the will of God is identical with the notion of reality. (Weil 2002a, 267)

This passage first references the methodological problem of how to isolate a given thing or event from the overall time-space geometry in which it is inextricably set,[17] but then it underlines that what occurs—shaping the thing or event and how it acts or what ensues—is at once both the workings of "reality" and a constant, immutable "conformity" with what God has originally willed (long ago and with no need to will again). Gravity acting upon a leaf is inferred here, and one of Weil's aphorisms states that "we must always expect things to happen in conformity with the laws of gravity unless there is supernatural [i.e., godly] intervention" (Weil 2002b, 1). Yet, Weil does not expect there to be such "supernatural intervention," neither that it should be sought, because "divine Providence is *not* a disturbing influence, an anomaly in the ordering of the world"—something flickering into life to change matter(s)—but rather is "the order of the world, . . . the regulating principle of this universe, . . . eternal wisdom, unique, spread across the universe" (Weil 2002a, 281; added emphasis).

To develop an earlier comment, therefore, the implication is that God has stood implacably back from the world/universe, not continually enchanting it with "his" goodness, and in so doing leaving open determinisms, necessities, and contingencies that might end up, to human witnesses, seeming nothing but badness. As Weil reveals:

> All the events which go to make up the universe in the total stream of time, each one of these events, each possible assemblage of several events, each connection between two or more events, between two or more assemblages of events, between one event and an assemblage of events—all that, to the same degree, has been permitted by the will of God. All that represents the particular intentions of God. The sum of the particular intentions of God is the universe itself. Only that which is evil is excluded, and even that must not be wholly excluded, from every single aspect, but solely insofar as it is evil. From every other aspect, it is conformity to the will of God. (Weil 2002a, 280)

This passage adds in the possibility, even the necessity, that evil will be present, willed to be present by God, although I detect a conflict here between Weil insisting that what might be termed "absolute evil"—imagined as equivalent to "absolute good"—cannot have been allowed into the universe by God, but that what may subsequently appear to (certain) humans as "evil," as suffering, hardship, totalitarianism, and more, *does* arise (and indeed *has* to arise). Elsewhere, she posits that "in this universe good outweighs evil," but also that "in its individual aspects there is, unfortunately, no room for doubting that evil is present" (268).[18] Or again, the intimation is that the universe as the originary whole is and cannot but be good, filled with good, but that—to return again to my title for this chapter—"everything . . . *less* than the universe is subject to suffering" (in Winch 1989, 134; added emphasis).

Such, then, are the contours of Weil's negative geometry, and Thibon amplifies:

> Simone Weil presents the problem of evil as follows: "How can we escape from that which constitutes gravity in ourselves?" By grace alone. In order

to come to us God passes through the infinite thickness of time and space; his grace changes nothing in the play of those blind forces of necessity and chance which guide the world; it penetrates into our souls as a drop of water passes through geological strata without affecting their structure, and there it waits in silence until we consent to become God again. Whereas gravity is the work of creation, the work of grace consists of "decreating" us. God consented through love to cease to be everything so that we might be something; we must consent through love to cease to be anything so that God may become everything again. (Thibon 2002, xxii)

The geometry of creation has been made by God, in effect replacing "him" so that he becomes nothing, and he leaves it alone with all the evils that may then stem from or shadow its objects dancing their "sort of dance" in and across time-space. The only option for "his" return, for God "passing" through "the thickness of time and space" unnoticed and without altering anything, is when humans consent—as noted above—to cease being a self, a thing, a center: to opt instead for an act of "decreation" (one of Weil's most difficult notions) that melts us, at the last, into a loving, truth-filled communion with God. Insofar that nobody, Weil and Thibon included, seems to regard themselves as able to complete such a mystical transition, the impression persists of Weil ultimately resigning herself (and others) to the enduring struggle of attending to the tainted things of this creation, many of which might strike as anything but enchanted or enchanting, doomed only ever to inhabit the "empty place[s] or hollow[s]" of a "surface" that can never be "entered" (Thibon 2002, xxiv).

Another construct pervading Weil's thinking is that of "the void," a term evoking a negative space devoid of life and meaning, through which she reenvisions her world/universe bereft of godly grace: wherein reality just *is*, doing its stuff, maybe evilly, without rhyme or reason, under the dull compulsions of "necessity and chance." This darkened void is distant from any sunlit pasture of things loved in their minutest details: it is the negative geography/geometry to set against any initial sense of Weil's positive geography/geometry, albeit the latter does not wholly disappear, perhaps remaining as a melancholic residue of what *ought* to be (and of what we, humans, *ought* to be capable). Thibon ponders Weil's theological negativity:

> Simone Weil chose the negative road. "There are people for whom everything is salutary here below which brings God nearer; for me it is everything which keeps him at a distance." Is not this [the] royal road of salvation which consists of finding and loving God in what is absolutely other than God (the blind necessity of nothingness and evil)? (Thibon 2002, xxxiv)

Perhaps Weil never wished to close that gap, to achieve that communion, but rather preferred to take a rockier route through the void, the barren spaces of often unspeakable negativity. Unsurprisingly, some have characterized Weil as a proponent of "negative theology," a position that "refers to theologies which regard negative statements as primary in expressing our knowledge of God, contrasted with 'positive theologies' giving primary emphasis to positive statements" (Braine 2017, n.p.). Accordingly, she approaches God through "negative qualifications on positive statements attributing so-called 'perfections' to God—for example, existence, life, goodness, knowledge, love or active power ('strength')" (Braine 2017, n.p.), precisely because she regards God as outside of time-space and hence ultimately "unimaginable" (and therefore beyond banally anthropocentric positive attributions).[19]

Closing

I hope that this chapter makes a useful contribution to reevaluating what is at stake in "(re)enchanting geography" (Woodyer and Geoghegan 2012), with its tip toward a new positivism, and in then rediscovering potentials for critiquing such a move (also Philo 2017a, b). I have accented the superficial similarity between Weil's universe of attentively loved details, lit up by God's love, and the broadest ethos of enchanted geographies minted in such a positive currency. But I have then dug deeper into the more contorted or dispiriting dimensions of Weil's void, lacking everyday boosts of godly "magic," and instead abandoned as a zone where evils proliferate, sufferings accumulate, and all manner of black storm clouds gather. The promise and glints of well-loved small things, moments, and occasions still remain, shrapnel of a positive geography, but there is no ignoring the threat and darkness of deeply troubling trajectories running through human history, society, culture, and politics—ones exhibiting the patterns of a negative geography (for Weil, ones marked by war, totalitarianism, fascisms, and racisms). An imagined geography of miniscule glints shaded by darkened patterns is also how I might depict my current sensibility, paralleling the dual tensioned poles in Weil's writings, and I am left wondering about whether there are geometrical resources here—to do with glints and voids, pinpricks of positivity all but marooned, it seems, in shrouds of negativity—that might be enlisted in Harrison's project of "relating the non-relational" (as taken further in his chapter for this volume). I should acknowledge that I have already noticed further complications lumbering into view: the chapter's title, for instance, suggests that even the smallest aspects, obviously embodying "less than the universe," may be loci of suffering and not ones where it will be easy or justified to seek solace (even if, for Weil, they do solicit our loving attention). I am not a "disciple" of Weil, however, and so I can learn from her even as I elect on occasion, intellectually and personally, to disagree.

A final observation before closing: I have actually cheered up while drafting this chapter and begun to feel more positive. It benefited me to be a scholar, to locate some words and ideas from the great library of ideas enabling me to understand better, or at least in a different register, the many possible articulations of the positive and the negative. I hope too that there can be some larger gains to be gleaned from the chapter, ones of value to others interested in theory, geography, and the negative.

Notes

I owe a mighty vote of thanks to Mitch Rose and David Bissell for their patience, encouragement, and gentle, sage wisdom. Paul Harrison and Angela Last have provided lovely comments. Big thanks to Hester, Taliesin, and Peter Philo.

1. Gold draws upon Lubich, and briefly Weil, to fashion a vision of "alternative economic geographies" addressing economies of *sharing* not *competition*.
2. Ingeniously, Last engages Weil and other contemporaries as providing an aesthetic and politicized address to the "cosmic," the grandest reaches of time and space, and

hence being precursors of those currently writing on themes of "the planetary," "the Anthropocene," "deep time," and equally expansive constructs (within which the figure of humanity becomes small, insignificant, vulnerable).

3. Last stresses the snare of "totalitarianism" throughout her 2017b paper, not least because here she considers the ostensibly antimaterialist "anti-totalitarianism" of Arendt, seeking to read (against the grain) matters of "matter" back into Arendt's writings. In both of her 2017 papers, Last engages thinkers for whom the totalitarian/fascist evils of the mid-twentieth century loom large. In her 2017b paper, Last also draws briefly upon Weil's critiques of Marx (Last 2017b, 75–76).

4. Sometimes in what follows I use words and quotes from Weil's writings as cited by secondary authors. For reasons of space, I will not necessarily comment upon or footnote details about the original Weil sources.

5. For what it is worth, a perspective not so distant from my, admittedly still more thoroughly Foucault-inflected, account in Philo (2012).

6. Anderson has himself engaged with scholars such as Ernst Bloch (1885–1977), "the German Jewish writer whose esoteric utopian Marxist philosophy profoundly influenced the Frankfurt School" (Jeffries 2016, 36): see Anderson (2006).

7. For an up-to-date compendium of writings about Weil, emphasizing the concept of "attention," see Rozelle-Stone (2017).

8. *The Need for Roots* was penned during the early months of 1943, the year of Weil's death. The manuscript was published in France in 1949 and then translated into English in 1951. It was republished in the Routledge Classics series in 2002, and attributions here are to this 2002 edition.

9. "Learning to become 'like matter' is not seen as a bad or apolitical path for Weil. . . . In Weil's case, 'inhuman' factory work or chronic migraines led her to experience herself as matter in a way that prompted political action" (Last 2017a, 154).

10. "We should identify ourselves with the universe," wrote Weil just before her "everything . . . suffering" statement (in Last 2017a, 151).

11. Last (2017a, 154) acknowledges Weil's appreciation for "people's need to feel rooted in a particular place and social context," the *true* roots for the living of a life, not those artificially invoked by the reactionary forces of "competitive nationalism."

12. It is tempting to read such claims with reference to arguments advanced by the geographer Gunnar Olsson about the languages, cultural symbolisms, power relations, and more saturating the points, lines, circles, and shapes of geometry for the Greeks, the Christian tradition, Western philosophy, European history, global circulations, and more (Olsson 1991, 2007).

13. Weil's appreciation of the beauty of material and human landscapes—geographies rather than geometries, perhaps—is emphasized by Abosch (1994, 83–86) as an entry point for discussing her understandings of beauty, order, and "God's love."

14. Last (2017a, 153) notes this priority that Weil lends to attention, framing it as "creative attention": "to 'feel the universe through each sensation,'" a possibility that Last elaborates as a wish "to become 'like matter'" (154).

15. I should underline that all items in double quotation marks here, as elsewhere in my exegesis of Weil's writings, reflect terms and phrases that are commonplace in the original (translated) texts. The absent God in Weil's cosmos is also noted by Last (2017a, 152) in a remark quoted earlier about "the universe as a divine (but abandoned) creation."

16. "This God who is 'silent in his love' is not indifferent to human misery after the manner of the God of Aristotle or Spinoza" (Thibon 2002, xxxv).

17. On this methodological point, Weil talks of humans taking "cuttings" from this continuum: "One cannot cut out from the continuity of space and time an event as it were like an atom; but the inadequacy of human language obliges one to talk as though one could" (Weil 2002a, 280).

18. I note the occasional reference to "*this* universe," implying that Weil could conceive of other universes where "absolute evil" might be the regulating principle and where, in consequence, the balance between good and evil may tip decisively toward the latter.

19. Abosch (1994, 104) sets Weil in the horizon of claims about "negative theology" made by Erich Fromm (1900–1980), the German-born psychologist-psychoanalyst associated at one time with the Frankfurt School (Jeffries 2016, 1, 17).

References

Abosch, H. 1994. *Simone Weil: An Introduction.* Translated by Kimberly A. Kenney. New York: Pennbridge.

Anderson, B. 2006. "'Transcending without Transcendence': Utopianism and an Ethos of Hope." *Antipode* 38, no. 4 (September): 691–710.

———. 2012. "Affect and Biopower: Towards a Politics of Life." *Transactions of the Institute of British Geographers* 37 (1): 28–43.

———. 2014. *Encountering Affect: Capacities, Apparatuses, Conditions.* London: Routledge.

———. 2017. "Cultural Geography 1: Intensities and Forms of Power." *Progress in Human Geography* 41 (4): 501–11.

Anderson, B., and P. Harrison, eds. 2010. *Taking-Place: Non-Representational Theories and Geography.* Aldershot UK: Ashgate.

Barnes, T. J. 2002. "Retheorising Economic Geography: From the Quantitative Revolution to the 'Cultural Turn.'" *Annals of the Association of American Geographers* 91 (3): 546–65.

Bennett, D. 2008. "Positivism/Positivist Geography." In *International Encyclopedia of Human Geography*, edited by R. Kitchin and N. Thrift. Oxford: Elsevier.

Bennett, J. 2001. *The Enchantment of Modern Life: Attachments, Crossings, and Ethics.* Princeton NJ: Princeton University Press.

———. 2010a. *Vibrant Matter: A Political Ecology of Things*. Durham NC: Duke University Press.

———. 2010b. "Vibrant Matters: An Interview with Jane Bennett." *Philosophy in a Time of Error* (blog), April 22, 2010. https://philosophyinatimeoferror.com/2010/04/22/vibrant -matters-an-interview-with-jane-bennett/.

Billinge, M. 1977. "In Search of Negativism: Phenomenology and Historical Geography." *Journal of Historical Geography* 3 (1): 55–67.

Bissell, D. 2009. "Obdurate Pains, Transient Intensities: Affect and the Chronically Pained Body." *Environment and Planning A* 41 (4): 911–28.

———. 2010. "Placing Affective Relations: Uncertain Geographies of Pain." In *Taking- Place: Non-Representational Theories and Geography*, edited by B. Anderson and P. Harrison, 93–112. Aldershot UK: Ashgate.

Braine, D. 2017. "Negative Theology." In *The Routledge Encyclopaedia of Philosophy (REP Online)*, edited by T. Crane and others. https://doi.org/10.4324/9780415249126-K053-1.

Carter-White, R. 2009. "Auschwitz, Ethics, and Testimony: Exposure to the Disaster." *Environment and Planning D: Society and Space* 27 (4): 682–99.

———. 2012. "Primo Levi and the Genre of Testimony." *Transactions of the Institute of British Geographers* 37 (2): 287–300.

Edensor, T. 2013. "Reconnecting with Darkness: Gloomy Landscapes, Lightless Places." *Social & Cultural Geography* 14 (4): 446–65.

———. 2015. "Introduction to Geographies of Darkness." *cultural geographies* 22 (4): 559–65.

———. 2017. *From Light to Dark: Daylight, Illumination, Gloom*. Minneapolis: University of Minnesota Press.

Edensor, T., and H. Lorimer. 2015. "'Landscapism' at the *Speed of Light*: Darkness and Illumination in Motion." *Geografiska Annaler* 97 (1): 1–16.

Eliot, T. S. 2002. "Preface." In Weil 2002a, vii–xvi.

Foucault, M. 1987. *Mental Illness and Psychology*. Translated by Alan Sheridan. Berkeley: University of California Press.

Gold, L. 2000. "Making Space for Sharing in the Global Market: The Focolare Movement's Economy of Sharing." PhD diss., University of Glasgow.

———. 2004. *The Sharing Economy: Solidarity Networks Transforming Globalisation*. Aldershot UK: Ashgate.

Gregory, D. 1978. *Ideology, Science and Human Geography*. London: Macmillan.

Gren, M. 1994. *Earth Writing: Exploring Representation and Social Geography In-Between Meaning and Matter*. Göteborg: Kulturgeografiska Institutionen.

Haraway, D. 2016a. *Staying with the Trouble: Making Kin in the Chthulucene*. Durham NC: Duke University Press.

———. 2016b. "Tentacular Thinking: Anthropocene, Capitalocene, Chthulucene." *e-flux journal* 75 (September). https://www.e-flux.com/journal/75/67125/tentacular-thinking -anthropocene-capitalocene-chthulucene/.

Harrison, P. 2007. "'How Shall I Say It?' Relating the Nonrelational." *Environment and Planning A* 39 (3): 590–608.

———. 2008. "Corporeal Remains: Vulnerability, Proximity and Living on after the End of the World." *Environment and Planning A* 40 (2): 423–45.

———. 2009. "In the Absence of Practice." *Environment and Planning D: Society and Space* 27 (6): 987–1009.

———. 2010. "Testimony and the Truth of the Other." In *Taking-Place: Non-Representational Theories and Geography*, edited by B. Anderson and P. Harrison, 161–79. London: Ashgate.

———. 2011a. "Flētum: A Prayer for X." *Area* 43 (2): 158–61.

———. 2011b. "The Broken Thread: On Being Still." In *Stillness in a Mobile World*, edited by D. Bissell and G. Fuller, 209–28. London: Routledge.

———. 2015. "After Affirmation, or, Being a Loser: On Vitalism, Sacrifice and Cinders." *GeoHumanities* 1 (2): 285–306.

Hill, M. R. 1981. "Positivism: A 'Hidden' Philosophy in Geography." In *Themes in Geographic Thought*, edited by M. E. Harvey and B. P. Holly, 38–60. London: Croom Helm.

Jeffries, S. 2016. *Grand Hotel Abyss: The Lives of the Frankfurt School*. London: Verso.

Last, A. 2017a. "We Are the World? Anthropocene Cultural Production beyond Geopoetics and Geopolitics." *Theory, Culture and Society* 34 (2–3): 147–68.

———. 2017b. "Re-reading Worldliness: Hannah Arendt and the Question of Matter." *Environment and Planning D: Society and Space* 35 (1): 72–87.

Lea, J. 2008. "Post-phenomenology/Post-phenomenological Geographies." In *International Encyclopaedia of Human Geography*, edited by R. Kitchin and N. Thrift. Elsevier: Oxford.

Ley, D. 1977. "Social Geography and the Taken-for-Granted World." *Transactions of the Institute of British Geographers* 2 (4): 498–512.

McCormack, D. P. 2017. "The Circumstances of Post-phenomenological Life Worlds." *Transactions of the Institute of British Geographers* 42 (1): 2–13.

Olsson, G. 1991. *Lines of Power/Limits of Language*. Minneapolis: University of Minnesota Press.

———. 2007. *Abysmal: A Critique of Cartographic Reason*. Chicago: University of Chicago Press.

Orange, H. 2018. "Artificial Light, Night-Work and Daycentrism in Post-Medieval and Contemporary Archaeology." *Post-Medieval Archaeology* 52 (3): 409–14.

Philo, C. 2012. "A 'New Foucault' with Lively Implications—or 'the Crawfish Advances Sideways.'" *Transactions of the Institute of British Geographers* 37 (4): 496–514.

———. 2013. "'A Great Space of Murmurings': Madness, Romance and Geography." *Progress in Human Geography* 37 (2): 167–94.

———. 2017a. "Squeezing, Bleaching and the Victims' Fate: Wounds, Geography, Poetry, Micrology." *GeoHumanities* 3 (1): 20–40.

———. 2017b. "Less-than-Human Geographies." *Political Geography* 60:256–58.

———. 2019. "Nothing-much Geographies, or towards Micrological Investigations." Paper presented at Annual Meeting of the Association of American Geographers, Washington DC, April 2019.

Pickles, J. 1985. *Phenomenology, Science and Geography: Spatiality and the Human Sciences.* Cambridge UK: Cambridge University Press.

Pred, A. 1977. "The Choreography of Existence: Comments on Hägerstrand's Time-Geography and Its Usefulness." *Economic Geography* 53:207–21.

Relph, E. 1976. *Place and Placelessness.* London: Pion.

Romanillos, J. L. 2011. "Geography, Death and Finitude." *Environment and Planning A* 43 (11): 2533–53.

———. 2014. "Mortal Questions: Geographies on the Other Side of Life." *Progress in Human Geography* 39 (5): 560–79.

Rose, M. 2012. "Dwelling as Marking and Claiming." *Environment and Planning D: Society and Space* 30 (5): 757–71.

———. 2013. "Negative Governance: Vulnerability, Biopolitics and the Origins of Government." *Transactions of the Institute of British Geographers* 39 (2): 209–23.

Rozelle-Stone, A. R., ed. 2017. *Simone Weil and Continental Philosophy.* London: Rowman & Littlefield.

Ruddick, S. 2010. "The Politics of Affect: Spinoza in the Work of Negri and Deleuze." *Theory, Culture and Society* 27 (4): 21–45.

Thibon, G. 2002. "Introduction." In Weil 2002b, vii–xl.

Thrift, N. 1996. *Spatial Formations.* London: Sage.

———. 2000. "Entanglements of Power: Shadows?" In *Entanglements of Power: Geographies of Domination/Resistance*, edited by J. P. Sharp. P. Routledge, C. Philo, and R. Paddison, 269–78. London: Routledge.

———. 2007a. *Non-Representational Theory: Space, Politics, Affect.* London: Routledge.

———. 2007b. "Overcome by Space: Reworking Foucault." In *Space, Knowledge and Power: Foucault and Geography*, edited by J. W. Crampton and S. Elden, 53–58. Aldershot UK: Ashgate.

Weil, S. 1951. *Waiting on God.* Translated by E. Crawford. London: Routledge & Kegan Paul.

———. 2002a. *The Need for Roots.* Translated by A. Wills. London: Routledge.

———. 2002b. *Gravity and Grace.* Translated by E. Crawford and M. von der Ruhr. London: Routledge.

Whatmore, S. 2002. *Hybrid Geographies: Natures, Cultures, Spaces.* London: Sage.

Winch, P. 1987. "Inattentive Readings: Review of Girard's *The Scapegoat* and Riches' *The Anthropology of Violence.*" *Times Literary Supplement*, March 1987.

———. 1989. *Simone Weil: 'The Just Balance.'* Cambridge UK: Cambridge University Press.

Woodyer, T., and H. Geoghegan. 2012. "(Re)enchanting Geography? The Nature of Being Critical and the Character of Critique in Human Geography." *Progress in Human Geography* 37 (2): 195–214.

3 A Love whereof Non- Shall Speak

Reflections on Naming; of "Non-Representational Theory"

Paul Harrison

A non- anon!

—Anon

and it is within speech, that speech must be led astray

—Roland Barthes, "Inaugural Lecture"

Investments and Summonings

ROSS: His absence, sir,

Lays blame upon his promise

—*Macbeth*, Act 3, Scene 4

I've often wondered where the name—if it is a name—"Non-Representational Theory" came from. It is an awkward term, too many syllables for comfort and from the beginning a confusion. Not that there was a beginning.

The first use of the term in Nigel Thrift's work I have been able to locate is on page 6 of "Strange Country," the introduction to his 1996 book *Spatial Formations*. After running through a list of likes and dislikes (a style for which Thrift's writing is somewhat notorious) concerning problems he had with current ways of approaching the social, we find this somewhat innocuous line: "The first and longest section of the introductory chapter lays out some of the main tenets of non-representational thinking which in turn have had a major influence on my work" (Thrift 1996, 6). Two lines later we are referred to "non-representational models of the world"

(6) which may be found in various bodies of work. Notably, according to the text, the Russian school of activity theory, ecological psychology, and theories of autopoiesis. So the beginning is not a beginning, but a gathering. At this moment "Non-Representational Theory" in the singular is nowhere to be found. Its time is yet to come. Instead, the very plurality of the work gathered by the uncapitalized term "nonrepresentational thinking" seems to be an important part of the argument, not only in its diversity but also in an appeal to its externality. It, whatever it is, "informs," from without. What Thrift sets out in the remaining pages of the chapter is a work of remarkably consistent eclecticism, one which ultimately builds toward a call for a "radical contextualism" (41–47).

By 1999 things have shifted. I do not know the timing of writing. It could be that "Steps to an Ecology of Place" was composed days or years after the publication of "Strange Country." Either way, it arrives in 1999 in the succinctly titled collection *Human Geography Today*. On the second page of the chapter the term is now in the singular, though notably uncapitalized (1999, 296). However just as things seemed to be coming together, a new confusion is added: "nonrepresentational 'theory'"—the 'theory' is in scare quotes as, Thrift writes, one of the purposes of "non-representational 'theory'" is apparently to "undo what we think of as theory" (297). Looking back now, at the end of June 2017, to two journal special issues that have arguably become key texts in the slim archive of "non-representational theory," *Environment and Planning D: Society and Space* (2000) and *Geoforum* (2002), it is surprising to see how little the term is actually used. Across two editorials and eight papers the phrase "non-representational" occurs twenty-six times. If we cut out the editorials, the number drops to sixteen. If we were to divide now between mention and use, admittedly a problematic division, the numbers would be lower still. It is also worth noting the continuing variability in naming including but not limited to "nonrepresentational theory" (Thrift and Dewsbury 2000, 411), "non-representational way of sensing" (Dewsbury 2000, 480), "non-representational theory" (Dewsbury et al. 2002, 428), "non-representational practice and performance" (McCormack 2002, 470), "non-representational 'theory'" (Harrison

2002, 489). Indeed from here on out, for a few years at least, names multiply, proliferating way beyond texts authored by Thrift and those based at the time in Bristol. Non-representational theories, nonrepresentational theory, non-representational "theory," Non-Representational Theory, the transposition and displacement of the "more-than-representational" (of which more anon), then just NRT and following this acronymic atrophy, a rather rapid fade into the background furniture and an appropriately ghostly nonexistence.

When was it first made singular? First extended the credit of a proper name? Was it first done by friends or enemies? By interested or concerned onlookers? Diligent or frustrated reviewers? Or by all. But with what intentions, with what investments? A name is never a simple thing. The singularization of nominalization, the substantiation of a thing in a name, is the necessary prerequisite for having friends and enemies, for becoming an object of regard, self or otherwise, a subject of record, of celebration, rallying, dispute, or disgust. Perhaps the narrative is already wrong. Personally I always disliked and have attempted wherever possible to avoid such direct nominalization. It always struck me as an aggressive act, a performative *coup de force*, summoning into existence something not ready, not able, or not willing to be born. Still an ungainly monster would be pulled into the light, called forth by mixtures of emotional, intellectual, political, personal, and disciplinary investments.

Interestingly in Catherine Nash's prescient 2000 *Progress in Human Geography* report, "Performativity in Practice: Some Recent Work in Cultural Geography," the singular "nonrepresentational theory" or "nonrepresentational geography" occurs some thirteen times. However seemingly aware of its half-formed nature, many of these occasions are explicitly mentions rather than uses, appearing within inverted commas as if to be taken under advisement. Something more tangible may be sighted in 2003 when J.-D. Dewsbury claims, in his paper "Witnessing Space: 'Knowledge without Contemplation'"—*Environment and Planning A*—that "nonrepresentational theory" as he terms it (four occurrences) has an "agenda" (2003, 1907), an "argument" (1911), and a "project" (1911), though the force of this incantation is somewhat softened by the qualifier "for me" (1911). In 2004 in his paper "Time-Stilled Space-Slowed: How Boredom Matters," Ben Anderson uses the term "non-representational" five times, the first use is a proper name: "in Non-Representational Theory" (Anderson 2004, 740). However this use is caveated in a footnote a few pages later: "There is a danger here of assuming a singular, fixed, entity named 'nonrepresentational theory'" (745n11). By 2005 the manifestation of Non-Representational Theory is all but complete. In "Making Connections and Think through Emotions: Between Geography and Psychotherapy," published in *The Transactions of the Institute of British Geographers*, Liz Bondi uses the term "non-representational theory" only once and "non-representational geography" a scant four times along with the plural "non-representational geographies" a further four. However a step change has occurred, the grammar is different. Now the plural refers less to multiple *modes* of thought than to multiple instances of a *singular* mode. This is a crucial turn, though by no means unprecedented as we have seen, but still a *critical* moment. Critical because in this change "nonrepresentational theory" undergoes the gestures of thought that characterize critique—objectification, evaluation, differentiation. And in turn, as if the action were happening across a double-sided mirror, a *psyche*, "non-representational theory" or "geography" now has agency; it makes happen, it objectifies, evaluates. In no discernible order it is differentiated, it differentiates, it differentiates itself. To take a few examples: "non-representational geography has no such qualms" (Bondi 2005, 438), "non-representational geography avoids" (438), "nonrepresentational geography has argued for" (445). It has made itself something, something has been made of it. Which is which is hard to tell. Still now it has a life. From here on out "non-representational theory" in the singular is the norm. Not from this particular paper—we have seen and could find many more premonitions from before this time—however it is, I think, from the mid-2000s that the chimera which is for better and worse "nonrepresentational theory" is made whole. From this time onward it is something and so it is something that projects outward and is projected upon. Indeed it becomes a somewhat uncanny actor in all kinds of arenas, near and far. And as something that acts it becomes something that should act when it has not. With a name comes responsibilities.

The year 2008 sees a homecoming, of sorts. With the publication of Thrift's singularly titled *Non-Representational Theory: Space, Politics, Affect* things become decidedly programmatic; "non-representational theory is resolutely" (2008, 7), "non-representational theory, therefore, concentrates on" (8) and, waxing Latourian, "the constitution of non-representational theory has always" (9). And so for Steve Pile in 2009: "non-representational theory" is resolutely singular and it moves under its own steam; "non-representational theory sees thought as being" (2009, 12), "unlike non-representational theory" (7), "non-representational theory is seeking" (18n9). We are only a short step here from the last name; NRT. I guess we'll never know where this acronym sprang from; a shorthand while taking notes, forged under the pressure of a word count or editorial command, a knowing imitation of ANT. Whatever, I curse the day. These three letters seal all that was promised and withheld in the most unthinking of black boxes. No doubt there is pleasure to be had in such a situation for both the one constraining and the one bound: the desires, dialectics, paradoxes, and logics of recognition are well known and documented if never quite finished in their inversions.

Around this time, the mid-2000s, the die is cast, a naming takes place, a threshold is crossed. What was once indefinite is no longer. Perhaps this is inevitable. It is not like it hasn't happened before, on much more significant and grander scales. But this paper is about the names of "non-representational theory." Or, rather, it is about part of that name. Somewhat ironically it is around the same time that the name of "non-representational theory" is institutionalized that the non- started to come into its own. As we shall see it was perhaps only in the light of a proper name, of the *coup* of singular nominalization, be it by baptism, coronation, or imposition (if these are not different aspects of the same event), that the shadow of the non- started to appear in all its insubstantiality. Smuggled in but now an unwelcome guest, an unreal mockery of the newly crowned.

In the Shadow of the Non-

MACBETH: *(seeing the* GHOST*)* Avaunt, and quit my sight! Let the earth
hide thee.
Thy bones are marrowless, thy blood is cold.
Thou hast no speculation in those eyes
Which thou dost glare with

—*Macbeth*, Act 3, Scene 4

The meanings, or rather the lack thereof, of the non- in the name "non-representational theory" was, I think, a source of disquiet. Though quite why or how this was the case is less easy to identify. Despite the diversity of critiques and commentaries in the years since 1996, of which there have been many, formal and informal, insightful and opportunistic, I want to suggest that they share a common object in the non-. Not that they are determined by this, far from it; the most cursory glance at the archive demonstrates otherwise. No, what is shared is a wariness about the non-. Blank, inert, unrevealing, the non- is concerning. What to do with it? What to make of it? What does it mean? What does it hide? This is the shared problematic. That this could be the case goes some way to explain the diversity of responses, responses that vary widely in their assessments and conclusions to the point of being incompatible. For example, in a few short years "Non-Representational Theory" was assessed or accused, more or less sympathetically, more or less directly, of being humanistic, antihumanistic, individualistic, anti-individualistic, universalist, nominalistic, normative, antinormative, crypto-normative, apolitical, politically complicit, radical, antirepresentation, representational, and so on. My concern here is not the veracity or efficacy of these accounts but simply to wonder at what could, in part, lie behind or allow for such variance in response to what was, we should recall, a remarkably small body of work.

As early as 2003 Jacobs and Nash comment that "if this ['non-representational theory'] is an escape from those categorical fixes" such as "age, sex, ethnicity, race and dis/ability," it also "risks unintentionally reinstating the unmarked, disembodied, but implicitly masculine, subject" (2003, 275). While this is only one point made in what is a much wider-ranging and

substantial paper concerning the shifting nature of thinking difference, it is a significant one. While carefully qualified by the "if" and "risks" by Jacobs and Nash—though these cautions are themselves somewhat undermined by the open invitation to speculate given by the "unintentionally"—this would be a claim expressed by multiple authors in multiple ways over the years; the non- as an instance of epistemological privilege, the non- as ideological ruse, the non- as forgetting of historical context, the non- as excuse for quietude, the non- as cover for moral or logical inconsistency (see for example Pain 2006; Thein 2005; Tolia-Kelly 2006; Cresswell 2006).

Naming nothing positive or definite other than perhaps the insufficiency of such naming, the non- threatened as much as promised. Double edged, palindromic, it could conceal as much as it was claimed to reveal, deceive as much as it made public. While as noted one should be wary about collecting such critical interventions under one banner, it seems to me that they all revolve around the apparent blankness of the "non-." From qualified unease through to outright distrust, all speculate on, invest in, project onto the non- of "non-representational theory." And so, with varying degrees of perspicuity all seek to diagnose what the "non-" is. All seek in one way or another to discern and tell the truth of what is hidden therein. For example Jacobs and Nash close their paper by stating the need to consider "embodiment as *not only, but also always* the product of representation, regulation, relationality and performative reiteration" (2003, 276 original emphasis) and suggest that this "not-only," a term that I think is an early transposition of the non-, is to be found in rethinking the nature of nature, a rethinking of the bio-socio-historical context of the materiality of the given.

Two years later, in 2005, in the first of three *Progress in Human Geography* reports he would write—"Cultural Geography: The Busyness of Being More-than-Representational"—Hayden Lorimer addresses a remarkably similar problem and proposes a remarkably similar solution while approaching the issue in quite a different manner. In the context of this narrative, what is fascinating about Lorimer's intervention is how he suggests that a significant part of the "problem" around "non-representational-theory" is due to an original misnaming: that the first name, the prefix or *prénom*, was not quite right. The first section of Lorimer's report gives a deft, albeit necessarily constrained, summary of work which could be said to be operating under the title "non-representational theory" at the time. What is it, Lorimer asks, if anything that holds this work together? His answer requires a replacement of the non-: "An alteration to the chosen title might help for starters. I prefer to think of 'more-than-representational' geography, the teleology of the original 'non-' title having proven an unfortunate hindrance" (2005, 84). The "more-than," as Lorimer will go on to detail, will refer to the excessive fullness of the world, the multitude of things as yet un-thought or un-accounted for. Reading the report again today I find it hard to pin down quite what, for Lorimer, constituted the "unfortunate teleology" of the "original 'non-'"; however, it seems fair to presume that it originates in its apparent lack of positive or determinate content, and so in the lack of things to name in or by its name. Thus, glancingly, Lorimer engages with the difficulties of the non-, its reticence, the way it holds back or refrains, its odd disclosure of non-discloser, the shadow it casts. However as quickly as it is begun this engagement is resolved or rather, ironically enough, negated, via renaming. From the undecidable to the innumerable, from ambivalence to plenitude. Who could say no to that?

Still despite Lorimer's efforts, worries about the non- did not cease. Indeed with alternatives now suggested in many respects they became more intense than ever. So in 2009 we find Pile noting his "apologies for being blunt" but all the same stating that "non-representational theory" is "straightforward hypocrisy," insofar as "it continually does what it says cannot be done: it cannot help but re-present and represent affect—and *in language*" (Pile 2009, 17, original emphasis). Two years later Kenneth Olwig had similar concerns, though expressed somewhat less directly and with less moralistic overtones, when he suggests that "the 'non-' in non-representational theory comes dangerously close to the 'non-' in non-sense" (2011, 857). The culprit or the ground zero of this crime? "It is this non-disclosed quality that makes it difficult for the reviewer to disclose the meaning of non-representational theory" (857). In stating an apparent paradox so succinctly I cannot but feel that an opportunity was missed.

In the entry for "non-representational theory" in the current online version of *The Dictionary of Human Geography* the non- does very little work, quickly effaced by a multitude of things; nonhuman animals, materiality, affects, embodiment, assemblages, all and more rush into this apparent void. The author of the piece, Anderson, addresses the non- directly only toward the end of the entry: "the prefix 'non-' in 'non-representational theory' names an attunement to moments of indeterminacy and undecidability, in which new events emerge to exceed and potentially disrupt given orderings" (2009 n.p.). Don't get me wrong, within the constraints of the form, I think it is an excellent piece. Anderson goes to some lengths to stress the plurality intrinsic to "non-representational theory" and emphasizes that it—"non-representational theory"—is not a "new paradigm that would supersede others," but rather consists in "a multiplicity of perspectives and takes its inspiration from a range of sources" (n.p.). Yet one cannot but get the feeling that the entry is working under the weight of a name. As if by now the name were now dictating the words, rather than the other way around. Of course it is naive to read a dictionary expecting a definition and yet this is what is asked of every entry therein. The epistemological form, paratextual framing, and grammatical norms of dictionaries—as well as encyclopedias, textbooks, review articles, and more—while indispensable, demand the declarative statement. In a circular logic, to be the subject of such work necessitates that the subject be or exist as such, and so the task of the entry writer is to positively and succinctly define the things named therein. Such works are the flip side of Socratic irony, the straight man in any double act. As with all the entries in such a dictionary, Anderson's undergoes such a trial. The passion of the dictionary entry writer! And yet perhaps more so than many other entries in the volume, in this case there is a persistent impression of dissimulation, of a sleight of hand. What is it the non- does or doesn't do? Why is it there, at the beginning? How to account for this initial and initiating hiccup or hiatus? To what, if anything, does the non- refer?

As if the whole problem, the whole problematic of "non-representational theory" were already given in the *prénom*, in the prefix, in the first syllable and the caesurae of a hyphen: "non-."

In such a setting an "attunement to moments of indeterminacy and unde-cidability," just like the rechristening of the "more-than" or a "not-only," cannot but give rise to suspicion. A sense of backfilling and of characters and traits being retconned into a plot-holed narrative. Of an epistemological promise of more tomorrow being used to staunch an ontological wound. And so as if the non- were itself a ruse, a snake, left deliberately undefined in order to extend future lines of credit. A ruse to be all too easily exposed by the criteriological requirements of objectification, evaluation, and differentiation.

The indeterminate neutral of the non- must be named, that is the criti-cal move. And to this end marrow must be added to its bones, heat to its blood. Above all intention, content, form, motivation, some *vouloir-dire*, must be found in its glare.

> MACBETH: Take any shape but that, and my firm nerves
> Shall never tremble. Or be alive again,
> And dare me to the desert with thy sword.
>
> —*Macbeth*, Act 3, Scene 4

A Personal Story of the Non-Personal. Or, Relating the Non-Relation. Again.

non-, prefix

1. Prefixed to nouns of action, condition, or quality with the sense 'absence or lack of', often corresponding semantically to 'not doing, failure to do' (where a verb is implied by the noun, as in *non-accomplishment*, lack of accomplishment, failure to accomplish) or to 'not being, failure to be' (where an adjective is implied by the noun, as in *non-activity*, lack of activity, failure to be active).

a.

non-accomplishment *n.*

> —OED online, emphasis in original

> MACBETH: And nothing is, but what is not.
> —*Macbeth*, Act 1, Scene 3

Perhaps this is the case, perhaps the non- is a lie. I will address such suspicions and accusations directly, or as directly as I can, below. For now I want to try something else. I want to suggest that the non- in "non-representational theory" is particularly averse to the form of the dictionary and, insofar as they share a set of discursive practices and norms, the encyclopedia entry, the textbook, and the review essay, all the while not doubting for a moment such works' necessity, value, and utility (or dismissing the largely unremunerated labor that goes into their construction). So to get to the rationale for this section: if the non- is not suited to dictionary definitions, albeit for reasons that we have yet to establish, why not try a different form? If the official biographies of "non-representational theory" cannot but seek positive nominalization, due their epistemological and discursive (and so, let's just say it, metaphysical) norms, why not try something else?

With some indulgence—which I understand is far from warranted—I would like to break with Thrift's second proposition of "non-representational theory," that "non-representational theory is resolutely anti-biographical and pre-individual. It trades in modes of perception that are not subject-based" (Thrift 2008, 7) and offer a personal account of the non- instead of a declarative discussion, a confession.

A warning before getting underway. We should be aware that in seeking to suspend, if only for a moment, be it successfully or unsuccessfully, the criteriological demands of such forms as the dictionary entry, we necessarily veer away from the founding moves and purchase of what are generally regarded as *critical* thought. It is somewhat unclear therefore exactly what is or what can be "traded" here, what criteria, metrics, or norms are to apply. Still while we have seen a little of what becomes of the non- as it passes through the sieve critical, what will become of the critical as it passes through the grate of the non- remains to come.

. . .

In many respects the non- of "non-representational theory" always struck me as noncontroversial, early on at least. In the early phrasing, at least as I experienced it as a PhD student in Bristol, with Nigel as my supervisor (though, of course, my reflections on this issue are my own, and my own alone), what the non- designated was relatively straightforward. It is true that it had taken me two years of reading to get to that point, through my master's degree and the first year of the PhD. But the lessons I learned then about the non- are still the ones I teach undergraduates now and which are written up, somewhat truncated, in the "practices" section of the introduction Anderson and I wrote for *Taking-Place: Non-Representational Theories and Geography* (note the plural—published, after much delay, in 2010). Without wanting to further reduce an account that is already a reduction, I will simply quote a line from that introduction: "Insisting on the non-representational basis of thought is to insist that the root of action is to be conceived less in terms of willpower or cognitive deliberation and more via embodied affordances, dispositions and habits" (Anderson and Harrison 2010, 7).

The non- then becomes a *version* of a Heidegger's Being-in-the-World, of an *Umwelt*, of one of Wittgenstein's "forms of life," of Bourdieu's *habitus*, of Varela, Rosch, and Thompson's *Embodied Mind*, with the slight difference that it is being actively brought into the present as a potential object for and of contextual variation, change, speculation, manipulation, action, rather than just description. It is interesting to go back to 1996, to "Strange Country," and note the presence on those pages of not only the figures mentioned above, but also Raymond Williams, Lev Vygotsky, and Cornelius Castoriadis, among others. There are also notable absences, perhaps most strikingly given the often-overlooked focus of that chapter on linguistics and doings, Judith Butler. However as I said, for me, this initial understanding of the non- was fairly noncontroversial. At least at first. Yes these claims had issues to work out and around—what exactly is meant by "cognitive deliberation"? Is this the thin end of a behaviorist wedge? What is the nature of "tacit" or "embodied" knowledge and its relation to wider structures? Is this simply a reframing rather than a resolution of structure-agency debates? Are in fact two domains, the "cognitive" and "non-cognitive" for example, being demarcated, suggested, implied, or not? Noncontroversial does not mean not challengeable, but the basics of this claim of the non- were, it seemed to me then as it still does now, intelligible, respectable, defensible, and had many sound though of course disputable arguments behind them.

And yet one question kept coming back. With insistence and intensity. Where, oh where, is the politics? When does theoretical reframing turn into critique? Where is the question of power in these claims? Where is the diagnosis? Where do you stand? What is your position? What does this mean? And when what may well have been insufficient answers were given the intensity of questioning only became more apparent. The responses were too vague; insofar as they were at all they were too general or too specific, they rewrapped the question into other questions; they constantly deferred. A statement or a proposition was lacking, and tellingly. To this day, and I do not want or expect a moment's sympathy, I have never recovered from these questions.

Strangely, to me at least, the dividing line between the noncognitive and cognitive (read and transposed, with multiple diffractions, reductions, amplifications, and interventions) onto the emotional and the affectual, the personal and the public, the universal and individual, became the sites where these debates would, at least on what are generally taken to be the larger stages, be played out. Some, and only some, of the relevant articles have been cited above. Of course my haphazard textualism and my inevitably but by no means unmotivated selective memory do not capture what was so much more apparent in this period, at conferences, at seminars, in hallways and offices, in emails, in homes, cafes, pubs. Personally, I do not want to recall these things as during this time my relation to the non- was shifting in ways I could have never foreseen, and in ways I would never have chosen.

I cannot remember when it happened. Of course I know the dates. I may, today, even think I know why. But, and I say this to you now hopefully after reading the above, dates are not always a reliable guide to events, and retrospective narrations are all too often convenient reframings of the present, or of a desired future, or a past. The date and the story and above all the name all too often obscure the event and can prevent us, willingly or not, from listening to its echoes, from living with its ghosts. When it comes to dates and stories *Nachträglichkeit* rules by not ruling, an incessant ambiguity haunting and hunting every positive determination. As if each date were already split from the inside, as if it split everything. Still, I have delayed enough, or enough for now. So a date, that is what is demanded of confession, no? Let's go with June 11, 1996.

Sometime in the early 2000s I became conscious of the fact that my relation to the non- was shifting. The non- was no longer constrained by what I had thought to be the relatively easily delimited realm of the precognitive and the reassuring arms of a fairly analytic mode of phenomenology. Not that I was particularly interested in or troubled by expanding this field into the pre- or postphenomenological realms, be it of affects and percepts, of flows and becomings, of assemblages and dispositions, or similar, possibly more empirical, expansions into quasi objects, nonhuman animals, or geology. Instead the non- started to show me its invisibility. From here on out, for me, so-called non-representational theory no longer designated a particular domain within the ontic, the good news of plenitude, the as yet undiscovered realms of the great outdoors, nor did it entail an ontological commitment to affirm the sense of things, however chaosmatic, wonderful, or enchanting they may be. Instead the non- came to mark or trace some potentially infinite unworking, of the impossibility of all of the above (and below).

Unmoored, the non- floated free. Ranging and raging across everything and anything, coloring one and all with its shadow. To try your patience, but in all honestly for the sake of brevity, I will quote from a paper written during this time and published somewhat later:

> The nonrelational is that which offers no purchase, which eludes in a passivity which if it may be said to resist at all has the inert resistance of a weakness beyond or outside power, like a "blank cry" the harkening of which "alone parts our lips" and which causes our "answer to fall short of any possible match, so that this very failure gives us speech." (Harrison 2007, 593)

A never-ending instant in which past and future flee into themselves and the ecstatic structure of the world breaks apart leaving in its wake a here and now emptied of depth, meaning, and potential. A here and now divested of the possibility of relation, refuge, or dwelling. As these structures recede what is revealed is not another possibility for the self, another becoming, but rather the extreme exposure and abandonment. (595)

So much for the—now I came to think about it—only ever promised or avowed joy of "nonrepresentational theory." That was long gone. Moreover the now interleaved promise of the "more-than-representational," of the proliferation of forms and life, set me in mind of lines from Macbeth's famous soliloquy: "Tomorrow, and tomorrow, and tomorrow, / Creeps in this petty pace from day to day" (5.5). No, now the non- held the promise not of affirmation but inseparably and inevitably its decline. Not only happiness but sadness, not joy but suffering, not plenitude but reduction. And so not only the possibility for new, yet to be invented modes of solidarity and agency but the quagmire of the unwilled, of the unchosen, of harm. Not more but less, ever more less. The non- as the mark of ruin that touches all, that has already left its mark, before any beginning and from which there is no escape. Or, as the OED has it, in the first entry for the prefix *non-*: "not doing," "failure to do," "non-accomplishment."

It may seem as if the non- had become a persecuting angel, a vindictive superego or something unwillingly internalized, whichever, something unnamable, or simply the remorseless undertow of the *Todestrieb*. And it felt like that, one or all of those, or something like them, and I am sure it will again. Perhaps also something close to Emmanuel Levinas's *il y a* ("there is"). The non- sounding the rustle and murmur of anonymous being, of the night, back into which all forms fall, and which haunts all daylight names. I spent many hours, sometimes weeks and, looking back now, months and years, observing this process of dissolution. Sometimes trying to wrest myself, or at least a self, free, sometimes encouraging it, mostly at its mercy. Like the student in Georges Perec's *A Man Asleep*, who wakes one day having forgotten how to live, or has remembered how not to: "Here you sit, and you want only to wait, just wait until there is nothing more to wait for: for night to fall and the passing hours to chime, for the days to slip away and the memories to fade" (Perec 2011, 142).

By now the non- was far detached from its original anchors. From here on out it had its own course, despite me. At this time my committal to non-committal was absolute, which left me in a somewhat precarious situation. Not that I was completely alone, or rather I was, but this didn't prevent— indeed it may have allowed for—unexpected forms of non- or asocial sociality. I was moving in marginal circles. Strange, awkward, wonderful, and somewhat terrifying encounters happened thanks to this modulation of the non-. Infrequent, but all the more valuable for that. Mutual recognitions of misrecognition, acknowledgments of an incapacity to acknowledge. Or so I started to hope, for myself as much as anyone. Brief intervals after talks, halfway between a lectern and a door, over stale conference coffee in anonymous meeting rooms, while walking through a cold, unfamiliar city, or hours later in some dive. Outside of recognition or empathy, a certain useless compassion could be found in the endless processes of disintegration. Or so I would come to silently tell myself, or so I was being given to learn. At these moments I was like Robinson, staring down at a footprint in the sand, struck dumb between fear and a hopeless hope, unsure if this trace was mine or an other's . . .

A-non: The Auto-hetero-bio-graphy of No-one

Once uttered, even in the subject's deepest privacy, speech enters into the service of power.
—Roland Barthes, "Inaugural Lecture"

I am certain that the above is true, but also that it does not conform to the requirements of a dictionary entry. Any truth that it has lies elsewhere. Equally, having written it, I am unsure if I have given an account that is "anti-biographical and pre-individual" and that "trades in modes of perception that are not subject-based," or not. Certainly there is a proliferation of "I's" and "me's," but I would hope we are not so naive, not critical enough, to think that we can name and know, without due reflection, what these terms represent. I, myself, am far from certain. Indeed the possibility of a confession being mine, being said in my name, is always the possibility of a lie. Be it the intended lie, that of a ploy, a sleight of hand, of dissimulation, or hypocrisy, or the unthinking or unthought untruth of ignorance, unconscious motivation, ideology, epistemological privilege, or ontological blindness. These possibilities and more are not only inherent in but inherent to any confession, as a confession. No matter how direct, blunt, or straightforward, a confession may always be suspect, as one which disguised, oblique, all but silent, may be judged most true. And vice versa. Depending on the context, on the criteria within which the words are to be received and grasped, meticulously examined or skim read, a confession will have always said too little or too much. It will always point elsewhere. For the author as much as the reader.

A confession is never only the confession of a secret, of this hidden fact or that furtive detail, this desire or that inclination, that symptom or trait, which have been waiting to be disclosed but also, before this, the possibility of secrecy itself. One does not confess just because one has secrets but because one is secretive. From oneself as much as to others. The only mirror we have, the only psyche, the only room for speculation, is made out of this displacement. Displacement of and in the first place.

As soon as a confession is phrased, as soon as it is dispatched, if only in the loop of short-term memory or even a half-second before, as soon as it is or could be, it goes astray. Whether given to the self, a priest, a critical audience, in public, or in secret, just to you. This going astray is not external to the confession, it is not a sad fate that befalls it from without, but rather its condition of possibility. A confession is always given, sent, en-tounged, inscribed, be it privately, intimately, in a subtle shift of mood, a touch, a staying silent, or publicly, in a speech, a tweet, a press release, or an authored chapter. Always underway, sent as such, it is always returning, and yet in each case, each instance, the subject only arrives in and as the confession's going astray. For the author as much as the reader. This is its, and my, chance, or mischance. Without this encryption, this *spacing*, this tragedy of destination, there could be no confession at all. One cannot both be and be coherent.

And so the circle of auto-affection is always already dislocated, always already auto-hetero-affection. The non- inheres and persists, however disavowed, in the intervals, the blanks, the gaps, in all the displacements that make speculation possible. The non- neither affirms nor denies, and while it can of course be named and in being named become another object or subject of speculative or critical thought, be that thought philosophical, sociological, psychoanalytic, geographic, or otherwise, it can never be held by such, or as such. The return of presence in negation it remains, and remains as the disorganization of such systems and structures; as that which must be disavowed for the surety of such systems and structures; as that which must be forgotten for the establishment of context, content, meaning, and intention. Unremembered, for the sake of objectification, evaluation, and differentiation. Or for the sake of a self who would confess. Still, like bubbles in the earth, like a hesitation or a caesura, the non- haunts. The profile of anonymous being, of an unlimited economy, of the swarming of a base or aleatory materialism, perhaps. Or as a goat, a spider, or a snake. As ashes or a summer's cloud.

Maybe the concerns expressed by those cited two sections ago concerning the non- were right: the non- is not amenable, it will not be put to use, or not fully; and it is not reassuring, or at least I don't think so, despite the opportunities that may be found in its name. No, outside of oppositional or binary logic, irreducible to a speculative dialectics or phenomenological reduction, flouting the laws of the excluded middle and noncontradiction with irony or great conviction, or both, the non- appears as hollow, bankrupt, monstrous, impossible.

And yet it is in and by the heteronomy of any *autos*, of any presence, which all techniques of investigation, frames of reference, and courts of judgment, including those of self-reflection and critical analysis, will, despite themselves, found and cite themselves. Found themselves in the disavowal of a site-without-unity, without identity, without sovereignty. Found themselves in the *coup de force* of nominalization, in the violence

HARRISON

of proper names. All speculation, reflection, analysis, all objectification, evaluation, and differentiation, all critique and all confessions, begin t/here, all find themselves by forgetting a beginning that is not a beginning, so they may begin.[1]

Coda: A Love of Which Non- Shall Speak

> But for us, who are neither knights of faith nor supermen, the
> only remaining alternative is, if I may say so, to cheat with
> speech, to cheat speech.
>
> —Barthes, "Inaugural Lecture"

In his recently published book *No One's Ways: An Essay on Infinite Naming* (2017), Daniel Heller-Roazen sets out to write a history of the non-. It would be foolhardy to attempt to summarize Heller-Roazen's text in the space that remains; it is a masterwork of comparative philology, with an itinerary running from Ancient Greek, Roman, and Arabic thought, through Christian theology, to Kant, Hegel, Heidegger, Boole, and Carnap. Instead, I want to give an all too brief précis of what I take to be the core claim. While non- words existed long before Aristotle, it is in the philosopher's work that Heller-Roazen finds the first formalization of the non-. Or almost, for, as Heller-Roazen tells it, the "non-" posed particular problems for Aristotle and those following him. Specifically, for the role the non- should or should not play in the development of a coherent theory of propositions and categorical logic. To wit, the issue of its nonspecificity.

By late antiquity the principles of Aristotle's theory of the proposition, as set out in *On Interpretation*, *Prior Analytics*, and *Categories* had acquired a "fixed shape"; the oppositional square, also called the Roman square or, more commonly today, the Traditional Oppositional Square. It is worth quoting Heller-Roazen's description of such a square at length, due to the precession of his prose:

> projected, for the purposes of teaching, onto the surface of an imagined
> square . . . In each of its four right angles, a predictive assertion is to be

inscribed. The upper two vertices will contain two universal statements: that is two statements bearing on a subject quibbled by the determiner "every." [For example,] "Every pleasure is good" will be written in the upper left, and "Every pleasure is not good" in the upper right. The two lower vertices of the square exhibit statements that will be considered "particular" in the sense that they bear on an indeterminate quantity of subjects, a quantity to be designated by the determiner "some." The sentence, "Some pleasure is good," will be inscribed in the lower left corner, and "Some pleasure is not good" will be written to its right. The horizontal lines of the square will thus trace a movement in quality, from "is" (*est*) to "is not" (*non est*), or, in other words, from affirmation to negation. The vertical lines of the square will convey a passage in quantity: from universal to particular, that is, from "every" (*omnis*) to "some" (*quaedum*). (24–25 original emphasis)

The horizontal lines of the square thus describe a relation between contrary propositions and the diagonal lines between the right angles a relation of contradiction. The upper horizontal lines are contrary in a strong sense in that both cannot be true (though both may be false), whereas on the lower horizontal line both cannot be false, but both may be true. In the case of the diagonals, contradiction was the preferred term, as one must be true and the other false (26). The rules are clear and well known; to enter into and play the game of propositions, or to play it properly, one must not contradict oneself (law of the contradiction—one must exist or not, something must be or not be), one must be self-contained (law of identity—one is oneself, for all a: a=a), and one cannot waver (law of the excluded middle—one cannot be and not be at the same time).[2]

Heller-Roazen's text explores the difficulties posed by and responses to the place of "non-names" into the workings of categorical logic and predictive judgment. For example, and to stay in the early stages of this development, how does or how could the square reform if the proposition in the top left-hand corner were stated as "Every pleasure is non-good"? The path for this investigation is opened by Aristotle himself, at the moment of the founding of this logic, as he did not reject such "non-names" as being unworthy of either grammatical or logical reflection. Key to this

HARRISON

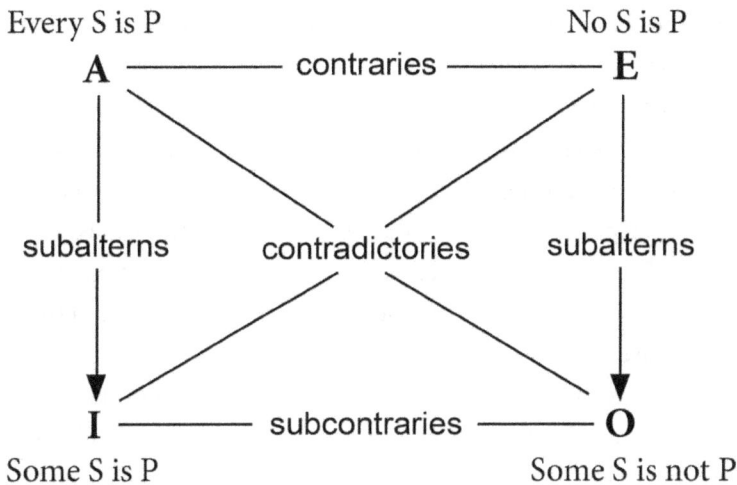

Every S is P   No S is P
A ──────── contraries ──────── E

subalterns   contradictories   subalterns

I ──────── subcontraries ──────── O
Some S is P   Some S is not P

Fig. 1. Traditional square of opposition. Terence Parsons. "The Traditional Square of Opposition." *Stanford Encyclopedia of Philosophy* (Summer 2017 edition), edited by Edward N. Zalta, https://plato.stanford.edu/entries/square/.

nonrejection is Aristotle's claim that non-names perform a unique type of naming, which he termed "indefinite naming." So, of the term "non-man," his primary example, Aristotle writes: "It is not a name, nor is there any current name for it. It is neither a phrase nor a negation. Let us call it an indefinite name [*onoma aoriston*]" (19). The unique but itself quite indefinite role that Aristotle gives the non- stems from its *not* being a pure or absolute negation nor a pure affirmation. The non- is not a not, nor is it a yes. Nor does the non- indicate a form of privation (think, for example, of the difference between the terms "blind" and "non-sighted"). Nor, as the ambivalence of the term "non-being" continues to demonstrate, is the non- easily reduced to questions of existence or in-existence. Instead, it hovers.

Having posed the question of the non- and not rejected it out of hand as erroneous or duplicitous, Aristotle leaves the issue aside. Thus, Heller-Roazen observes that, at this time at least, "the word 'indefinite' [as in 'indefinite-' or 'non-' names] constitutes less the name of a concept than the index of a difficulty, which troubles the theory of terms, sentences, and regularities of truth and falsity that are to hold between forms of stated opposition" (32). Of course not everyone agreed with Aristotle. Between his comments on the non- and now many have sought in various ways and for various reasons to make the non- into a no or a yes, or a form of privation; to sublate, subsume, transpose it, to dismiss or envelop it. Heller-Roazen charts these debates, displacements, and disavowals with diligence. Throughout the text he is careful to refrain from passing judgment; however, in the closing sections of the book, he begins to speculate on the future of the non-.

Reflecting today Heller-Roazen wonders if in the passing of the doctrine inherited from Aristotle "in which the *non-* had its modest place," and "after some have set off for artificial symbolism in place of 'colloquial language' . . . a new possibility might be envisaged" (250 original emphasis). Reminding us again that non- words were in use well before Aristotle, Heller-Roazen points to their ongoing multiplication today. We could reflect on, for example, non-violent, non-governmental, non-binary, non-conformist, non-European, non-philosophy, non-citizen, non-binding, non-human, non-profit, non-person, non-representational, non-state, non-resident, non-event. And while it touches on much, this list does not touch on non-names that pass less noticed, through different prefixes and etymologies, all the while holding a similar grammatical status and a similar ambivalence. For example, the un- of uncanny, unknowing, unbelievable, as with dis-, de-, a-, and so on (all the way up to and including deconstruction, perhaps). And this is to limit an already small sample to only those most readily apparent in English (more or less). As I understand him, Heller-Roazen is asking us what does or what could this dissemination of the non-, a dissemination that was always there, give us to think?

There is no suggestion of an underlying logic here nor even a new one, much less a method. Only contexts, grafts, and displacements. Perhaps, at last, we should be done with confining language "in the image of arithmetic" as we should be done with confining it to the role of correspondence. Instead a suggestion of something altogether more shifting, un-revealed, withdrawn, held in reserve. Not for the sake of coming to light, but an infinite and indefinite resistance to, and an un-working of, exactly that: "In fragments of discourse, in words, declined, case by case, according to grammars that are still to be uncovered, an unfamiliar logic and illogic will make itself more audible. It will be our own" (251).

"It will be our own." Outside any sovereignty, ghosting any claim to the throne, it will be our own only in its movement of dis-possession, negative and active, persistent and an-archic, in making us strange to any disposition that we claim.

Perhaps now to respond, in a way, to those questions I never could, and still cannot, I will quote Roland Barthes once again: "But language—the performance of a language system—is neither reactionary nor progressive: it is quite simply fascist for fascism does not prevent speech; it compels speech" (Barthes 2000, 461). Compels the making of statements, assertions, the naming of names. Today, as then, I would prefer not to. Is this critique? I do not know. Still, for now, as then, to the ever undoing of proper names; a non, anon, a non- . . .

Notes

First and foremost, my sincere and heartfelt thanks to Mitch and David, for their patience, care, and diligence. I couldn't have asked for such wonderful and understanding colleagues. Thanks also to Ben, John, Vickie, Rachel, and Adam for commenting on drafts of this chapter, and to Charlotte for her support throughout.

1. A site-without-unity, perhaps *Ereignis* (Heidegger), or, the unconscious (Lacan), a plane of immanence (Deleuze), a differend (Lyotard), a between-two (Irigaray), *différance* (Derrida), *il y a* (Levinas), the abject (Kristeva), *Nachträglichkeit* (Laplanche), non-identity (Adorno), the aleatory (Althusser), whatever (Agamben), *khōra* (too many to name), to give just a few of the names that have been given, all different, all anachronous, all responding, all irreducible to each other, all irreducible to either the sensible or the intelligible, to presence or absence, to the internal or the external, at least as traditionally understood.

2. As both Parsons (2017) and Heller-Roazen (2017) note, the bases for the square are to be found in Aristotle's *On Interpretation* (17^b17–26) and *Prior Analytics* (I.2, 25^a1–25). The traditional square of oppositional is now generally considered outdated, and there are questions as to how well the square itself maps onto Aristotle's writing. Equally, there has been a multiplication of logico-geometrical frames, including logical hexa-

gons, cubes, dodecahedrons, and more. However, despite this, the square's influence is little short of prodigious, being recognizable in many forms all the way up to and beyond Greimas's semiotic square. Such developments, while fascinating, do not undercut the point being made here, which concerns the intrinsic ambivalence of "non-names" in a game of propositions and so in the court of evaluative judgment.

References

Anderson, Ben. 2004. "Time-Stilled Space-Slowed: How Boredom Matters." *Geoforum* 35 (6): 739–54.

———. 2009. "Non-Representational Theory." In *Dictionary of Human Geography*, edited by Derek Gregory, Ron Johnston, Geraldine Pratt, Michael Watts, and Sarah Whatmore. London: Blackwell.

Anderson, Ben, and Paul Harrison, eds. 2010. *Taking-Place: Non-Representational Theories and Geography*. London: Ashgate.

Aristotle. 1963. *Categories and De Interpretation*. Translated by J. L. Ackrill. Oxford: Oxford University Press.

———. 1989. *Prior Analytics*. Translated by Robin Smith. Indianapolis: Hackett.

Barthes, Roland. 2000. "Inaugural Lecture, Collège de France." In *A Roland Barthes Reader*, edited by Susan Sontag, 457–78. London: Vintage.

Bondi, Liz. 2005. "Making Connections and Think through Emotions: Between Geography and Psychotherapy." *Transaction of the Institute of British Geographers* 30 (4): 433–48.

Cresswell, Tim. 2006. "'You Cannot Shake That Shimmy Here': Producing Mobility on the Dance Floor." *cultural geographies* 13 (1): 55–77.

Dewsbury, John-David. 2000. "Performativity and the Event: Enacting a Philosophy of Difference." *Environment and Planning D: Society and Space* 18 (4): 473–96.

———. 2003 "Witnessing Space: 'Knowledge without Contemplation.'" *Environment and Planning A* 35 (11): 1907–42.

Dewsbury, John-David, Paul Harrison, Mitch Rose, and John Wylie. 2002. "Enacting Geographies." *Geoforum* 33 (4): 437–40.

Harrison, Paul. 2002. "The Caesura: Wittgenstein's Interruption of Theory, or, Why Practice Eludes Explanation." *Geoforum* 33 (4): 487–503.

———. 2007. "'How Shall I Say It . . . ?' Relating the Non-Relational." *Environment and Planning A* 39 (3): 590–608.

Heller-Roazen, Daniel. 2017. *No One's Ways: An Essay on Infinite Naming*. London: Zone.

Jacobs, Jane, and Catherine Nash. 2003. "Too Little, Too Much: Cultural Feminist Geographies." *Gender, Place, and Culture* 10 (3): 265–79.

Lorimer, Hayden. 2005. "Cultural Geography: The Busyness of Being More-than-Representational." *Progress in Human Geography* 29 (1): 83–91.

McCormack, Derek. 2002. "A Paper with an Interest in Rhythm." *Geoforum* 33 (4): 469–85.

Nash, Catherine. 2000. "Performativity in Practice: Some Recent Work in Cultural Geography." *Progress in Human Geography* 24 (4): 653–64.

Olwig, Kenneth. 2011. "Book Review: Taking-Place; Non-Representational Theories and Geography." *Progress in Human Geography* 35 (6): 856–58.

Pain, Rachel. 2006. "Paranoid Parenting? Rematerializing Risk and Fear for Children." *Social & Cultural Geography* 7 (2): 221–43.

Parsons, Terence. 2017. "The Traditional Square of Opposition." In *The Stanford Encyclopedia of Philosophy Archive* (Summer Edition), edited by Edward N. Zalta. https://plato.stanford.edu/archives/sum2017/entries/square/.

Perec, Georges. 2011. "A Man Asleep." In *Things: A Story of the Sixties, with a Man Asleep,* 127–221. London: Vintage.

Pile, Steve. 2009. "Emotions and Affect in Recent Human Geography." *Transactions of the Institute of British Geographers* 35 (1): 5–20.

Thien, Deborah. 2005. "After to beyond Feeling? A Consideration of Affect and Emotion in Geography." *Area* 38 (2): 213–17.

Thrift, Nigel. 1996. *Spatial Formations.* London: Sage.

———. 1999. "Steps to an Ecology of Place." In *Human Geography Today,* edited by Doreen Massey, John Allen, and Philip Sarre, 220–43. Cambridge UK: Polity.

———. 2008. *Non-Representational Theory: Space, Politics, Affect.* London: Routledge.

Thrift, Nigel, and John-David Dewsbury. 2000. "Dead Geographies—And How To Make Them Live." *Environment and Planning D: Society and Space* 18 (4): 411–32.

Tolia-Kelly, Divya. 2006. "Affect—and Ethnocentric Encounter? Exploring the 'Universalist' Imperative of Emotional/Affectual Geographies." *Area* 38 (2): 213–17.

4 Ethics for the Unaffirmable

The Hesitant Love of a Cultural Translator

Vickie Zhang

Ever since I was a child, I have had the same recurring dream. In it, I am running to some place, where I know something will happen. I am always at a loss to name what that thing will be, but dream-me does not seem to mind; she remains driven by absolute conviction in my arrival. As I set off to my destination, my body glides free, freer than my real-life body could ever be capable. I set sail with the wind, but it never lasts long; the wind always changes. I feel it before I recognize it: fatigue accruing in my muscles, my still-moving legs turning to stone as the surrounding air becomes thick like tar. In waking life, these heavy conditions would force reevaluations, new judgments; I have, after all, always detested running. Incapable of lucidity however, dream-me never doubts the imperative to keep moving. Instead, I become caught in an infinite spiral, as the weight of action slowly crushes my dreaming body. But I have never known what happens upon my arrival, because the journey is asymptotic; my only respite is waking life, when I am finally released from the scene of entrapment.

This chapter is a meditation on affirmation, responsibility, and endurance in the context of critical academic practice. It reflects on the nature of critique, understood as a "negative" practice, and responds to the recent move to affirmative and postcritical styles of research in geography and the social sciences (Noys 2010; Anker and Felski 2017). Contrasting the affective demands of critique with those of affirmation, my focus is the impact of academic labor on the researcher's body—the feelings, good and bad, that accompany our knowledge-making practices. Birthed through months in an impasse—a decompositional, in-between space of indecision (Secor and Linz 2017)—this chapter detours through racialized childhood memories to confront my discomforts about undertaking research in China as an Australian of diasporic Chinese descent, as a native-English-speaking child of migrants, as a junior academic at a Western institution. Turning to the emotional expanses of the self, I consider an approach to research ethics—as relations between self and others—that recognizes the ambivalent baggage freighted by personal histories and habits (Askins and Blazek 2017; Proudfoot 2015; Bondi 2014). Conscious of an underengagement with race in cultural geography (Mahtani 2014) and blindness to bodily difference in nonrepresentational theories (Colls 2012), my writing is guided by a postcolonial desire to "use writing-theorizing as a way of transforming the body" (Noxolo 2009, 63). This piece thus hopes to not just "slow the quick jump to representational thinking and evaluative critique" in academic conventions (Stewart 2007, 4), but also to reshape a persistent scene of doubt that returns to me like a refrain.

My starting point is the ascendancy of affirmative approaches across the social sciences and humanities, where an "affirmationist" set of engagements have emerged as the disposition for our times. Speaking to both the "high affirmationism" of immanentist poststructuralist philosophy and the "low affirmationism" of theory in the humanities and social sciences, philosopher Benjamin Noys characterizes such approaches through tendencies to acknowledge "historical density, complexity and materiality," "the creation of unashamedly metaphysical ontologies, the inventive potential of the subject, the necessity for the production of novelty, and a concomitant suspicion of the negative and negativity" (2010, ix). In human geography, this move to affirmation is evident in a wide range of approaches that seek to "ontologize," foregrounding the inherent and inexhaustible productivity of a lively world of relations and the excesses of materiality and affect (Anderson and Harrison 2009; Thrift 2008; Thrift and Dewsbury 2000; Whatmore 2006). Inspired by vitalist philosophies of becoming, postcritical and postcolonial critique, compositional theories, and postphenomenological thought, affirmationist approaches hold together diverse valences of academic practice, from descriptive trackings of difference to action-oriented cultivations of possibility.

Correspondingly, influential thinkers in the humanities and social sciences have moved to cultivate explicitly affirmative praxes that foster dispositions to protect and care for (Latour 2004), repair and love (Sedgwick 2003), and be enchanted by (Bennett 2001) the objects with which we live and work. Geographers have sought to animate wonder, enthusiasm, and awe toward topics both ordinary and strange, including those conventionally considered undesirable, undervalued, or unnoticed. Dovetailing with care in feminist literature and a Foucauldian "care of the self," this work has importantly opened up a range of affective dispositions away from the detachment—feigned or otherwise—demanded by critical negativity (see Anker and Felski 2017; Felski 2015). Explicitly joyful, playful, and experimental approaches have been offered to human geographers in a contemporary academic climate where "extant pressures upon academics and the nature of being critical have the potential to leave many geographers feeling helpless, depressed and defeated" (Woodyer and Geoghegan 2013, 195). Similarly, Nigel Thrift speaks of "the prospect of constructing a Machine for 'sustaining affirmation' . . . of launching an additional source of political nourishment and responsiveness and imagination in a time when so many forces militate against it" (2008, 4). In this context, it seems that affirmation has even become aspirational, working at the level of mood to cultivate more hopeful and endurant dispositions (Anderson 2006).

And yet, there has been concern for what might be going missing in this move to the "more-than" of affirmation. Working from a suspicion of what is disavowed in the celebration of life, Paul Harrison (2015) describes affirmation as a "double yes," an affirmation of affirmation, drawing a line from key theorists in the present moment (e.g., Bennett, Braidotti, Connolly) to Nietzsche's *amor fati*. The first "yes" of affirmation recognizes the primacy of becoming and change in a productive world. But why, Harrison demurs, the second "yes"? "Why does another, second, apparently voluntary, 'yes' need or desire to catch up with the first?" (2015, 296). Underscoring that the affirmation of affirmation is a *choice*—that the second "yes" stems from

ZHANG

an a priori judgment of affirmation as a desirable stance—Harrison reflects that "I cannot help feeling the deck has been stacked before the game has begun, for what monster would ever choose anguish over generosity, fatalism over love, the past over the future, *ressentiment* over joy?" (Harrison 2015, 195). Similarly, Chris Philo senses that, with the rise of "more-than-human geographies" oriented to the "and, and, and" of a lively world, we may be forgetting that "there is maybe a whole other, more expansive, trajectory to explore, a flip-side, an antipode . . . alert to what diminishes the human, cribs and confines it, curtails or destroys its capacities" (Philo 2017, 257–58). Moving from the spectacular to the ordinary, undercurrents of a refusal to let go of negativity have emerged, aiming to repair the political possibility of bad, "ugly," or negative feelings (e.g., Cvetkovich 2012; Halberstam 2011; Muñoz 2006; Ngai 2004; Osborne 2019; Wilkinson and Ortega-Alcázar 2019).

Picking up threads of this negative tradition, I begin this chapter by returning to postcolonial literary theorist Gayatri Chakravorty Spivak and her directives for the "good" cultural translator (and, by analogy, geographer). I write through Spivak's prescriptions, explaining what she means when she speaks of "love" as necessary to the work of translation. I take Spivak's argument to be exemplary of the negative critical tradition, one that I suggest is paradoxically founded on a particular kind of affirmation: the *affirmation of negativity*. I explain why Spivak sees critical negativity as fundamental to the work of cultural translation, elaborating the nonreciprocal relation of surrender at the heart of her account. Working with Spivak's text, I aim to contribute to the small literature in geography that focuses on the learning that comes from inhabiting the gap between languages (Crane, Lombard, and Tenz 2009; Drozdzewski 2018; Krzywoszynska 2015; Watson 2004), and a more metaphorical sense of translation as shuttling between cultural worlds, broadly understood (Germes and de Araújo 2016; Hancock 2016; Jazeel 2007; Sidaway et al. 2004).

In the section that follows, I compare the critical concept of translation offered by Spivak with a different version of love, drawing on queer theorist Eve Kosofsky Sedgwick's analysis of critique as paranoid. My use and juxtaposition of these thinkers' positions on love, and my turn to Spivak's "double bind" in the conclusion, are heavily inspired by Carolyn Pedwell's (2014) discussion of the roles of reparation, translation, and ambivalence in contemporary cultural theory. Here, I position Sedgwick's notion of the reparative position as an emblematically "affirmative" stance. Sedgwick's analysis is particularly pertinent as it explicitly addresses critique and affirmation through its performative effects on the academic subject. Sedgwick famously describes critique as "paranoid," as a strong negative affect that, through the anticipatory production of subjectivity, tends toward the reproduction of further critiques (Sedgwick 2003). In its place, Sedgwick draws on the psychoanalysis of Melanie Klein to argue for a shift toward the "reparative position": an anxiety-mitigating process of repair that Sedgwick gives the name of "love." Compared to the paranoid and suspicious tendencies of critique, love denotes the act of assembling for critic and audience alike "a more satisfying object" with which to identify and be nourished, a practice co-founded on the care of the self and the productive potentials of pleasurable affects (Sedgwick 2003, 128). Although Sedgwick's version of affect differs from the Deleuzian version more prominent in nonrepresentational theories—notably in the evocation of several named affects rather than a "single" force called affect (see Sedgwick and Frank 1995)—both approaches share a motivating belief in the productivity of capacity-building affects, aiming to make space for a radically expanded repertoire of action that experimentally harnesses "pleasure, hope and the possibilities of ameliorating social problems in the present" (Brown et al. 2011, 2), and "spaces which flirt and flout, gyre and gimble, twist and shout" (Thrift and Dewsbury 2000, 412) in the poesis of academic practice. Put simply, affirmation's wager is that the "margin of maneuverability" (Massumi 2015, 2) in a situation means that an arena of ethico-political action can also be a scene of feeling good.

Reflecting back on my own history of translation, I then pause. I stop to wonder whether either Spivak's or Sedgwick's affirmations of love are suited to my task as a translator of "China." Finding myself at an impasse— caught between equally compelling arguments for and against affirmation and critique—the final sections of the chapter address the topic of love in relation to my own fraught history of translation as a Chinese Australian. Ultimately unsatisfied with the terms offered by either Spivak or Sedgwick, I draw attention to a blind spot that the two share in their desire to establish a normative relation to their objects of interest, wondering what it means to turn love into a political principle. Instead, I set out for an alternative, turning to Roland Barthes, Paul Harrison, and Spivak's later writings to sketch an alternative disposition for navigating academic life. What I hope to afford through this—to myself, as much as anyone else—is a more hesitant style of becoming: an ethical stance founded not on the a priori judgement of the affirmation, but on the ineliminable responsibility of the decision.

Allow me to start with a story:

> I watch on silently as my mother haggles with the man at the street market, his fake wares spread out on blanketed trestle tables. Louis Vuitton bags, Ralph Lauren polo shirts, Rolex watches. It's the early 2000s, China has just acceded to the World Trade Organization, and my family is in Guangzhou to visit my maternal grandparents. It's my first time in China; I'm about to turn ten. At the open-air market, my mum has vigilantly instructed me not to utter a single word, because if I do, the unmistakably accented inflections of my household Cantonese will reveal us as overseas Chinese, apparently flush with overseas cash, and my overseas mother will lose the delicate game of back-and-forth she is playing with the stallholder, nervously attempting to wrench the asking price down to buy the watch or blouse that she would never allow herself in Melbourne. I'm tucked away by her legs, paralyzed with paranoia. *Be still*, my preadolescent brain reasons, *because if anyone finds out we're from Australia, Mum not only will get scammed, but I will also get kidnapped, because Chinese criminals are always on the lookout for small overseas children, and no public space is safe, so I should always stay close to her and never ever talk to or even look at strangers.* It is the middle of another muggy and scorching Guangzhou summer, and I have never sweated so much in my life. I am tense, on edge the whole time; I do not like this strange place.

Translation as Surrender

I would like to begin this piece with an analogy between the task of the social scientist who works in milieus foreign to herself, and the "necessary but impossible" task of the translator, as described by Gayatri Chakravorty Spivak in *The Politics of Translation* (2009). Asking: "How does the translator attend to the specificity of the language she translates?" Spivak proclaims: "I must overcome what I was taught in school: the highest mark for the most accurate collection of synonyms, strung together in the most proximate syntax" (2009, 201). Writing against a presumed transferability of content across bodies of meaning, Spivak asserts the impossibility of translating between one idiom and another. This untranslatability rests, of course, on differences internal to history and culture that manifest in language. But it is also an incommensurability complicated by histories of imperialism and colonization, which render vastly different discursive positions available to the disparately located speaker, translator, and reader (Spivak 1988). Instead, Spivak draws attention to the space outside of the text itself, to "the possibility that things might not always be semiotically organized" (2009, 209). Interested in conceptualizing the agency of the agent who uses language—"even though intention is not fully present to itself" (2009, 201)—Spivak focuses on the way language-in-use is modulated through the disruptive workings of rhetoric and randomness. She argues that rhetoric does not work like logic; instead, rhetoric refers to the way in which the speaker or writer uses and acts with language, workings that give "vital clues" about the agency of the speaker. Without sufficient intimacy with the language and culture of the original, a translator is unable to read the rhetoric of the speaker "in the silence between and around words" (Spivak 2009, 203). Without the imaginative capacity to conceptualize agency in the rhetorical silences, the cultural translator, no matter how technically proficient, is incapable of conceiving of the other as a user, rather than an object, of language. Addressing the native English speaker in particular, Spivak holds no prisoners: in the absence of understanding and care for the agency of the other in language, a "neocolonialist construction of the non-Western scene is afoot" (2009, 203).

How, then, might the impossible task of translation proceed? Faced with semiotic disorganization, Spivak relegates product to process. She argues that a "good" translation emerges from an act of *surrender*, an act of "love" in which the translator yields to the scene of the text in pursuit of the rhetorical edge of language. She declares: "The task of the translator is to facilitate this love between the original and its shadow, a love that permits fraying, holds the agency of the translator and the demands of her imagined or actual audience at bay" (Spivak 2009, 202). This puts translation in an affective realm: to "surrender" is to transform not just the text, but also to transform *oneself* in the approach. Practically speaking, this transformation of the self occurs not just at the proximate scene of reading or writing; to even begin, Spivak argues, a translator must be *prepared*. A good translator must earn her right to translate by becoming intimate with the sphere of the other, familiar not just with the language itself, but also the presuppositions of the speaker, the intricacies of the host medium, the "histories of the language, the history of the author's moment, the history of the language-in-and-as-translation" (Spivak 2009, 209). Given the translator's status as the reteller of another's texts, the translator "must have a tough sense of the specific terrain of the original" (Spivak 2009, 211) so she can discriminate on *this* basis, rather than the terms set by discourse of her own idiom. It is no small task, but it is necessary.

There's a knock on my open bedroom door. It's 8 a.m., and even though it is Saturday, it is still a school day, and I am in my single bed, trying to will myself back to sleep. It is futile, of course—the more I try to return to sleep, the more awake I become. The contours of the eggshell-white room in my memory tell me that we are already living in the "new house," an off-the-plan suburban home on the then-outskirts of Melbourne. My mum knocks again, imploring me to wake, and although I hear her, my preteen-self steadfastly refuses to show any sign of stirring. Instead, I hold my body rigid with feigned slumber, in the naive hope that she might extrapolate that I somehow couldn't wake up *at all*, and would thus, out of panic or delay, cancel my attendance to Mandarin School that morning.

Weekend language school: that torturous topic of migrant-child derision. Although we speak Cantonese at home, it never strikes me that the southern dialect is remotely like its mutually unintelligible standardized counterpart. Instead, I am chronically unable to link characters to sounds, to the world of meaning fragmentedly glimpsed through my parents; chronically unable to link my identity as an Australian to my parents' desire for me to speak Mandarin Chinese. Waking every Saturday filled with dread, I endure my source of childhood trauma with years of unremitting protestation and incompetence.

Saturday morning runs on loop for years and I have long given up hope of escape when, suddenly, something shifts. As if life were a dream, in a moment that still feels miraculous, our government-run language school abruptly announces that it must relocate. Sensing a once-in-a-lifetime opportunity, my brother and I hastily escalate our lobbying and tantrums— *"Fifteen more minutes of driving each way! Think of the petrol money! Higher fees! We're learning nothing anyway! Ahhh!"*—until our exhausted parents finally relent. I can barely believe my luck: *it* is finally over and, like the proverbial day after an undergraduate exam, I promptly forget all the Mandarin I have learnt in the seven years to that date.

Love's Surrender

Spivak refers to love sparingly in her chapter, most prominently in the oft-quoted declaration that frames her essay, that "the task of the translator is to facilitate this love between the original and its shadow" (2009, 202). However, I would like to unpack the undernarrated referent of this term further. "To surrender in translation is more erotic than ethical," Spivak asserts (2009, 205). Subtended by desire, her language for the translator's task is less about love as a feeling and more about love as a particular relation. The translator's love is a commitment to *surrender* to the others whose idioms we might wish to retell, and to the work of making that retelling possible. Given this understanding of love through structural attachment, Lauren Berlant poses a question in a different context that feels pertinent. On the borrowing of love as an idiom to organize the political, she asks:

Is this "version of love a love we would feel as love? Or is it a structure or principle that would animate us while we might be having other strong and or diffused feeling events hooking us to the world, and the world to us?" (Berlant 2011, 687). Drawing out the idiom of vernacular love, one perhaps knows from experience that a moment of desire is an insufficient foundation for love to flourish. Recognizing that desire and love, though related, should be viewed separately, Berlant highlights the nonsovereign origins that characterize desire. She describes desire as an attachment that emerges from outside of you but, through a certain recognition through repetition, comes to feel like it comes from within. For this feeling to become love, it requires a scene stable enough for recognition of desire's inhabitation there, to "make a world for desire's endurance" (Berlant 2012, 7). Indeed, a hallmark of love—romantic, platonic, or otherwise—is its persistence as a scene of repetition to which one can return, even as the experience of it may be ambiguous, inconsistent, and ambivalent.

With its acknowledgment of the global and cultural hierarchies that position subjects differently in relation to each other, Spivak's politically motivated love is a love that, while demanding the nonsovereign self-suspension associated with love, denies the possibility of being founded upon reciprocity. That is, it unsettles the structure of the normative couple-version of love in which one might rightly expect the object of your love to offer you love back. In his discussion of the ethics of reflexive feminist fieldwork in geography, Mitch Rose addresses a similar desire for reciprocity in ethical relation. There, Rose recognizes a "desire for equality" between the academic and her collaborators, which, although careful not to premise itself on sameness, involves "an underlying desire for correspondence, an ambition to meet on level ground and speak through (as far as possible) the social, cultural, racial, sexual, and ethnic differences that divide them" (Rose 2016, 142–43). Instead, Rose suggests that the relation between the writer and her object is necessarily unequal, that the academic is unavoidably situated in a relation of ontological dependence. Like Spivak, Rose inverts the ethical relation to foreground not the positive subject of "speaking for" but the negativity required to "hear from" the other.

While Rose's essay, evoking the figure of the ancient Egyptian scribe, stakes its ethical claim in the more nostalgic orientation of acknowledgment, Spivak's task for the translator looks to the time to come, emphasizing an unequal reciprocity that makes a greater set of demands on the academic. Aware that affirmation can easily turn to appropriation, Spivak's translator requires an abiding disposition "toward the (im)possible effort of moving toward the imagination the 'quite other,' or radical forms of alterity whose contours cannot yet be fully known" (Jazeel 2014, 95). To surrender in translation is to surrender to the call of the other, to the work that would make this hearing possible prior to, and regardless of, the matter of reciprocity. As such, the translator's task would insist upon a certain critical paranoia, in the sense that "of all forms of love, paranoia is the most ascetic, the love that demands the least from its object" (Sedgwick 1986 in Sedgwick 2003, 132). Spivak's affirmation is that some attempts to relate make greater demands than others, given the positions in which one stands, the distances across which one translates, and the histories in which one lives. The love of the translator insists that we make such demands of ourselves, so that we do not—implicitly, inadvertently, intentionally—misread the stories we claim to be telling.

Spivak's critique is clear. Her instructions for the cultural translator are, perhaps contrary to reputation, surprisingly practical. I understand her task; I agree with its necessity. It should be *all systems go* from here, a flurry of organization activity as I get to work. And yet, I pause. As the future stretches ahead of me in the task's infinite ask, I feel myself caught by an unexpected question. A moment of discomfort emerges as I become paralyzed at the front door, arm raised but unable to knock. Heat rises in my face; my eyes cast downward; my hands begin to fidget. If the translator's love still counts as love, it is a difficult love: a love without cushion, a love that cannot ask for reciprocity, a love that does not eagerly lend itself to affirmation. The stilling discomfort morphs into a self-reflexive moment: a moment of critique, a moment of shame. Before I can ask myself *how* to

ZHANG

prepare for the translator's task, I suddenly catch myself wondering: *am I prepared to make the necessary preparations for the task?* Looking back at my fraught history with "Chineseness," I hesitate: do I want to do this *at all*?

High school is finally over, and there are hijinks to celebrate its passing. It's "muck up day"—an Australian tradition reveling in the end of thirteen years of formal education. I spend the evening putting the finishing touches on the outfits for my friends and me. We're dressed up as the schoolgirls from the faux-French children's cartoon *Madeleine*, complete with self-made bright yellow capes and white Peter Pan collars. Today, we're packed cross-legged on the wooden floor of the long and narrow auditorium as tongue-in-cheek graduation awards are announced from the stage: American teen-movie style goodbye gifts voted on by our classmates to mark the end of our high school days. We're at a government selective girls' school, a strange, state-sponsored outlier of socially mobile education in a striated education system. Meeting each announcement with whooping and cheering, nineties pop classics lend a thick air of ready nostalgia to the occasion as my friend, our school captain, ascends to the stage to pick up the award for "Most Likely to Become Prime Minister" (a claim about which we are only half-joking). "Best Dressed" passes to a commendable recipient as I pause to ponder what constitutes good taste.

As we travel down the list, my heart beats faster in anxiety and anticipation. The award for "Most Asian White Person" is announced by my MCing classmate—an awkward thing to call an "award" perhaps, but a long-standing tradition passed down through generations of unashamedly multicultural girls at our school. The recipient is declared and there is an uproarious laughing-with of recognition as a blonde classmate runs up to the stage in excitement. I suddenly realize the moment I've been waiting for is coming next. A lump rises into my throat, and I become hyperparanoid about the gaze of those around me: an outlier group of white girls—"skips," like Skippy the kangaroo—who have been my closest friends since we all arrived four years ago. "The award for 'Whitest Asian' goes to . . ." the MC proclaims, basking in the moment with a dramatic pause. The stillness seems to last an eternity as I feign nonchalance, determined not to show disappointment if it is to come. "The award for 'Whitest Asian' goes to *Vickie Zhang*!" she declares. I relax, a grin cracks across my face as my chest slowly puffs out in pride. *Yes!*

A Difficult Love: Affirmation or Critique?

Critique is predicated on movements to shame. It is indeed this reliance "on shame in critics about their own culpability and denials" that has, for thinkers like Jacques Rancière, divested critique of hopeful potential (Anker and Felski 2017, 11). As Sedgwick (2003) describes, critique is a prolific machine that captures energy in the paranoid habit of producing further critiques, energies which Sedgwick, Gibson-Graham, and Bruno Latour, among others, have prominently aimed to redirect to affirmative projects. Founded upon moments of paranoia, hypervigilance, and shame in critic and critiqued alike, critique is "a strange and multifaceted creature: mistrust of others, but also merciless excoriation of self" (Felski 2015, 10). Functioning initially as a form of *self*-critique, Sedgwick's suggestion is that critique is too negative, too paranoid, too self-congratulatory, too miserable, too unthinkingly caught up in its own destructive feedback loop. In its capture of assertion, the teleology of critique reveals itself to be, in fact, a peculiar variety of affirmation: as the *affirmation of negativity*. With this understanding, Spivak might be seen as the ur-critic of reflexive critical negativity, demanding a "hyper-self-reflexivity" that even the most critical of academics "fail to live up to" (Kapoor 2004, 628). Her critical practice, proceeding from the need to constantly acknowledge one's complicity through a "persistent dredging operation" (Spivak 1999, 1), has led to accusations of paralyzing the intellectual (Kapoor 2004). Mirroring a concern in affirmative practice for the endurance of the subject, the accusation is that Spivak can take reflexivity too far.

As suggested in the introduction, the shift in the social sciences and humanities toward "postcritical" academic approaches appears to have exiled negative styles of engagement (like Spivak's) in favor of affirmative modes. And yet, it bears repeating that Spivak's critique is not for its own sake; rather, it aims to foster a practice of self-critique that is "expressly carried out in order to clear the way for an ethical relationship with the Other" (Kapoor 2004, 643). Allied to good feelings, affirmative approaches appear to be less capable of conceptualizing a love that can coexist with discomfort, ambivalence, or negativity, as its temporal horizon condenses into that of a positive affective immediacy. As Eleanor Wilkinson and Iliana Ortega-Alcázar (2019) recognize, the affirmative tendencies of "more-than-human" or "more-than-representational" approaches to "good" affects have occluded from view not just the political potential of negative or bad feelings, but also those whose function is more difficult to categorize as good or bad. Like Spivak, I am reluctant to let go of the discomfiting workings of critique when it functions as autocritique, as it is precisely its negative moments—its small destructions of subjectivity and habit—that make a different relation possible. After all, what would it mean to let go of the "negative" feelings of shame? Like desire, shame is nonsovereign; we do not choose to be ashamed. As an intensifier, shame prompts a self-evaluative moment. Shame potentializes a moment of self-transformation; but, as Elspeth Probyn (2005) underscores, this possibility is only actualized if shame is acknowledged. If, even if only implicitly, negative feelings like shame have no place in affirmation, then the question of how this willful absence might redraw relations to objects matters. Are such feelings minimized, suppressed, forgotten, ignored—or do they never emerge in the first place? After all, shame always emerges in the context of interest. If shame "illuminates our intense attachment to the world, our desire to be connected with others" (Probyn 2005, 14), then the only way to eradicate shame would be to eradicate interest.

And yet, I pause here again. It also bears repeating that shame is difficult to bear, that its decompositions debilitate and destroy in ways that cannot be cast as purely productive. Although he otherwise opts for an unambiguous affirmation of affirmation, Latour offers a helpful metaphor, musing that critique is a "most ambiguous *pharmakon*" (2004, 239). That is, the value of critique is ultimately a matter of *relative*, not absolute, dosage. Likewise, then, for affirmation and repair. Despite the affirmative practices with which her writings are associated, Sedgwick's original formulation was clear that the paranoid (critical) and reparative (affirmative) positions are "changing and heterogeneous relational stances" to be taken up as judged to suit the situation (Sedgwick 2003, 128). Her enduring contribution to critique debates was the recognition that the "problem is with any theoretical maneuver that becomes *automatic,* translated from a problematic into a deadened habit" (Anderson 2011, 129)—a critique that arguably applies just as much to the automatism of affirmation as it does to critique. However, as literary theorist Robyn Wiegman argues, despite this rhetoric, even Sedgwick herself "avoided grappling at length with the less salvific implications of reparation" by ultimately presenting it as a more or less "decided critical good" (Wiegman 2014, 17). Wiegman further speculates that reparation and affirmation, though usually presented as caring for the *other,* might be just as much about repairing the academic *self* hoping to sustain her own attachments. That is, reparative practices often exist for the sustenance of the self, not the other. As a result, where Spivak's critical affirmation calls for surrender to the other, Sedgwick's reparative affirmation looks to care of the self.[1]

It seems, then, that there is no straightforward answer to either affirmation's desirability, although both are presented by their proponents as necessary. Despite its increasing influence, affirmation is evidently not a catchall solution; as Carolyn Pedwell remarks, if repair functions partly as a guilt-reducing defense mechanism (as it does for Melanie Klein, on whom Sedgwick draws), then while it "may be appropriate for some subjects in some intellectual and political contexts, it might be very inappropriate, incommensurable and simply absent in others" (2014, 55). And yet, on the flip side, I cannot shake my instinctive misgivings about critique's difficult demands, to the nonreciprocal, self-sacrificing, demanding love it espouses. It seems that neither critique nor affirmation are the automatic answers they are variously offered to be. Both positions feel similarly untenable and, yet, equally necessary.

Minimal Critique: An Affirmation

Finding myself at an impasse, I attempt in the final sections of this chapter to venture a hesitant response to this predicament, suggesting what might be occluded in accounts of critique and affirmation that aim to assert an ideal disposition to their objects of interest. Unable to find in affirmation or critique an ally for my circumstances, I set out in search of a position that I feel—and not just wish-I-could-feel, or feel-I-should-feel—but a position that I *really feel* able to affirm, in my quest to become a "good" translator of "China." It is here that I account for the stories I have been recounting in parallel; these memories represent the experiential terrain that catalyzed the searching desire of this piece, returning to me during a period of personal crisis. Offering an angle of approach that evades affirmation's rhetorical style, I draw on more recent writing by Spivak to amplify a different stance for the academic, one that looks past affirmation and critique to acknowledge the exigency and aporia of the decision. To prepare the ground, I begin with Roland Barthes and his efforts to avoid the rhetoric of conflict and assertion.

If a problem with critique and affirmation alike is their automatism, then the first move to shame in critique and the first "yes" of affirmation suggest movements that can be diverted from their apparently predestined ends. Tarrying with these moments, I would like to draw an analogy with Barthes's (2005) discussion of "the Neutral" to produce an alternative anchor for what might be called a persistently negative, minimal affirmation. Preferring figuration to didactic prose, Barthes offers only a minimal definition of the Neutral—a "thing" not a word—that "baffles" the paradigm of the "yes/no (+/-) model": for/against, positive/negative, affirmation/critique (Barthes 2005, 42). Compared to the translator's mandate to go "all in" on surrender, the Neutral offers an almost opposite version of action. If surrender is nonsovereign *action*, then the Neutral's desire is for the possibility of sovereign *nonaction*, as an act of undoing knowledge in search of an affective silence, an attempt to escape relations of opposition. Perhaps paradoxically, Barthes explains that the move toward the Neutral will necessarily retain the work of negation, to counter what he calls the "arrogance" of language and discourse: the "*yes* (the affirmation) . . . implicitly inscribed in all of language," where "to utter a word is immediately to affirm its referent" (2005, 44). The negativity of the Neutral is therefore not the negativity of critique, but a minimal negation whose only aim is to "suspend, to thwart, to elude the paradigm" (2005, 7). It is a position whose desire is to be without position: recognizing that this can exist only in the "ceaseless struggle" of a minor, negating movement that counters the assertive disposition inherent to discourse (2005, 44). For Barthes, the Neutral is a matter of ethics; it represents the desire to find "the other of conflict" (8) that is lost in the assertive discourse of either/or. Like Barthes, I am drawn to the Neutral as I see in it "a manner—a free manner—to be looking for my own style of being present to the struggles of my time" (2005, 8).

Fast forward a decade. It's early autumn, late on a Monday night, and my assistant Jianan and I are sitting in a cold security office at a residential block next to a recently closed coal mine. Having delayed my trip until it could be delayed no longer, I suddenly find myself on fieldwork in a small city in the middle of China.

It's only our first few days in the area, but already nothing has quite gone to plan. My trusted local contact turns out to be of little help, and we have turned to approaching people on the street. Locals are rightly wary, and I'm perhaps fairly suspected of being a spy. The whirlwind year since my last visit has led me to forget how alienating China has always felt for me. Language difficulties add to my problem, as I realize that I don't speak a word of the strong dialect of my air-drop location, and many locals do not speak the national standard either. I'm freshly heartbroken, gripped by a world-shattering force that refuses to clear despite the oceans I've traversed. The sky is permanently thick with smog and my skin misses the crisp Australian sun. Although the two older men we are interviewing in the cold office are warm and talkative, I feel the strain of past months engulf me, as the accrued inertia catches up to my fatigued body. My lips still are moving, in conversation, but I feel myself crossing an interpretative threshold, zoning out of conversation and no longer present to the room.

It's soon close to 11 p.m., and Jianan and I are edging to leave, eyes glazing over, yawning, when a man stumbles into the sparse concrete office. He looks to be in his early forties, face slightly red. I am snapped back into my body as my heart begins to pump at double speed, wondering who this man is and whether he is here to catch us in the act, as if we really *were* undercover spies. I don't realize he's drunk quite yet; it's not until several minutes later that I catch a whiff of *baijiu* on his breath. For now, surprised to see us, two unknown young women, the man pauses, eyebrows raised. He asks us why we are here. Sensing my hesitation, Jianan takes the lead, cheerfully explaining, "We're university students, here to collect data for a graduation thesis." Still apprehensive, the man asks us where we've come from. My stomach involuntarily tightens. We inform him that we've just arrived from Beijing a few days before. Expression unchanged, the man presses again, more aggressively, "Why are you here?" Confused this time, Jianan repeats herself again: "We're university students, here to collect data for a gradu-ation thesis." Our two friendly interviewees are looking on with bemused expressions, but the man shakes his head, leaning in closer: *"Why are you here?"* By now I'm alert, if baffled, skin prickling with suspense and confu-sion. Jianan changes tack, but the man seems to hear nothing of her expla-nation. It's getting awkward. Jianan turns to me blankly, not sure what else to say. Suddenly remembering that we have prepared a written statement about the project, Jianan scrambles to find a copy, and presses the sheet of paper upon the man. *"Here!* Just read this."

The drunken man takes the flyer, laser-focuses his gaze on the lines of text, and then looks up soberly. "Oh, you are university students, undertak-ing research for a graduation thesis," he states blankly. "Why didn't you say so?" Inexplicably satisfied, the man flops down into the cracked leather armchair opposite us, making himself comfortable for the night. The ten-sion suddenly clears, and the mood lightens again, but, for me, a threshold has been crossed. The encounter resonates with my existing anxieties, leaving me with a deep sense of disquiet that stays with me in the weeks and months to come. Somewhere in the midst of his insistent probing, I have an out-of-body experience. With each repetition, the drunk man's questions start to take on philosophical overtones. *Yes*, my exhausted body begins to think; *why* am *I here?*

A Translator's Love

Back on the doorstep, my hesitating knuckle is still dangling limply in the air. My other hand clutches a half-bitten self-critique cookie, one that has left a faint bitterness in my mouth. Standing paralyzed, my mind races through memories of the past, as I begin to doubt my suitability for the translator's task. Spivak talks of an intimacy with the other as necessary to translation, but what kind of love sits at the heart of my relation, I wonder? Do I have access to the joys of love?

Reflecting on my scene of translation, I think of the infectious zeal with which Gregory Veeck offers useful tips and tricks picked up on his journey learning Chinese, and the palpable joy with which he writes about his annual research field trips and working toward "a lifelong goal of retiring to a small village in China to grow vegetables while my grandchildren run fat and happy in the fields of northern Jiangsu" (Veeck 2001, 35). Unable to relate, I turn instead to Ien Ang, a Dutch-Australian scholar of Chinese-Indonesian descent, as she explains how "I did not quite have the freedom to see this country as exotic because I have always had to see it as somehow my country, even if only in my imagination" (Ang 2001, 23). I empathize with Yi-Fu Tuan, as he reflects on how, "in the United States, I am seen as a hyphenated American," darkly joking that a "hyphenated American is one who seeks to have the hyphen dropped so as to become simply an American" (Tuan 2007, 160).

If translation involves the surrender to love, and love requires an enduring scene of desire, then what kind of anchor might sustain my impulse to cleave to my Chinese other? Perhaps there *is* a compelling case to be made for moods of enchantment as a fundamental part of healthy scholarly endeavor; that is, that one might indeed desire an affirmative disposition to their objects of interest, not just for the capacity-enhancing productivity of joy, but as ballast against the subjection of sustaining an attachment. Perhaps this is easy for others, in a way that has never felt unconflictingly possible for me. *Maybe I am just not the right person for the job.*

But then, rather than isolating love as a simple issue of object-attachment—a matter of just you and me—Berlant suggests that it may be more helpful to look "at the whole field of what it takes to sustain an attachment to the world" (2011, 687). In that case, perhaps the translator's desire might rub up on other convictions and solidarities that might see one through. As scholars, this might lead back to the role of their discipline and its institutions in providing the love that would close the loop of reciprocity—as a love triangle not a pair, because one might not be drawn so intensely into this relation, at least partly, if not for one's profession. But what remains to say on this matter, when everything that needs to be said feels like it has already been said under "neoliberal university" (Caretta et al. 2018; Mountz et al. 2015). That is, however, only the more deserving side of the story, the one I can confidently file under "structural." Shadowing these worries are uglier feelings. Perhaps I am just selfishly looking for a cover to justify an unwillingness to find the time to properly learn another's language and rhetoric. Or, maybe, my hesitation is merely borne of enduring habits of racialized aversion and desire, ones which I admit remain hard for me to shake. Who gets intuitive access to the joys of love, I wonder? It is really a matter of will and choice, or is there more to it? *Maybe I really am just not the right person for the job.*

If critique as reflexive self-critique is about opening to scrutiny the lived circumstances of the body, then from this vantage point I can finally pinpoint the source of my instinctive reluctance to Spivak's task for the translator: I recognize that I am insufficiently prepared to translate, but also hesitant to undertake the labor of preparation, glimpsing the fraught emotional territory I am asking myself to traverse; uncertain from where I might draw the desire for that task; wondering "why bother?" given the precarious future ahead. Piece by piece, a pessimistic domino show becomes set up before me, as my sense of failure threatens to turn into fatality, a fatality that stands a whisper from futility (Thacker 2015, 14). All that is left, it seems, are two conflicting bad choices: to undertake a reluctant, perilous surrender, or to give up the task, to exit the theater, to wake up from the dream. I am caught in the middle.

The Double Bind, or, a Training in Love

Facing the ambivalence of my experiential juncture, I find myself at the forking of two paths that split the "wedding ring" of affirmation's double "yes." Laying out affirmation's logical structure, Harrison explains that the second "yes" of affirmation—the affirmation of affirmation—is the "yes" of *amor fati*, Nietzsche's love of fate. Associated with a stoic stance, it is a domestication of acceptance, a move to affective resolution, a small kind of mastery. Crucially, to read such an affirmation through the logic of choice is to misread its nature, as *amor fati* is founded not on sovereign will but is rather an existential state of grace. Although *amor fati* requires one's participation, one cannot *choose* to be touched by it: "Simply put, I cannot will myself to love what I do not, just as I may not choose what I do love" (Harrison 2015, 292). Rather than regulate what may or may not be worthy of affirmation, Harrison draws attention to the sacrificial economy at its heart: that for there to be a winner (she who can affirm that before her), there must also be a loser (she who cannot); for there to be life, there must also be death. At the heart of affirmation's doubled celebration is a "bio-will-to-power," an "active forgetting" that, by deciding "what can be dispatched without consequence" in an act of liberation for *some*, rushes to ignore the fuel to its flame—that, in order to affirm, "something or someone has been forgotten, disavowed, or sacrificed" (Harrison 2015, 297). Put differently, as Daniel Cockayne and Derek Ruez (2018) suggest, "affirmative critique often ignores those who are unable to situate themselves as joyful in the face of the violences of representational politics encountered in research and everyday life" (n.p.).

Finding myself unable to love the translator's fate, I am unable to accede to the second yes of affirmation, in an unfortunate scenario where the conditions of my past do not allow my two yesses to easily coincide. At play here are two versions of love: love of the other and love of the self. As Eleanor Wilkinson notes, self-love has been a vital source of survival to many feminist, queer, and critical race scholars, as an "act of withdrawal recognizes the need for safe space, and acknowledges that attempts to create connections across difference can often be a painful and dangerous task" (2017, 61). Self-love has been, and remains, utterly vital. But self-love is not a relation to an other. It can be fundamental in paving the way there, by providing endurance for the depleted self, but it does not itself replace the work of striving toward a relation if that is what one hopes to achieve. The latter remains the task to come, a possibility that resides in the necessary act of exposure, in the risk of a new relationality. Without the good fortune of a second yes to that by which I might nonetheless prefer to *abide* (see Jazeel 2018), the translator's task presents me with an unenviable double bind: hesitating between an affirmable desire to protect the self and an unaffirmable desire to surrender to the other.

Trapped between two languages, two paradigms, two paths, two loves, I am in a double bind. Spivak explains that "when we find ourselves in the subject position of two determinate decisions, both right (or both wrong), one of which cancels the other, we are in an aporia, which by definition cannot be crossed, or a double bind" (2012, 104). As an aesthetic experience, one enters the double bind before one recognizes it; it is a communicational matrix that demands neither your consent nor your affirmation. A double bind cannot be solved through synthesis or compromise, nor can it be exited without that "exit" constituting a choice in itself. As a device for thought, the double bind does not exist to prescribe the "correct" path, as if one were possible in advance; rather, it functions to illuminate the stakes of the decision, where responding to one message will preclude responding effectively to the other. The double bind is interested not in the a priori affirmation, but, rather, in the *immanent decision*, in the ongoing training of one's *own* ethical reflexes. It discloses the contingency of the need to decide, in the regretful knowledge that something will go missing, one way or another.

Every love is different, but my love asks me to love a part of me that I have never loved. Perhaps the rhetoric of love can accommodate this ambivalence. It might even transform it. Either way, there is nothing to celebrate in the double bind's demand. After all, ethics cannot be suspended a priori; choices must be made, over and over and over again. Although I am unable to truly find solace in the terms set by affirmation, I have come to realize that this is not simply a personal failing. It is, instead, an artifact of the normative framing of affirmation—a framing that, grounded in idealizations of love, can ignore the more conflicted versions of love that bodies must come to endure and navigate, where love-of-the-other and love-of-the-self do not always coincide, and choices must be made between them. As Spivak continues, although the double bind offers no real sense of affective resolution, it emphasizes that roads must nonetheless be traveled, that decisions must be made: "For, as we know every day, even by supposedly not deciding, one of those two right or wrong decisions gets taken, and the aporia or double bind remains. Again, it must be insisted that this is the condition of possibility of deciding. In the aporia or the double bind, to decide is the burden of responsibility" (2012, 104–5).

Notes

I would like to thank Jingzhong Ye, Hong Zhu, Zhenjie Yuan, Effy Xing Qi, Ben Anderson, Paul Harrison, Sarah Knuth, and Mitch Rose for the hospitality they each showed me on the long journey across four continents that accompanied this chapter. My sincerest appreciation to David, Mitch, and Paul for encouragement and succor, to Ben, Danny Butt, and especially Thomas Jellis for thoughtful comments on drafts, to Lijianan Zhang for the joy of her company on field work, and to audiences at the "Public Moods" workshop in Durham and the "Negative Geographies" session at the 2019 AAG in Washington DC. I gratefully acknowledge the support of an Australian Government Research Training Place Scholarship, Endeavour Research Fellowship, and the University of Melbourne's Elizabeth and Vernon Puzey Scholarship.

1. Briefly translating this discussion into the Deleuzian terminology more familiar to cultural geographers, perhaps love is less about affirmation and more about learning. Drawing together Deleuze's disparate discussions on love, particularly in *Proust and Signs*, Timothy Laurie and Hannah Stark (2017) suggest that love for Deleuze involves an apprenticeship in signs. Love moves the subject beyond itself to *learn* about others, engendering a sensitivity to the depth and life of signs emitted by others "in worlds that we cannot always control and cannot completely know" (Laurie and Stark 2017, 75). Yet, Deleuze and Guattari also warn against too-rapid change. Advocating an "art of dosages, since overdose is a danger," they advise that "you don't [destratify the organism] with a sledgehammer, you use a very fine file" (Deleuze and Guattari 1987, 160). Love in Deleuze's writing might thus be seen as a more probing, experimental force that "should not be understood or mobilised as a sudden and violent certainty about the world. Love persists only through curiosity, through humility in the face of the unknown" (Laurie and Stark 2017, 76). As Harrison notes, however, there appears to be little room for reflexivity in Deleuze's ontology and version of the subject, because its version of life-as-becoming "destroys any prospect of reflective thinking, because it destroys any subject position in which to think" (Morgan 2007, 126, quoted in Harrison 2015, 301). Accordingly, it remains unclear what scope (or

ZHANG

desire) there is in current Deleuze-inspired geography for a style of love that is open to the insistent self-critique described by Spivak and foregrounded in this piece.

References

Anderson, Ben. 2006. "'Transcending without Transcendence': Utopianism and an Ethos of Hope." *Antipode* 38 (4): 691–710.

———. 2011. "Shame, Paranoia and Other Affects. In Forum: Sedgwick's Geographies: Touching Space." *Progress in Human Geography* 35 (1): 127–31.

Anderson, Ben, and Paul Harrison. 2009. *Taking-Place: Non-Representational Theories and Geography*. Surrey UK: Ashgate.

Ang, Ien. 2001. *On Not Speaking Chinese: Living Between Asia and the West*. London: Routledge.

Anker, Elizabeth S., and Rita Felski, eds. 2017. *Critique and Postcritique*. Durham NC: Duke University Press.

Askins, Kye, and Matej Blazek. 2017. "Feeling Our Way: Academia, Emotions and a Politics of Care." *Social & Cultural Geography* 18 (8): 1086–105.

Barthes, Roland. 2005. *The Neutral: Lecture Course at the Collège de France 1977–1978*. New York: Columbia University Press.

Bennett, Jane. 2001. *The Enchantment of Modern Life: Attachments, Crossings, and Ethics*. Princeton NJ: Princeton University Press.

Berlant, Lauren. 2011. "A PROPERLY POLITICAL CONCEPT OF LOVE: Three Approaches in Ten Pages." *Cultural Anthropology* 26 (4): 683–91.

———. 2012. *Desire/Love*. Brooklyn NY: Punctum.

Bondi, Liz. 2014. "Feeling Insecure: A Personal Account in a Psychoanalytic Voice." *Social & Cultural Geography* 15 (3): 332–50.

Brown, Gavin, Kath Browne, Michael Brown, Gerda Roelvink, Michelle Carnegie, and Ben Anderson. 2011. "Sedgwick's Geographies: Touching Space." *Progress in Human Geography* 35 (1): 121–31.

Caretta, Martina Angela, Danielle Drozdzewski, Johanna Carolina Jokinen, and Emily Falconer. 2018. "'Who Can Play This Game?' The Lived Experiences of Doctoral Candidates and Early Career Women in the Neoliberal University." *Journal of Geography in Higher Education* 42 (2): 261–75.

Cockayne, Daniel, and Derek Ruez. 2018. "From Affirmative to Ambivalent Critique: Difference, Politics, and the Possibility of the Plural." In *American Association of Geographers Annual Meeting 2018*. https://aag.secure-abstracts.com/AAG%20Annual%20Meeting%202018/abstracts-gallery/12581.

Colls, Rachel. 2012. "Feminism, Bodily Difference and Non-Representational Geographies." *Transactions of the Institute of British Geographers* 37 (3): 430–45.

Crane, L. G., M. B. Lombard, and E. M. Tenz. 2009. "More than Just Translation: Challenges and Opportunities in Translingual Research." *Social Geography* 4 (1): 39–46.

Cvetkovich, Ann. 2012. *Depression: A Public Feeling*. Durham NC: Duke University Press.

Deleuze, Gilles, and Félix Guattari. 1987. *A Thousand Plateaus: Capitalism and Schizophrenia*. Minneapolis: University of Minnesota Press.

Drozdzewski, Danielle. 2018. "'Less-than-Fluent' and Culturally Connected: Language Learning and Cultural Fluency as Research Methodology." *Area* 50 (1): 109–16.

Felski, Rita. 2015. *The Limits of Critique*. Chicago: University of Chicago Press.

Germes, Mélina, and Shadia Husseini de Araújo. 2016. "For a Critical Practice of Translation in Geography." *ACME: An International Journal for Critical Geographies* 15 (1): 1–14.

Halberstam, Jack. 2011. *The Queer Art of Failure*. Durham NC: Duke University Press.

Hancock, Claire. 2016. "Traduttore Traditore, the Translator as Traitor." *ACME: An International Journal for Critical Geographies* 15 (1): 15–35.

Harrison, Paul. 2015. "After Affirmation, or, Being a Loser: On Vitalism, Sacrifice, and Cinders." *GeoHumanities* 1 (2): 285–306.

Jazeel, Tariq. 2007. "Awkward Geographies: Spatializing Academic Responsibility, Encountering Sri Lanka." *Singapore Journal of Tropical Geography* 28 (3): 287–99.

———. 2014. "Subaltern Geographies: Geographical Knowledge and Postcolonial Strategy." *Singapore Journal of Tropical Geography* 35 (1): 88–103.

———. 2018. "Singularity. A Manifesto for Incomparable Geographies." *Singapore Journal of Tropical Geography* 40 (1): 5–21.

Kapoor, Ilan. 2004. "Hyper-self-reflexive Development? Spivak on Representing the Third World 'Other.'" *Third World Quarterly* 25 (4): 627–47.

Krzywoszynska, Anna. 2015. "On Being a Foreign Body in the Field, or How Reflexivity around Translation Can Take Us beyond Language." *Area* 47 (3): 311–18.

Latour, Bruno. 2004. "Why Has Critique Run out of Steam? From Matters of Fact to Matters of Concern." *Critical Inquiry* 30 (2): 225–48.

Laurie, Timothy, and Hannah Stark. 2017. Love's Lessons: Intimacy, Pedagogy, and Political Community. *Angelaki* 22 (4): 69–79.

Mahtani, Minelle. 2014. "Toxic Geographies: Absences in Critical Race Thought and Practice in Social and Cultural Geography." *Social & Cultural Geography* 15 (4): 359–67.

Massumi, Brian. 2015. *Politics of Affect*. Cambridge UK: Polity.

Mountz, Alison, Anne Bonds, Becky Mansfield, Jenna Loyd, Jennifer Hyndman, Margaret Walton-Roberts, Ranu Basu, Risa Whitson, Roberta Hawkins, and Trina Hamilton. 2015. "For Slow Scholarship: A Feminist Politics of Resistance through Collective Action in the Neoliberal University." *ACME: An International Journal for Critical Geographies* 14 (4): 1235–59.

Muñoz, José Esteban. 2006. "Feeling Brown, Feeling Down: Latina Affect, the Performativity of Race, and the Depressive Position." *Signs: Journal of Women in Culture and Society* 31 (3): 675–88.

Ngai, Sianne. 2004. *Ugly Feelings*. Cambridge MA: Harvard University Press.

Noxolo, Patricia. 2009. "'My Paper, My Paper': Reflections on the Embodied Production of Postcolonial Geographical Responsibility in Academic Writing." *Geoforum* 40 (1): 55–65.

Noys, Benjamin. 2010. *The Persistence of the Negative: A Critique of Contemporary Continental Theory*. Edinburgh: Edinburgh University Press.

Osborne, Natalie. 2019. "For Still Possible Cities: A Politics of Failure for the Politically Depressed." *Australian Geographer* 50 (2): 145–54.

Pedwell, Carolyn. 2014. "Cultural Theory as Mood Work." *New Formations* 82:47–63.

Philo, Chris. 2017. "Less-than-Human Geographies." *Political Geography* 60:256–58.

Probyn, Elspeth. 2005. *Blush: Faces of Shame*. Minneapolis: University of Minnesota Press.

Proudfoot, Jesse. 2015. "Anxiety and Phantasy in the Field: The Position of the Unconscious in Ethnographic Research." *Environment and Planning D: Society and Space* 33 (6): 1135–52.

Rose, Mitch. 2016. "A Place for Other Stories: Authorship and Evidence in Experimental Times." *GeoHumanities* 2 (1): 132–48.

Secor, Anna, and Jess Linz. 2017. "Becoming Minor." *Environment and Planning D: Society and Space* 35 (4): 568–73.

Sedgwick, Eve Kosofsky. 2003. "Paranoid Reading and Reparative Reading, or, You're So Paranoid, You Probably Think This Essay Is About You." In *Touching Feeling: Affect, Pedagogy, Performativity*, 123–51. Durham NC: Duke University Press.

Sedgwick, Eve Kosofsky, and Adam Frank. 1995. "Shame in the Cybernetic Fold: Reading Silvan Tomkins." *Critical Inquiry* 21 (2): 496–522.

Sidaway, James D., Tim Bunnell, Carl Grundy-Warr, Robina Mohammad, Bae-Gyoon Park, and Asato Saito. 2004. "Translating Political Geographies." *Political Geography* 23 (8): 1037–49.

Spivak, Gayatri Chakravorty. 1988. "Can the Subaltern Speak?" In *Marxism and the Interpretation of Culture*, edited by Cary Nelson and Lawrence Grossberg, 271–313. Basingstoke UK: Macmillan.

———. 1999. *A Critique of Postcolonial Reason*. Cambridge MA: Harvard University Press.

———. 2009. "The Politics of Translation." In *Outside in the Teaching Machine*, 200–225. New York: Routledge.

———. 2012. *An Aesthetic Education in the Era of Globalization*. Cambridge MA: Harvard University Press.

Stewart, Kathleen. 2007. *Ordinary Affects*. Durham NC: Duke University Press.

Thacker, Eugene. 2015. *Cosmic Pessimism*. Minneapolis: Univocal.

Thrift, Nigel. 2008. *Non-Representational Theory: Space, Politics, Affect*. London: Routledge.

Thrift, Nigel, and John-David Dewsbury. 2000. "Dead Geographies—And How to Make Them Live." *Environment and Planning D: Society and Space* 18 (4): 411–32.

Tuan, Yi-Fu. 2007. *Coming Home to China*. Minneapolis: University of Minnesota Press.

Veeck, Gregory. 2001. "Talk Is Cheap: Cultural and Linguistic Fluency during Field Research." *Geographical Review* 91 (1/2): 34.

Watson, Elizabeth E. 2004. "'What a Dolt One Is': Language Learning and Fieldwork in Geography." *Area* 36 (1): 59–68.

Whatmore, Sarah. 2006. "Materialist Returns: Practising Cultural Geography in and for a More-than-Human World." *cultural geographies* 13 (4): 600–609.

Wiegman, Robyn. 2014. "The Times We're In: Queer Feminist Criticism and the Reparative 'Turn.'" *Feminist Theory* 15 (1): 4–25.

Wilkinson, Eleanor. 2017. "On Love as an (Im)properly Political Concept." *Environment and Planning D: Society and Space* 35 (1): 57–71.

Wilkinson, Eleanor, and Iliana Ortega-Alcázar. 2019. "The Right to Be Weary? Endurance and Exhaustion in Austere Times." *Transactions of the Institute of British Geographers* 44 (1): 155–67.

Woodyer, Tara, and Hilary Geoghegan. 2013. "(Re)enchanting Geography? The Nature of Being Critical and the Character of Critique in Human Geography." *Progress in Human Geography* 37 (2): 195–214.

ZHANG

5 The Politics of Volunteering in Loss and at a Loss

Autobiographical Reflections on Grief, Vulnerability, and (In)Action

Avril Maddrell

Many people think that grief is privatizing, that it returns us to a solitary situation and is, in that sense depoliticizing. But I think it furnishes a sense of political community of a complex order, and it does this first of all by bringing to the fore the relational ties that have implications for theorizing fundamental dependency and ethical responsibility.

—Judith Butler, *Precarious Life*

Introduction

This volume explores how events of rupture, exhaustion, interruption, hesitancy, and loss can be recognized as a component of our political inclinations and engagements. In relation to the first part of this agenda Romanillos asks, "Are contemporary geographical imaginations able adequately to address those difficult, if unfashionable, mortal conditions of vulnerability, decline and exposure—to those geographies on the other side of life? . . . . to grasp or apprehend the agonized face, the exposed, absent or vulnerable body" (Romanillos 2015, 574). The answer to this is yes, or at least a partial yes, especially through sensitive critical studies of embodied-emotional-affective geographies. As part of that "yes," my own work on the spatialities, places, landscapes, and practices of death, mourning, remembrance, and living with loss, addresses what many see as the ultimate negatives of mortality and bereavement. Here, I bring into dialogue experience-grounded research on grief and volunteering, exploring their relationality and analyzing these fields through the lens of feminist theory and methods, notably Judith Butler's work on the politics of loss and precarity and Pamela Moss on intimate writing as a research method. This chapter scopes the varied politics of inaction and being in-action in the face of everyday death and bereavement and is situated in the meshing of more-than-representational experiences, practices, and beliefs, particularly the emotional-affective, and feminist geographies, which draw attention to the politics of embodiment, the personal, relationality, the everyday, and the domestic. My aspiration is to build on what has been identified in this work as "an attunement to the ways in which our lives are sutured and shaped, made and undone, through different kinds of negativity" (Romanillos 2015, 575; see Maddrell 2013) and to suture this, in turn, to the political. At first glance, the negative impacts of death and bereavement have all the hallmarks of disempowerment, and this is indeed the experience of many in the face of the inevitability of the march of time, an incurable life-shortening illness, a tragic accident, the erosion of malnourishment, the excoriation of war or famine. Yet death and grief can, in some circumstances, be shaped by agency. Death itself can be a political act, and those facing death can act politically in relation to the timing and means of death, or their bodily disposal, exemplified by contemporary advocacy in the United Kingdom for ecoburials and legal test cases in support of euthanasia, access to new drugs, or open air pyres. Thus, even the everyday death and the disposition of "ordinary" people can be (bio)political: the personal is political and politics are personal; they blur the public-private divide (Hanisch [1969] 2006; Wastl-Walter and Staeheli 2004). Furthermore, the embodied is not just (bio)political, it is geopolitical (Fluri and Piedalue 2017): geopolitics link international power relations and local services, local lives, local deaths (see Maddrell and Sidaway 2010). Likewise, those confronted by loss may respond in ways that ignite or catalyze new agencies, prompting lobbying or activism as part of their wayfinding in living with that loss—not least in the face of injustice, violence, or tragedy, whether personal, local, national, or international.

In this chapter, I draw on my own experiences of bereavement and volunteering as a lens through which to analyze the relation between the negative of loss, inaction, and impotence in the face of finitude, and the politics of subsequent inaction and acting, being in-action. Feminist analyses show everyday (in)actions to be both more political and more potent than is often acknowledged within public discourse and academic debate. Here, I aim to extend understanding of what constitutes the political through the interrogation of a particular confluence of grief and volunteering via an autobiographical account. Grounded in part in phenomenological traditions and rooted in a wealth of feminist and queer studies of embodiment and emotional-affective experiences, autobiographical approaches and work on intimate experience (Valentine 2008; Moss 2017; Moss and Donovan 2017) can incorporate and shed light on both individual and collective experience and agenda (Falconer Al-Hindi et al. 2017). Although a rich and burgeoning area of qualitative scholarship, this approach, nonetheless, represents a particular methodological and ontological politics within the context of academic writing. Thus, autobiographical writing can itself be a political act: through an insistence on the validity of the personal and a refusal to silence or abstract the experiential, and through an assertion of the conceptual purchase of the intimate and the analytical potential of writing autobiographically. As Donovan and Moss (2017, 4) note: "Writing as an analytical method especially warrants attention, for it is through writing (which can be an intimate act itself) that intimacies of everyday living may be brought into dialogue with how to access and work with emotions and affect ethically and politically." This meshing of personal experience with reflective and analytical writing can powerfully connect the personal-emotional-affective-embodied-existential with the relational-collective-socioeconomic-political, as illustrated by Madge's (2016, 2017) interrogations of pregnancy and life-threatening illness explored through intimate diaries, poetry, and photography. However, despite growing recognition of the value of such corporeal and relational ontologies associated with Braidotti's (1994) researcher as nomadic processual subject, with all its messiness and rawness, autobiographical work has personal and professional risks inherent in sharing, exposing, vulnerabilities in an academic context (see Maddrell and Olson 2019; Mountz et al. 2015). Autobiographical work also risks the appearance of privileged or indulgent self-reflection (Donovan and Moss 2017), but at the same time encompasses the "productive potential of intimacy" (Moss and Donovan 2017, 232). It is this productive potential of intimate autobiographical material, in sociocultural as well as intellectual arenas, which makes the risks associated with sharing vulnerabilities worthwhile, in professional and other contexts.

Before turning to an autobiographical fragment, some reflections on death, bereavement, impotence, action, and inaction that set the scene for that experiential account.

Reflections on Impotence, Action, and Politics in the Face of Everyday Loss

Death and grief are personal embodied emotional-affective experiences which also impact on others, human and nonhuman. As Judith Butler (2006) explains, "we are implicated in lives that are not our own" (26) and this creates "a vulnerability to a sudden address from elsewhere that we cannot pre-empt" (29). Reflecting on impotent inaction in the face of brutality to animals observed during research, Garcia (2019, 50) argues for a transition "from politics of disavowal to an ethics of avowal." This interplay of tragedy-impotence-action is also at the heart of Butler's (2006) *Precarious Life* and of Solnit's (2004) *Hope in the Dark*, both responses to post-9/11 U.S. geopolitics and the war in Iraq, which offer, in turn, insights into more "everyday" contexts of loss and carrying on.

The term "impotence" is overwhelmingly associated with sexual incapacity in Western society. This medical condition is associated variously with physiological and psychological disease, dying, and bereavement (e.g., treatment for prostate cancer or depression), but a more generalized sense of personal impotence is experienced by individuals, families, communities, and professionals in the face of certain illnesses and deaths, notably suicide, homicide, accidents, untreatable conditions, miscarriage, and what are deemed to be "untimely" deaths, especially of the young or vulnerable. Ann Varley's (2008) eloquent account of parental dementia and the loss of home also highlights the processual nature of predeath grieving in such circumstances. In such cases, impotence centers on being confronted by mortality and a disempowering and disabling inability to act or change the situation. This sense of impotence frequently underscores grief, whether that grief is triggered by events in the distant international arena or experienced close to home. Such experiences of loss can engender a sense of liminality, of being on a threshold, caught in suspension, betwixt and between; ruptures creating new fissures, apertures, and mobilities, offering different viewpoints, openings, and choices, new ways of being and moving forward (see Maddrell 2009).

While understanding death in extraordinary circumstances is highly important, and weighty work has been done on extraordinary events and sites of death (e.g., Foote 2003; Knowles, Cole, and Giordano 2014), the everyday is also important, also political. As the work of Staeheli et al. (2012) makes plain, the complexities of citizenship are worked out and best understood in daily life and experience. This leads us to the personal and collective politics of "everyday" First World bereavement, grief, and (in)action. In focusing on the "everyday," this chapter explores aspects of loss, vulnerability, impotence, and agential acting and inaction, which, in turn, prompts reflections on the politics of action and resilience through volunteering in vulnerability. Just as Butler called for considered action, rather than ill-considered re-action in the international arena, this is a commentary on the intersections of personal inaction, of being immobilized by grief, experiencing enforced hiatus, and when grief calls for action, or compels certain sorts of being in-action.

First, an autobiographical reflection on loss and carrying on. This piece is not a diary extract—it was written retrospectively and is therefore inevitably characterized by processes of framing, sieving, and editing. Nonetheless, and despite the passage of time, there is an emotional charge in writing and sharing this piece, and the reading of it may also be emotionally charged. This is hardly surprising given that such intimate writing is a form of memorialization for the deceased (Henkin 2017).

Seventeen Babies a Day—in Loss and at a Loss

My work on the emotional-affective geographies of death, the spatial practices and politics of death, dying, and bereavement, mourning, and remembrance grew out of my own and my family's experience of bereavement as
a result of deaths across three generations in a period of about eighteen
months, the last being the stillbirth at term of our second child. This
already beloved child, the much-vaunted sibling for our first, another child
whose imminent birth had been a sign of hope in our already grief-stricken
extended family, had died in utero. We were impotent in the face of the
death of our child, but we had to act. I had to give birth. Birth is not passive, "labor" never an adequate term, even for the best of births, the task
of giving birth to a beloved-but-deceased, impossible, but necessary. An
experience of overwhelming pain and grief. A recurring sense of incredu-
lity that nothing could be done, mixed with brief moments of consolation.
A precious lock of dark hair and prints of feet and hands, all we could take
home. The gaping hole in our lives more than the presence of an absence.

Previously confident in bodily capabilities, in maternity health care, we
lost our innocence—naivety—about antenatal and postnatal death in rich
countries like ours. Given a leaflet from the SANDS (Stillbirth and Neonatal
Death Society) charity, we discovered that, rather than an experience
consigned to Victorian melodramas or conditions of extreme poverty,
seventeen babies a day died in the United Kingdom before, during, or
shortly after birth.[1] The risks of miscarriage in the first trimester of pregnancy are well known (if not always discussed); the risks associated
with the final weeks of pregnancy are typically deemed as information
unnecessary for parents to know: "It will only cause worry." Likewise,
only after the event was the social silence around stillbirth broken, as
we were repeatedly told, "It happened to my friend / cousin / neighbor."

Mourning oscillated between utter immobilization and the performative
mobilities of ritual and relationality. We were eviscerated by loss, and at
a loss. We entered a liminal phase, on maternity-paternity leave without
a baby; loving our firstborn, but suffering from an excess of parenthood.

With support from family, friends, colleagues, and health-care professionals, we carried on. Vital support also came from strangers. Other

parents who had experienced a similar loss became intimate confidantes; support group meetings, an oasis of mutual understanding. While still in loss and at a loss, we in turn joined the ranks of the small volunteer committee running a county branch of SANDS, in part as a memorial to our beloved, but also reflecting a desire to give to others, to return and perpetuate the support we had benefited from within this dynamic community of loss. This sense of obligation to others required action when we were mired in the inertia of a consuming grief. Working with others we undertook training, hosted support groups, organized the local group's annual service of remembrance, contributed to practitioner training, lobbied, and coordinated fund-raising sales and awareness-raising events.

Still holding on, in time, we were ultimately blessed by the live birth of our third child—thanks in no small part to NHS specialist antenatal care and timely intervention.

Living with and through the interleaved emotions of joy, grief, and much between, life at this time was further complicated by professional uncertainty. Having stepped down from a permanent academic post "for a year" in order to prioritize recalibrating our new family life with the youngest, five years went by in the hypercompetitive, neoliberalizing UK university sector. Professionally I subsisted on hourly paid lecturing, a short-term fractional teaching contract, and some small research grants before finally being offered a permanent post again. During this prolonged process, including numerous applications and rejections, professional vulnerability intermeshed with, and compounded and complicated, ongoing processes of grieving.

Meanwhile, as a volunteer SANDS "befriender," activities included peer-to-peer support by phone, hosting meetings in our home, and making home visits to newly bereaved parents across the county. These phone calls, meetings, and visits were not without cost: emotional exhaustion and interrupted or missed meals, family time, professional work. But when recently bereaved parents told me that talking with someone who had shared the experience helped them face the rest of the day, gave them hope that they might "get through," or that they had a new sense of the possibility of a tenable future they could move toward, I knew, without doubt, that this was some of the most important "work" I would ever do.

This brief autobiographical narrative does not seek to exaggerate our loss, which is sadly common in many parts of the world, nor lionize what was modest voluntary work. The history of the SANDS charity testifies to the *extraordinary* work the founders undertook for years in order to achieve legislative and health-care-practice changes, as well as establishing a national charity, peer support networks, and educational materials. Likewise, professional precarity is a reality for many in academia, especially early career scholars (see, for example, Caretta and Webster 2016). Rather, my intention is to share the ways in which I-we are undone by grief and how the competent can be disempowered and made impotent when confronted by finitude and loss; to understand bereavement as something that can both stall and catalyze action as well as to affirm the power of shared relational experience. As Butler notes, grief lays bare our relation to others and our imaginaries of self "in ways that challenge the very notion of ourselves as autonomous and in control . . . Let's face it. We are undone by each other. *And if we're not we're missing something*" (Butler 2006, 23, my emphasis). As outlined above, this "undoing" reflects my own experience and exemplifies a personal time-space of ontological insecurity, brought about by the disorder of loss and uncontrollable events (Giddens 1991). Elsewhere I have alluded to the seismic ruptures this loss engendered, the emotional and ontological flux that "shocked me to my core and made me question everything about my beliefs, world view and life-decisions" (Maddrell 2016, 3). Bereavement represents one of Giddens's "fateful moments" when self-identity is forged through the interplay of structure and agency, action and inaction, and, under certain conditions, creates ontological insecurity, prompting people to "question the meaningfulness and reality of the social frameworks in which they participate" (Mellor 1992, 13).

My hope is that this autobiographical fragment, for all its limitations, speaks of, and to, the inevitable vulnerabilities of bereavement per se, signals something of the imbricated nature of the living and the dead, a relationality that is dynamically mapped onto who we are, our habitus, and who constitutes our community (Maddrell 2013, 2016). Furthermore, that it illustrates a relational braiding of negative and positive, woven through, held together, by simply carrying on, learning to live with loss through the reconfigured embodied material, emotional-affective, and spiritual space-time, shaped by old and new relationalities and practices. This was to see the world and one's relational place in it afresh, to know, as Derrida (2001) points out, that some losses are part of your life "right unto" your own death; they are more than inscribed on the surface, they reshape the genetic code of personhood. What shows on the surface reflects changes in the physical-emotional-psychological core of individual identity and communities:

> For some mourners and some deaths, grief is a mantle worn for a season and then shed in due course, for other mourners and other deaths, grief is both inhabited and inhabiting, strands of which can be woven into one's very being, forever changing emotional and affective DNA, shaping and influencing experience of the world. This is not to essentialize grief or the bereaved as grief-stricken and incapacitated, not least as grief can be an inspiration and catalyst, but rather to recognize the intertwining of loss in one's ever-emerging self and relations with others, as well as places and practices. (Maddrell 2016, 172)

Benefiting from and contributing to a voluntary support group were central threads to my experience of loss, and the following section explores the relationship between volunteering and bereavement in more detail, before reflecting on the political citizenship of volunteering activities such as this as an example of a "politics of the negative."

Volunteering in the Face of Impotence and Finitude

> If we stay with the sense of loss, are we left feeling only
> passive and powerless, as some might fear? Or are we, rather,
> returned to a sense of human vulnerability, to our collective
> responsibility for the physical [and emotional] lives of one
> another?
> —Butler, *Precarious Life*

Voluntarism is typically seen as mediating between state services and the market, with acts of volunteer work being undertaken through formal and informal routes, the former being associated with the structures of a voluntary organization, and the latter, outside of any such structures (Milligan and Conradson 2006). These activities are also emplaced, and geographers have paid attention to the varying character and operations of the voluntary sector in particular localities and regions (Conradson and Milligan 2006), with more recent attention being given to the embodied experience of volunteers (Griffiths and Brown 2017). This last work, drawing on Gibson-Graham's (2008, 8) conceptualization of volunteering as a "performative ontological project," meshes with the discussion above on intimate research writing as a form of corporeal relational ontology. Indeed, voluntary work can be identified as a form of making, (re)positioning, and "writing" self, and writing *about* self is an effective way to ethically and politically reflect on the emotional-affective meanings and cadences of that process.

Associated with altruism, although in reality often representing more a complex interrelation of reciprocal benefits, volunteering per se is typically prompted by dynamic assemblages of intersecting personal and communal motivations including a desire to support a specific cause, to help others, to use as a stepping-stone toward paid work, and to address social isolation, loneliness, or a sense of lack of purpose (see for example, Goeke 2019; Maddrell 2000; Veludo-de-Oliveira, Pallister, and Foxall 2015). Bereavement is known to stimulate explicit activism (Maddrell 2013), for example, campaigns for improved road safety and drug awareness, increased funding for medical research, and campaigns against death in police custody. Less well-known is the relationship between bereavement and volunteering. Bereavement has been identified as a key motivation for volunteering in two key ways: firstly, for personal therapeutic benefits, as reported by volunteers in charity shops/thrift stores and in the hospice sector (see below), and secondly, some bereaved volunteers are inspired to support medical research or hospice fund-raising shops because of a family association with a particular disease or end-of-life care service: "I lost both of my parents to cancer, so it is close to my heart" (Volunteer 16, Shop Q, Oxford) (Maddrell 2000, 130). However, bereaved volunteers and their contribution to the voluntary sector remain an understudied cohort (Scott, Butler, and Wilson 2017, 55). More detailed studies of the motivations, experiences, and contributions of those volunteering in response to bereavement are merited, and this chapter can be seen as a contribution toward addressing this lacuna, as well as a response to calls for biographically situated and "more lively and creative" accounts of the forms and experiences of voluntary activities, participation, and social action (Conradson 2003; Milligan, Kearns, and Kyle 2009; Smith et al. 2010).

The bereaved also do significant voluntary work to support others who are bereaved. An examination of support services for the bereaved shows that as much as 80 percent of such services are provided by the voluntary sector (Osterfield 2009); and further, that the overwhelming majority of these services are provided by volunteers (Scott et al. 2017). Emerging studies show that bereaved people are central to the network of volunteers that offer support to the dying and bereaved, notably through work in hospices and bereavement support services. This is exemplified by a study of Cruse Scotland bereavement charity volunteers, which revealed that the predominant reason for volunteering was their own experience of bereavement. Echoing my own experience, one volunteer in this study attested, "It gives me the chance to meet new people. It gives me a purpose. It allows me to help people through something I've experienced myself and found impossibly difficult—losing someone you love through bereavement" (Volunteer 18; Scott et al. 2017, 57). While some individuals have gained a public profile for their heroic fund-raising and campaigning in response to their own life-limiting conditions or bereavement, most volunteering undertaken in this context is "under the radar" of public attention. Occasionally such everyday practices are given a spotlight in the mainstream media for the purposes of awareness-raising, as was the case of Christine Grew, whose experience of volunteering for a local hospice was published in a popular women's magazine to promote the "Open Up Hospice Care" campaign. Christine's account, entitled "It's Wonderful to Give Something Back" (Wooton 2017), outlined the interrelated experience of hospice care for her late husband and herself and her subsequent contribution as a volunteer at the hospice.

These narratives are also found in a recent international study examining the relationship between grief and hospice volunteer work, which offers some useful findings that are relevant to the following discussion. Firstly, it challenges the frequent assumption made by charities (including many hospices) that one's own grief must reach a stage of "resolution" before it is possible to offer support to others; instead, volunteering in a hospice is identified as a potential "pathway" *through* grief for some bereaved folk. Secondly, it reveals that bereavement can trigger an expansion of the self and be a biographical turning point that inspires social responsibility and activism (Baugher 2015), that is, to contribute to addressing wider social, economic, and political needs. These existential shifts center on discovering and developing caring capacities and emotional capital, transforming suffering and extending compassion through a sense of continuing bonds with the dead (see Klass, Silverman, and Nickman 1996), and grief-triggered self-reflection and learning (Baugher 2015). Seeing these responses as a "silver lining" to the negative of loss is a simplistic response to be resisted, not least because motivations and experiences can be complicated and messy. Nonetheless, "experiences of grieving are transformative for many because of the unique opportunities the death of a loved one creates for developing caring capacities and for wondering more deeply about impermanence, mortality and human connectedness" (Baugher 2015, 309).

While volunteering is often characterized in terms of altruism, or may be seen in terms of Mauss's (1967) economy of gifting, in addition to the more symbiotic exchanges and reciprocal benefits discussed above, many forms and acts of volunteering can also be seen as an *everyday politics of gifting* that interweaves action, education, campaigning for change, and social networks of support. Political analysis of volunteering has tended to focus on the mediating role of the third sector, or the politics of funding, which reflects a common underestimation of volunteering as less-than-activism and less-than-political. This can be seen in the work of Eliasoph (2013), who separates volunteering from activism, characterizing the latter as informed and informing campaigning for social, environmental, and political change, as opposed to largely unreflective and uncritical volunteering, which aims simply to address a shortfall in society through action. However, such constructions of activism as political and volunteering as nonpolitical represents a dichotomy grounded in particular U.S. socioeconomic, cultural-political relations. Moreover, even in the United States this dichotomy is oversimplified—and highly gendered—not least in a society where political activity has commonly been constructed as "unfeminine," causing many middle-class women involved in public service activities to eschew the term "political" (Blackstone 2004). Detailed examination of U.S. women's cancer charities highlights how activism is a complex concept and practice, one that is often blurred with, rather than distinct from, volunteering and social networks (Blackstone 2004). In this context even those who eschew the label of "political" or "activist" undertake meaning-making work, education, and empowerment activities and campaign for change; that is, they embody and practice many of the attributes of political activism.

While some definitions firmly situate activism within the arena of "*vigorous campaigning*" (*Oxford Dictionary* 2017, italics added), others provide a wider meaning: "Activism is the process of campaigning in public *or working for an organization in order to bring about political or social change*" (*Collins Dictionary* 2017, italics added). Contrary to traditional definitions of activism as a form of staged public and typically collective behavior, feminist and allied approaches underscore the "quiet politics" of activism (Askins 2011, 2015; Pain 2014) and the "implicit activism" (Horton and Kraftl 2009) of small resistances in mundane contexts, private and public. Thus, attention to the arena of local and domestic volunteering evidences the slippage between activism and volunteering, further challenging simplistic notions of these activities as political and nonpolitical, respectively. Significant to the discussion here, wider definitions of activism include *working for* social and political change (albeit through an organization and in public, both of which might be further debated). Crucially, these wider definitions accommodate the recognition of volunteer work as a *political act*, and as a form of *activism* per se. Returning to my own experience, what started out as peer-to-peer support group activities centered on the domestic spaces of homes and personal phones, came to include public awareness-raising and fund-raising events, contributing to training sessions for health-care professionals, and the local support group being part of a consultation process underpinning an update of national practitioner guidelines. While the group's chair, I was also called upon to mediate between distraught parents and local authority cemetery managers over the removal and disposal of memorial artifacts from children's graves. This led to being consulted by, and misquoted in, the local press on this matter, which inevitably required further mediation and conflict resolution between the parties involved. This is a small illustration of some of the ways in which apparently less-overtly political acts, such as informal "domestic" volunteering, what might be described as an act of everyday "ordinary citizenship" (Staeheli et al. 2012), can become highly public and implicitly-explicitly political, whether in the form of "*quiet campaigning,*" service-based *acti*vism, or conflict resolution, that in turn can influence everyday lives, professional practices, sociocultural understanding, and even policy.

Conclusion

> To foreclose vulnerability . . . is to eradicate one of the most
> important resources from which we must take our bearings
> and find our way.
> —Butler, *Precarious Life*

This chapter, centered on the meshing of autobiographical experience as research resource and broader research on bereavement and on volunteering, has sought to exemplify ways in which "life transitions—birth, death, trauma and illness—amplify the transformative potential of embodied knowledge" (Moss and Donovan 2017, 233); it has explored the value of—and possible need for—autobiographical interrogation, in order to situate knowledge (Haraway 1988), but also as an ethical form of experiential interrogation; and has shown how the "productive potential of intimacy" and intimate writing, with its intertwined politics of disclosure-exposure-vulnerability has, through its generative ontology, the potential for transformative affirmative politics (Moss and Donovan 2017, 232). This chapter has also illustrated how what might be described as intimate and relational *volunteering-alongside*, such as bereavement support to others while being in and working through bereavement oneself, challenges many of the assumed binaries associated with voluntary work, public and private space and actions, and the nature of the political, particularly in evidencing a particular form of implicit activism. It has also exemplified how autobiographical examination of key intimate life cycle events and processes, such as death and bereavement, shed light on highly significant but relatively neglected sites and experiences of the politics of the negative. These arguments underscore calls to accept the amorphous and ambiguous nature of political engagements. Bereavement-inspired political engagements, with all their intimate embodied vulnerabilities and spatial-temporal contingencies at the overlap of personal-public, can clearly contribute to Butler's ambition to achieve "an alternative framing of mourning as a resource for democratic politics" (McIvor 2012, 410).

Butler stresses both the importance and limitations of relationality, the ways we are undone by our relation to others, but also how we are also *done*, made, renewed by others—and, potentially, by the negative aspects of loss. These engagements and experiences—and the sharing of them—may expose aspects of frailty, vulnerability, and impotence, but somehow, in time, these same can act alchemically, channeling a dynamic blend of ontological securities and insecurities, catalyzing a spur to being agential—*to act where and when one can*. Volunteering in response to loss is one such example of acting and doing. In bereavement, these actions represent a form of mobility, an emotional mobility of fresh perspective and of "being moved, carrying on, taking the next step," but such actions are also sutures, anchoring points within the dynamic and dialectical interface of grief and consolation (Maddrell 2009, 687). In turn, these mobilities and moorings within the ebb and flow of living with loss can be a source or revivification of community and citizenship, new priorities, and sources of resilience, as well as an element of consolation in its truest sense (see Hannam, Sheller, and Urry 2006; Jedan, Maddrell, and Venbrux 2019). Volunteers who have been bereaved themselves can offer support and insights to peers, practitioners, and policy-makers that is powerful because it is grounded in authentic embodied experience. This is the apparently mundane stuff of active grassroots citizenship which, when mobilized for mutual support, resistance, or change, can constitute the day-to-day micropolitics of implicit-explicit activism. These are just some of the bittersweet trajectories of the rich and varied politics of the interweaving of the relational and dialectical "negative-positive" in contemporary domestic experiences of loss and carrying on. After Gillespie and Lopez (2019) and Falconer al Hindi et al. (2017), this chapter is an example of *inhabiting* research and being a vulnerable witness to my own biographical experience of a life-changing negative, as well as some of the life choices that followed, including the political—namely volunteer-activism and the act of writing about the dearly-felt and -held but intangible emotional-affective intimate. As Moss (2017) highlights, there are always tensions in autobiographical writing, such as what is necessary or desirable to include or not, and the situating and meshing of intimate and vulnerable accounts in relation to established (and more traditionally recognized) scholarship. Similarly, the emotional labor associated with research on death, dying, grief, and suffering is rarely placed center stage in that research (Gillespie and Lopez 2019; although see Madge 2016 and Sidaway 2008 for exceptions). Nonetheless, there is inherent ontological and political value in the ruptures and sutures of sharing and evidencing vulnerabilities that are usually hidden or unarticulated within academia. Likewise, there is a value in exploring the relation between research and researcher in this processual and generative ontology, as well as the collective embodied personal-political networks of support-activism in bereavement-inspired volunteering. Ultimately, the doing, the undoing, the acting, the being, and the emotional labor of sharing vulnerabilities in the past through volunteer work and now on these pages was-is inherently political. I can only hope my current academic interventions on grief and living with loss—such as this one—have a fraction of the "impact" of taking a timely support-line call from a fellow bereaved parent then.

Notes

1. SANDS works to support those affected by the death of a baby, improve bereavement care, and reduce baby death. In the United Kingdom seventeen babies a day died shortly before, during, or after birth in 1998; in 2017 the number was fifteen per day.

References

Askins, Kye. 2011. "Geopolitics and Activists: People, Power and Place." In *The Ashgate Companion to Critical Geopolitics*, edited by Klaus Dodds, Merje Kuus, and Joanne P. Sharp, 527–42. Aldershot UK: Ashgate.

———. 2015. "Being Together: Everyday Geographies and the Quiet Politics of Befriending." *ACME: An International Journal for Critical Geographies* 14 (2): 470–78.

Baugher, John Eric. 2015. "Pathways through Grief to Hospice Volunteering." *Qualitative Sociology* 38 (3): 305–26.

Blackstone, Amy. 2004. "It's Just about Being Fair: Activism and the Politics of Volunteering in the Breast Cancer Movement." *Gender and Society* 18 (3): 350–68.

Braidotti, Rosi. 1994. *Nomadic Subjects: Embodiment and Sexual Difference in Contemporary Feminist Theory*. New York: Columbia University Press.

Butler, Judith. 2006. *Precarious Life: The Powers of Mourning and Violence*. London: Verso.

Caretta, Martina Angela, and Natasha Alexandra Webster. 2016. "What Kept Me Going Was Stubbornness: Perspectives from Swedish Early Career Women Academics in Geography." *Investigaciones Feministas* 7 (2): 89–113.

Collins Dictionary. S.v. "Activism." Accessed October 30, 2017. https://www.collinsdictionary .com/dictionary/english/activism.

Conradson, David. 2003. "Doing Organisational Space: Practices of Voluntary Welfare in the City." *Environment and Planning A* 35 (11): 1975–92.

Conradson, David, and Christine Milligan. 2006. "Reflections on Landscapes of Voluntarism." In *Landscapes of Voluntarism: New Spaces of Health, Welfare and Governance*, edited by Christine Milligan and David Conradson. Bristol: Policy.

Derrida, Jacques. 2001. *The Work of Mourning*. Chicago: University of Chicago Press.

Donovan, Courtney, and Pamela Moss. 2017. "Muddling Intimacy Methodologically." In Moss and Donovan 2017, 3–30.

Eliasoph, Nina. 2013. *The Politics of Volunteering*. Cambridge UK: Polity.

Falconer Al-Hindi, Karen, Pamela Moss, Leslie Kern, and Roberta Hawkins. 2017. "Inhabiting Research, Accessing Intimacy, Becoming Collective." In Moss and Donovan 2017, 147–59.

Fluri, Jennifer L., and Amy Piedalue. 2017. "Embodying Violence: Critical Geographies of Gender, Race, and Culture." *Gender, Place & Culture* 24 (4): 534–44.

Foote, Ken. 2003. *Shadowed Ground: America's Landscapes of Violence and Tragedy.* Austin: University of Texas Press.

Garcia, Maria Elena. 2019. "Grieving Guinea Pigs: Reflections on Research and Shame in Peru." In *Vulnerable Witness: The Politics of Grief in the Field*, edited by Kathryn Gillespie and Patricia J. Lopez, 40–53. Oakland: University of California Press.

Gibson-Graham, Julie Katherine. 2008. "Diverse Economies: Performative Practices for 'Other Worlds.'" *Progress in Human Geography* 32 (5): 613–32.

Giddens, Anthony. 1991. *Modernity and Self Identity: Self and Society in the Late Modern Age.* Cambridge UK: Polity.

Gillespie, Kathryn, and Patricia J. Lopez. 2019. "Introduction." In *Vulnerable Witness: The Politics of Grief in the Field*, edited by Kathryn Gillespie and Patricia J. Lopez, 1–27. Oakland: University of California Press.

Goeke, Pascal. 2019. "Transformative Philanthropy in Practice: Urban Volunteers and the Power and Limits of the Gift." *Social & Cultural Geography.* https://doi.org/10.1080/14649365.2019.1672778.

Griffiths, Mark, and Eleanor J. Brown. 2017. "Embodied Experiences in International Volunteering: Power-Body Relations and Performative Ontologies." *Social & Cultural Geography* 18 (5): 665–82.

Hanisch, Carol. (1969) 2006. "The Personal is Political." *Writings by Carol Hanisch.* Accessed June 6, 2019. http://www.carolhanisch.org/CHwritings/PIP.html.

Hannam, Kevin, Mimi Sheller, and John Urry. 2006. "Editorial: Mobilities, Immobilities and Moorings." *Mobilities* 1 (1): 1–22.

Haraway, Donna. 1988. "Situated Knowledges: The Science Question in Feminism and the Privilege of Partial Perspective." *Feminist Studies* 14 (3): 575–99.

Henkin, Samuel. 2017. "Bearing Witness to Geographies of Life and Death: Intimate Writing and Violent Geographies." In Moss and Donovan 2017, 173–79.

Horton, John, and Peter Kraftl. 2009. "Small Acts, Kind Words and 'Not Too Much Fuss': Implicit Activisms." *Emotion, Space and Society* 2 (1): 14–23.

Jedan, Christoph, Avril Maddrell, and Eric Venbrux. 2019. *Consolationscapes in the Face of Loss: Grief and Consolation in Space and Time.* Abingdon UK: Routledge.

Klass, Denis, Phyllis Silverman, and Steven L. Nickman. 1996. *Continuing Bonds: New Understandings of Grief.* Philadelphia: Taylor & Francis.

Knowles, Kelly, Tim Cole, and Alberto Giordano. 2014. *Geographies of the Holocaust.* Bloomington: Indiana University Press.

Maddrell, Avril. 2000. "'You Just Can't Get the Staff These Days': The Challenges and Opportunities of Working with Volunteers in the Charity Shop—an Oxford Case Study." *International Journal of Non-Profit and Voluntary Sector Marketing* 5 (2): 125–39.

———. 2009. "A Place for Grief and Belief: The Witness Cairn, Isle of Whithorn, Galloway, Scotland." *Social & Cultural Geography* 10 (6): 675–93.

———. 2013. "Living with the Deceased: Absence, Presence and Absence-Presence." *cultural geographies* 20 (4): 501–22.

———. 2016. "Mapping Grief: A Conceptual Framework for Understanding the Spatialities of Bereavement, Mourning and Remembrance." *Social & Cultural Geography* 17 (2): 166–88.

Maddrell, Avril, and Elizabeth Olson. 2019. "Witnessing Grief: Feminist Perspectives on the Loss-Body-Mind-Self-Other Nexus and Permission to Express Feelings." In *Vulnerable Witnesses: The Politics of Grief in the Field*, edited by Kathryn Gillespie and Patricia F. Lopez, 162–73. Oakland CA: University of California Press.

Maddrell, Avril, and James D. Sidaway. 2010. "Introduction: Bringing a Spatial Lens to Death, Dying, Mourning and Remembrance." In *Deathscapes: New Spaces for Death, Dying and Bereavement*, edited by Avril Maddrell and James D. Sidaway, 1–16. Abingdon UK: Routledge.

Madge, Clare. 2016. "Living through, Living with and Living on: Creative Cathartic Methodologies, Cancerous Spaces and a Politics of Compassion." *Social & Cultural Geography* 17 (2): 207–32.

———. 2017. "Creative Intimacy: Using Creative Practice to Express Intimate Worlds." In Moss and Donovan 2017, 73–85.

Mauss, Marcel. 1967. *The Gift: Forms and Functions of Exchange in Archaic Societies.* New York: W. W. Norton.

McIvor, David W. 2012. "Bringing Ourselves to Grief: Judith Butler and the Politics of Mourning." *Political Theory* 40 (4): 409–36.

Mellor, Philip A. 1992. "Death in High Modernity: The Contemporary Presence and Absence of Death." *Sociological Review* 40 (1): 11–30.

Milligan, Christine, and David Conradson. 2006. "Contemporary Landscapes of Welfare: The 'Voluntary Turn'?" In *Landscapes of Voluntarism: New Spaces of Health, Welfare and Governance*, edited by Christine Milligan and David Conradson. Bristol: Policy.

Milligan, Christine, Robin Kearns, and Richard G. Kyle. 2009. "Unpacking Stored and Storied Knowledge: Elicited Biographies of Activism in Mental Health." *Health and Place* 17 (1): 7–16.

Moss, Pamela. 2017. "Death, Dying and Decision-Making in an Intensive Care Unit: Tracing Micro-Connections through Auto-Methods." In Moss and Donovan 2017, 203–13.

Moss, Pamela, and Courtney Donovan. 2017. "Intimate Research Acts." In Moss and Donovan 2017, 227–36.

———, eds. 2017. *Writing Intimacy into Feminist Geography.* Abingdon UK: Routledge.

Mountz, Alison, Anne Bonds, Becky Mansfield, Jenna Lloyd, Jennifer Hyndman, Margaret Walton-Roberts, Ranu Basu, Risa Whitson, Roberta Hawkins, Trina Hamilton, and Winifred Curran. 2015. "For a Slow Scholarship: A Feminist Politics of Resistance through Collective Action in the Neoliberal University." *ACME: An International Journal for Critical Geographies* 14 (4): 1235–59.

Osterfield, Jenny. 2009. "Volunteers Working in a Bereavement Service." In *Volunteers in Hospice and Palliative Care: A Resource for Voluntary Services Managers*, edited by Ros Scott, Steven Howlett, and Derek Doyle, 163–75. Oxford: Oxford University Press.

Oxford English Dictionary. S.v. "Activism." Accessed October 30, 2017. https://en .oxforddictionaries.com/definition/activism.

Pain, Rachel. 2014. "Seismologies of Emotion: Fear and Activism during Domestic Violence." *Social & Cultural Geography* 15 (2): 127–50.

Romanillos, José L. 2015. "Mortal Questions: Geographies on the Other Side of Life." *Progress in Human Geography* 39 (5): 560–79.

Scott, Ros, Debbie Butler, and Steward Wilson. 2017. "Volunteering in Bereavement: Motivations and Meaning." *Bereavement Care* 36 (2): 55–57.

Sidaway, James D. 2008. "The Dissemination of Banal Geopolitics: Webs of Extremism and Insecurity." *Antipode* 40 (1): 2–8.

Smith, Fiona M., Helen Timbrell, Mike Woolvin, Stuart Muirhead, and Nick Fyfe. 2010. "Enlivened Geographies of Volunteering: Situated, Embodied and Emotional Practices of Voluntary Action." *Scottish Geographical Journal* 126 (4): 258–74.

Solnit, Rebecca. 2004. *Hope in the Dark: Untold Histories, Wild Possibilities*. Chicago: Haymarket.

Staeheli, Lynn A., Patricia Ehrkamp, Helga Leitner, and Caroline R. Nagel. 2012. "Dreaming the Ordinary: Daily Life and the Complex Geographies of Citizenship." *Progress in Human Geography* 36 (5): 628–44.

Valentine, Gill. 2008. "Living with Difference: Reflections on Geographies of Encounter." *Progress in Human Geography* 32 (3): 323–37.

Varley, Ann. 2008. "A Place Like This? Stories of Dementia, Home and the Self." *Environment and Planning D: Society and Space* 26 (1): 47–67.

Veludo-de-Oliveira, Tânia M., John G. Pallister, and Gordon R. Foxall. 2015. "Unselfish? Understanding the Role of Altruism, Empathy, and Beliefs in Volunteering Commitment." *Journal of Nonprofit & Public Sector Marketing* 27 (4): 373–96.

Wastl-Walter, Doris, and Lynn A. Staeheli. 2004. "Territory, Territoriality and Boundaries." In *Mapping Women, Making Politics: Feminist Perspectives on Political Geography*, edited by Lynn A. Staeheli, Eleonore Kofman, and Linda J. Peake, 141–51. Abingdon UK: Routledge.

Wooton, K. December 5, 2017. "It's Wonderful to Give Back." *Yours Magazine*.

6 Liminal Geographies of Exhaustion

Exhausted Bodies, Exhausted Places, Exhausted Possibilities

David Bissell

"It certainly feels as though ours is the age of exhaustion," writes Anna Schaffner (2016, 3). Her historical account of the concept of exhaustion describes our current era as "characterized above all by weariness, disillusionment, and burnout" (3). Though it might be tempting to understand exhaustion as a modern affliction bound up with the intensification of capitalism and bombardments of new technologies, Schaffner explains how the concept has a complex history. She reminds us how, at certain times, "theorists and also patients may emphasize primarily its physical symptoms, while in others the focus might be on its mental and spiritual ones" (10). At some points exhaustion has been judged to be a sign of weakness, while at other times it has been seen as a badge of honor. Recognizing that "exhaustion can be understood not only as an individual physical, mental, or spiritual state, but also as a broader cultural phenomenon" (5), Schaffner's account highlights how exhaustion is a multivalent concept. Rather than just flagging one specific phenomenon or condition, it names an array of related but distinct concerns. For instance, to exhaust can mean "to tire" in the bodily sense of making someone feel tired. But it can also mean "to empty" in the sense of using up reserves completely. Furthermore, it can also mean "to expel" in terms of the removal of a by-product.

Situating the relevance of the concept for this collection, what each of Schaffner's diverse forms of exhaustion have in common is the theme of the negative. She explains how exhaustion is so often "defined negatively by what it is not and what a person afflicted by it lacks: its conceptual opposites include, above all, energy but also vitality, strength, optimism, engagement, and care for the future" (7–8). Schaffner's wide-ranging historicization of the concept is comprehensive, although not without controversy.[1] However, as the passages above indicate, her account of exhaustion centers in on bodies and different beliefs about exhaustion. This is perhaps not surprising, given that the set of experiences she discusses such as "weariness, disillusionment, apathy, hopelessness, and lack of motivation" (5) all signal corporeal states. Yet within Schaffner's account are signposts that suggest that exhaustion might have potentials as a distinctive concern for cultural geographical thought. Schaffner's starting point is the extraordinary circumstance of the retirement of Pope Benedict XVI in 2013, describing how his reasons for retirement were "physical and spiritual exhaustion." Although at first blush this rationale seems to point to very human-centered experiences, her description emphasizes how it is the former pope's bodily relationship with his spatiotemporal environment that matters. Clarifying this point, she says that he bore the "burden of an office that had become too heavy for him; he said that the world was changing and was doing so at a pace with which he could not keep up" (2016, 2). This curt description indicates how exhaustion must be conceived in terms of its spatial and temporal dimensions. Here the spatial features in terms of a body incapacitated by a heavy object, and the temporal features in terms of a body out of time with the demands of a changeable world. In short, Schaffner's description indicates that exhaustion has important geographical potentials.

Given its apparent ubiquity it is surprising that exhaustion is a concept that has received relatively limited direct geographical engagement. Where it is invoked, it is often a side effect of another more dominant object of analysis. Such is the complexity of exhaustion that it cannot be reduced to "pure form," Schaffner suggests. She says that we tend to encounter states of exhaustion "embedded in more complex symptom clusters, the constellations and names of which . . . are prone to change" (2016, 2). Such constellations of exhaustion can be identified in varied geographical scholarship. For humanist geographers, the perils of resource exhaustion featured in critiques of positivist and a-social geographies. As Ley and Samuels (1978, 1) wrote of the mechanistic models of mid-twentieth-century geographical thought, "the convergence of science and technology, once the Promethean harbinger of utopian society, began to emerge more as a central villain in the exhaustion and despoliation of man's own environment." The bodily dimensions of exhaustion feature in more recent geographical work. Sustained recent engagements with the concept include Moss's (2014) work on posttraumatic stress disorder experienced by military bodies. Situated in work on feminist emotional geographies, Moss explores the efficacy of differently capacious sites for addressing battle exhaustion. In my own work on the experiential dimensions of mobilities (Bissell 2009, 2015), the concept of exhaustion has helped me to think about the transitional dimensions of bodies in transit, wherein exhaustion changes capacities for affecting and being affected. In the context of sports geographies, Bale (2011) notes how practices such as running centrally involve bodily exhaustion. Exhaustion also comes to the fore in geographical writing on labor. For instance, through Cresswell's (2006, 89) discussion on problems of Taylorist workplace practices, exhaustion appears in accounts of being overworked. Through extensive ethnographic work, Whitelegg (2005) describes the exhausting experience of being a flight attendant. The endemic temporalities of exhaustion feature prominently in Wilkinson and Ortega-Alcázar's (2019) work on how young people experience welfare reforms under conditions of austerity. For academics too, Mandel (2003) discusses the exhaustion of fieldwork practices, a fatigue that manifests as irritability, changing relations between herself and participants. Lastly, and closer to home, Askins (2008) describes how the changing forces of university life can manifest in exhaustion for academics.

Though exhaustion features in different ways in the geographical research signposted above, for most, a specific situation or phenomenon tends to be the focus of these accounts, rather than the concept of exhaustion itself. In response to and building on this geographical foundation, this chapter outlines what a cultural geographical engagement with the concept of exhaustion might involve. Where its familiar correlates in weariness and burnout point to a specific spectrum of bodily experiences, the aim of this chapter is to expand the concept of exhaustion by exploring its multiple valences to indicate how it could be taken up by geographers in different ways.

Geographical Context

Cultural geography over the past two decades has been strongly influenced by poststructuralist styles of thinking about the relationships between people and places, which has led to new objects of analysis and changed the status of fieldwork and the data that it generates. There are three conceptual influences that need emphasizing in the context of this discussion. Theories of practice and performance have prompted a renewed focus on the creative, open-ended nature of embodied practices, previously neglected in cultural geographical work that prioritized discursive interpretations of representational forms. Second, and relatedly, theories of affect have prompted cultural geographers to reassess the constitution of bodies, both human and nonhuman, as relational and processual, rather than determinate and fixed. Third, actor-network approaches and theories of new materialism have prompted cultural geographers to reassess the role and agencies of nonhuman objects and forces in social formations. In short, the sizeable body of geographical research that has been influenced by this confluence of theoretical streams provides a compelling riposte to the accusation of "dead geographies" made over two decades ago (Thrift and Dewsbury 2000). Now, arguably more than ever, cultural geographical work is concerned with dazzlingly vibrant, shape-shifting objects of analysis.

Yet as explained in the introduction to this collection, such a turn to embracing the creative, forceful, and agentive dynamics in which the human is but one relationally formed constituent of a much wider ecology of affecting forces introduces pressing questions around the status of the negative in such affirmative, additive, geographical work. While cultural geographical work inspired by the turn to practice might be the clearest demonstration of this affirmative tendency, others have noted that this is actually part of a tendency that runs much deeper. As literary theorist

Steven Connor observes, "nearly all our theories about art, value, politics, the nature of human interactions, tend to assume a norm of well-nourished, fully-charged, maximally alert beings" (2004, 56). Nigel Thrift reinforces this point, acknowledging that "not everything is focused intensity. Embodiment includes tripping, falling over, and a whole host of other such mistakes. It includes vulnerability, passivity, suffering, even simple hunger. It includes episodes of insomnia, weariness and exhaustion, a sense of insignificance and even sheer indifference to the world" (2008, 10).

Paul Harrison has provided the most sustained response to affirmative cultural geographies through interventions that have drawn attention to the negative that is lost in focusing on the "bliss of action" (Deleuze 1988, 28). Through a series of linked discussions around the themes of vulnerability, susceptibility, suffering, lassitude, sleep, and boredom, Harrison's work (see especially 2007a, 2009) explores the conceptual implications of "radical passivity" for the way that cultural geography thinks about the limits of bodily existence. Where much contemporary cultural geographical work has approached the question of corporeality in terms of its skills, capacities, and competencies, Harrison's work insists that "corporeality must also be approached outside its capacities and powers and through its impossibilities and its 'not-being-able-to'" (2008, 432). It is from within this dimension of Harrison's work that I consider how exhaustion as a concept might offer intriguing potentials for rethinking some of cultural geography's central objects of analysis.

This chapter explores the concept of exhaustion in three ways. In turn, it explores how we might think about exhausted *bodies*, exhausted *places*, and exhausted *possibilities*. Thus, while it begins with a discussion of exhaustion in relation to corporeality, pushing the concept further in terms of how it might help us think about places and possibilities expands the geographical remit of the concept. I conclude that exhaustion foregrounds the liminal dimensions of the politics of the negative in terms of its capacity to push our understanding of limits, thresholds, and transitions. Where the concept of liminality in geography has conventionally been used to describe neglected places or landscapes (Andrews and Roberts 2012) or marginalized populations when evaluated against a normative yardstick (Skelton 2010), I draw inspiration from Marcus Doel's (1994) idea of "liminal materialism" where the idea of liminality points to destabilizing thresholds (see also Abrahamsson and Simpson 2011). My wager is that while exhaustion has been addressed more directly through other disciplinary approaches such as biomedicine, medical anthropology, history, and sociology, geographers can provide an important set of responses that foreground exhaustion's strange spatialities.

Exhausting Bodies

One way of approaching the concept of exhaustion is to consider it as an effect of bodily laboring. Here, exhaustion is biophysical and a result of practical activity, where bodies are pushed to their limits through the practices that they undertake. Thus, exhaustion can be phenomenologically sensed through somatically felt bodily sensations. Historian Anson Rabinbach's (1992) account of the rise of the machine-like laboring body through the intensification of the industrial system during the nineteenth century provides one of the most compelling ways of understanding how bodies can be exhausted by the practical activities that they engage in. Through an examination of how the bodily effects of laboring were understood through the scientific, literary, and political discourses of the day, Rabinbach locates the origins of the idea of "labor power" squarely in the Industrial Revolution. It was then that the human body became understood as a "human motor" within the industrial machine. Highlighting its cog-like nature, Rabinbach writes that the body was increasingly "the medium through which the forces of nature are transformed into the forces that propel society" (1992, 2–3). Bodily exhaustion came to matter within this industrial system quite simply because it was one of the elements that threatened productivity. As dominant discourses of the time shifted over the course of the modernist industrial period, Rabinbach describes how anxiety over depleted bodily energy became particularly prominent during the latter part of the nineteenth century. This was significant because where, previously, it was idleness that was the biggest threat to industrial modernity, at this moment it is exhaustion that needed to be mitigated.

Rabinbach explains how exhausted, fatigued bodies became a thoroughly medicalized problem, thus becoming subjected to close scientific analysis. What is particularly interesting about the medicalization of exhaustion is that, according to Rabinbach, it became the "most apparent and distinctive sign of the external limits of body and mind" (1992, 6). As such, the industrial system was effectively revealing the incapacities and constraints of what the human body could achieve for productivity gains in a system that required their energy. This also indicates that, as an "endemic disorder of industrial society" (1992, 2), exhaustion was about the depletion of bodily energy, echoing the dominant scientific discourses of the time. This "thermodynamic" understanding of what constitutes a body is a historical product of industrial modernity inspired by nineteenth-century physics. Bodies were thus understood in terms of their energy equivalence, for example having more or less energy at any point. This image is clearly exemplified through Rabinbach's description of the body as a "human motor," a phrase that barely differentiates it from the industrial machines that it effectively was a part of. Indeed, as Rabinbach surmises, "the great discoveries of nineteenth century physics led . . . not only to the assumption of a universal energy, but also to the inevitability of decline, dissolution and exhaustion" (1992, 3–4).

This thermodynamic understanding of exhaustion as a lack of internal energy is one of the most persistent ways that this phenomenon is approached today (Schaffner 2016). However, changes in the mode of production over the twentieth century have given rise to different effects on the laboring bodies caught up in them and, as such, the idea of bodily exhaustion has changed. As geographical work has shown, one of the most significant shifts has been the transition from an industrial Fordist mode of production to a post-Fordist mode of production. To make sense of these transitions, geographers have drawn particular inspiration from autonomous Marxist theorists whose writings have been attentive to the bodily consequences of such shifts. Among these writers, Franco Berardi (2009) provides one of the most compelling accounts of the bodily impacts of the transition to a "post-industrial" system. Where labor in the industrial system was characterized by muscular exhaustion, Berardi argues that labor in the postindustrial system—or what he refers to as semiocapitalism—is characterized by mental exhaustion. Partly influenced by psychoanalytical theories, he proposes a number of reasons for this. Primary among them is that the production of value in the postindustrial system does not rely on physical bodily energy, as the industrial system did, but rather emotional, linguistic, cognitive, and imaginative energy. Where previously these were all capacities that were valued by people because they were an escape from the boredom and pain of physical labor, these capacities became put to work by capital during the latter part of the twentieth century where value became increasingly created through the production of subjectivities, rather than material objects. In tandem with deregulation and the rollback of many social protections, Berardi's key point is that the progressive "mentalization" of work has given rise to a new kind of enslavement and, thus, a new form of alienation.

Berardi's argument has a distinctly geographical dimension emphasizing, as it does, how the transition from an industrial to a postindustrial system has changed the spatialities of bodily exhaustion, not just in terms of the location of exhaustion in bodies themselves, but where those bodily exhaustions take place. Where physically exhausted bodies engaged in industrial labor are able to leave their work at the factory gates at the end of the working day to indulge in the pleasures of places for rest and relaxation (such as working clubs and union communities), mentally exhausted bodies in the postindustrial system have no choice but to continue to work on their subjectivities. For Berardi, the exhaustion of postindustrial continuous laboring is manifested in two ways. First, through a sense of being overwhelmed to the point of collapse (see also Han 2015), and second, through depression. As Berardi summarizes, "capitalism is based on the exploitation of *physical energy*, and semiocapitalism has subjugated the *nervous energy* of society to the point of collapse" (2010, 4, emphasis added).

The acknowledgment that post-Fordist production induces a qualitatively different mode of exhaustion is not unique to Berardi. Henri Lefebvre's

(1984) Marxist analysis has consistently drawn attention to how, over the course of the twentieth century, the time of capital increasingly threatens "free" time, such as how journeys between suburbs and workplaces effectively extend the working day (see also Bissell 2018). His spatialized argument is accentuated and taken up with greater empirical precision by Melissa Gregg's study of post-Fordist working practices, where a key consequence of the digitalization of work through new technologies has been its "presence bleed" (2011, 22) into home and leisure domains previously the preserve of other functions. Gregg explains how the prevalence of flexible working practices for workers in the contemporary "knowledge economy," particularly through the rise of mobile devices and online connectivity, has meant that work increasingly encroaches into family and leisure time, demanding perpetual alertness that becomes exhausting. So where Rabinbach's account of bodily exhaustion focuses on the depletion of energy during the rise of the industrial mode of production, the problem of exhaustion becomes differently construed under the changed conditions of contemporary post-Fordist labor. For Berardi, this can be chiefly described in terms of the mental exhaustion of knowledge workers. Berardi's bleak diagnosis is, necessarily, polemic, and much work in geography has attempted to explore the knottier, geographically specific interstices between different types of laboring and their different experiences of bodily exhaustion. Feminist geographers in particular have a long history of drawing attention to the significance of unpaid domestic labor, which can be every bit as physically exhausting as paid industrial labor, as Hanson and Pratt's (1988) work powerfully demonstrates (see also McDowell 1993).

The complexity of bodily exhaustion under post-Fordism is taken in a different direction by those writing more explicitly through theories of performance. Literary scholar Lauren Berlant draws attention to the affective complexity of bodies to explore how experiences such as exhaustion might not necessarily be registered in ways that we might expect from other more humanist perspectives. Inspired by antifoundationalist theories that acknowledge how bodies are the composite effects of a teeming mass of inhuman forces, Berlant points out that "to impute a mirroring relation between affective activity and emotional states underdescribes the incoherence of subjects" (2008, 4). This apparent paradox is explored through her concept of "cruel optimism," which describes the ordinary situation where the processes of life-building and life-attrition are indistinguishable. Berlant is interested in why we cling to forms of life, including ways of working, that are exhausting us, rather than making a break. Backgrounded against more explicitly Marxist-inspired understandings of bodily exhaustion, Berlant provides a more complex understanding of the workings of contemporary power. Rather than understanding the power to exhaust in terms of domination through an intensified industrial mode of production, or even, more locally, a particular industrial production line, as in Rabinbach's analysis, Berlant's principal objects of analysis are immaterial, focusing on desires, attachments, and affections. Attending to these objects of analysis alters the distribution and patterning of power, which helps understand seemingly perverse situations such as when we might maintain an attachment to a fantasy, even when the effects of that attachment become exhausting (see Cockayne 2016; also Straughan, Bissell, and Gorman-Murray 2020). In its most everyday sense, as Berlant notes, "at the same time that one builds a life the pressures of its reproduction can be exhausting" (2007, 778).

To summarize, one way of thinking about exhaustion is focusing on bodies. It is perhaps unsurprising that much of the current writing that explores bodily exhaustion takes the changing practices of laboring as their empirical concern. From the critical perspective offered by different articulations of Marxist-inflected thought, much of this literature is concerned with tracing how the changing demands of labor are depleting the bodies caught up in these processes, raising important political and ethical questions. From the perspective of the dominant economic system, exhausted bodies are problematic owing to their incapacity to generate surplus value. Updating the medicalized concerns central to Rabinbach's account of exhaustion in the nineteenth-century industrial workplace, Jonathan Crary's (2013, 11) dark polemic that charts the rise of the contemporary 24/7 society indicates how exhaustion has, once again, become a "site of crisis" because of its threat to the continuity of production. Yet Berlant encourages us to think about how bodily exhaustion is political owing to its potential as a form of refusal in the face of an exploitative economic system. Rather than thinking of resistance as an active, calculated response to a dominant power, Berlant suggests that it is precisely the loss of a body's active and calculating capacities that marks a small interruption to the subject required by capital: a subject that is "called to consciousness, intentionality, and effective will" (2007, 778). These are the small pleasures of "episodic intermission from personality, of inhabiting agency differently in small vacations from the will itself, which is so often spent from the pressures of coordinating one's pacing with the pace of the working day, including times of preparation and recovery from it" (2007, 779).

Exhausting Places

This second section expands this bodily focus by broadening out to consider how place is a central but overlooked concern for understanding exhaustion geographically. Places are, of course, more than just meaningful locations (Agnew 1987). They have multiple kinds of capacities to do things. Rather than seeing places as an inert backdrop upon which the social life of humans plays out, cultural geographers have had an ongoing preoccupation with understanding the varied ways that different places have their own capacities and powers to act on different bodies in different ways. Foregrounding place, then, invites us to consider the affecting nature of places; in other words, how they act and impress upon us. A recognition of the agentive capacities of place develops our understanding of exhaustion because it invites us to think about how places themselves are centrally implicated in exhaustion, rather than exhaustion resulting just from the activities that bodies undertake. Of course place is quietly present in different guises in the first section of this chapter, such as the place of the industrial factory in Rabinbach's account, or the place of the home in Berlant's inference of domestic labor. But the focus was on bodily practices themselves and the exhausting labors of performing them. In this section

I trace two distinct but related bodies of work that highlight how places exhaust. First, I describe how a key thread of twentieth-century urban theory foregrounds the capacity of places to exhaust. Second, I describe how a thread of avant-garde practice has more playfully explored how places might be exhausted. While these bodies of work are preoccupied with quite different problems, what joins them is a more passive sense of bodies in the thrall of affecting places.

Writing at the turn of the twentieth century, at a time of dramatic social change, Georg Simmel was fascinated by the rapid growth of cities, stimulated by the development of industry and the associated rural to urban migration. He was especially interested in understanding the impact of this rapid transformation on city dwellers themselves. In his landmark essay "The Metropolis and Mental Life," Simmel describes how the intensification of "violent stimuli" in the new metropolis depletes people's energy (2002, 11). He writes, "just as an immoderately sensuous life makes one blasé because it stimulates the nerves to their utmost reactivity until they finally can no longer produce any reaction at all, so, less harmful stimuli, through the rapidity and the contradictoriness of their shifts, force the nerves to make such violent responses, tear them about so brutally that they exhaust their last reserves of strength and, remaining in the same milieu, do not have time for new reserves to form" (2002, 14). Inhabiting the same era that Rabinbach's account of bodily exhaustion focuses on, it is perhaps no surprise that Simmel draws on a similar "thermodynamic" understanding of bodies depicted in terms of their relative energy levels. However, what is distinctive about Simmel's account is that it is the sensory stimulation of the city itself that is exhausting, rather than the labor of bodily practice. The only way for an urbanite to cope with such rapid shifts of stimulus, according to Simmel, is through the development of a blasé gaze—a kind of aloof rational intellectualism that provides defense against the debilitating exposure to the city's incessant ever-changing stimulations. In contrast to the emotional and deeply personal relationships that characterized rural life, Simmel's point is that the intense sensory stimulations of urban life necessitated a new sort of interpersonal relationship, characterized by superficial and instrumental encounters that maximize individual utility. Therefore, where Rabinbach's account stresses how bodies became mere laboring cogs in the machine of industrial production, Simmel's blasé gaze provides a practical response for how individuals might protect their "inner life against the domination of the metropolis" (2002, 12).

The role of bodily practices is therefore positioned differently in Simmel's account of the urban dweller attempting to survive the stimulations of the new metropolis. Rather than being the cause of exhaustion, bodily practices help to guard against exhaustion. Simmel's focus on the bodily practice of the blasé gaze and the associated indifferent attitude created through streamlining social interactions paved the way for much symbolic interactionist theory, especially those writing during the mid-twentieth century, which sought to explore the patterned techniques through which individuals negotiated strangers in public space. Erving Goffman's (1972, 385) concept of "civil inattention" has a direct parallel with Simmel's blasé gaze. Goffman was interested in the way that, in certain situations, especially those where unacquainted people are together, a range of bodily practices which he tellingly calls "involvement shields" can perform a symbolic demonstration of their unavailability while signaling an awareness of the other.

Simmel's exploration of how bodily techniques defend against the potentially exhausting nature of being exposed to the rapidly changing stimuli in the metropolis shares certain similarities with contemporary cultural geographical writing on dwelling, deepening our appreciation of the relationship between exhaustion and exposure further. While its poststructuralist theoretical orientation diverges from Simmel's nascent symbolic interactionism, contemporary cultural geography has been interested in grappling with the ontological question of what dwelling is. Drawing principally on Heidegger as a starting point, the significance of this concept for many cultural geographers is that dwelling is an activity that actively configures space and social relations, rather than passive consumption, as it has been more traditionally conceived. This is part of a more general movement away from focusing on supposedly top-down forms of power, toward understanding social life as the emergent effect of a more distributed configuration of agencies.

Paul Harrison (2007b), however, provides a more nuanced interpretation of Heidegger's writings on dwelling. He points out that dwelling as a set of practices alerts us to an existential tension between scattering and self-containment. As such, and echoing Simmel's concerns, albeit through different conceptual registers, dwelling becomes a concept that highlights the tensile relations of enclosure and exposure. Harrison emphasizes that geographers' dominant interpretation of Heidegger is already a movement of enclosure. Because of this, geographers have tended to reinforce how *Dasein*, or being in the world, is first and foremost an activity of gathering, requiring resolute self-possessiveness. However, for Harrison, there is an overlooked flipside of dwelling that Heidegger's "centripetal" sense of enclosure pushes against. Leaning on the conceptual support of Levinas, Harrison describes how the enclosing movements of dwelling are actually a response to our more primary exposure in the world to the other. Harrison argues that this underappreciated exposure is a centrifugal openness to exteriority and an "incessant disquieting incoming of the other" (2007b, 640), of alterity. So, for Harrison, dwelling is first and foremost the development of an orientation from this "unforeseeable but ever proximal incoming of the other" (2007b, 642).

In summary, we can think about how places exhaust by turning to geographically informed literature that emphasizes how bodily vulnerability is a result of our primary exposure to the world, rather than emphasizing how vulnerability is derived principally through bodily exertion. This exposure is differently theorized for Simmel and Harrison, but there are important similarities. Simmel's argument is more pragmatic. His interest is in how the city dweller exposed to the overwhelming sensory bombardment develops a series of protective practical strategies to guard against exhaustion. Harrison's argument is more ontological. However, his interest is in demonstrating how the practical necessity of dwelling practices are a response to a much more primary condition of our exposure to the other. This means that our dwelling practices can only ever be provisional, because they are always and incessantly vulnerable to the force of the outside, and therefore have to be continually repeated (Rose 2012).

As a counterpoint to this argument, we can turn to a third strand of thought that develops a different relationship between place and exhaustion by thinking about exposure in a different way. Written in 1975, Georges Perec's (2010) *An Attempt at Exhausting a Place in Paris* follows in the footsteps of other French avant-garde thinkers who were interested in experimenting with performances and texts that potentially had the capacity to critique and softly subvert the gnawing sense of estrangement that the capitalist city was creating. Perec was concerned that part of the problem of urban life is how so much of what happens in the city goes unnoticed and unremarked upon. He finds this problematic because we can become preoccupied with only the exceptional "newsworthy" events, and this can cause us to overlook all manner of social problems that take place in the "infra-ordinary" realm of everyday life. Where Simmel's focus was describing practices that could help to insulate bodies from the exhaustion of exposure, Perec inverts this through a practice that experiments with becoming more exposed to place (see also Riding 2017).

In *Exhausting a Place*, Perec visits Place Saint Sulpice in Paris over three days. His aim is to attempt to record everything that he witnesses going on in that place, such that the place itself becomes exhausted. He first documents letters and symbols, slogans, the objects around him, then trajectories of buses passing through, then colors. These are a more systematic prelude to the observations that follow, which attempt to record everything that he sees happening. For instance, on day one, part of his account includes the following: "An 86 goes by, empty. A 70 goes by, full. Jean-Paul Aron goes by, again: he coughs" (2010, 22). Significant here is that Perec's ostensible aim is to develop a practice that attempts to exhaust *place*, rather than himself. This invites us to consider how, in contrast to Simmel, exhaustion might be understood in an inhuman manner. The melancholic overtones that can derive from reading his account seems to lay in the fact that, as Perec learns, it is of course impossible to exhaust a place. His experiment attunes us to how new things keep happening, even if they appear similar.

Aligning with Doreen Massey's (2005) more recent geographical writings that have underscored the incessant multiplicity and developmental qualities of space, Perec becomes aware of not only the partiality of his perceptions in this place, but also the limits of perceptual capacities as he senses the multitude of things that he is likely missing. Perhaps also affirming Simmel's observations of the exhausting nature of being exposed to the stimulations of the city, a little before six on the evening on the first day, Perec simply writes: "*(fatigue)*" (2010, 22).

In short, rather than focusing on how exhaustion can be an effect of bodily laboring practices, this discussion of the relationship between exhaustion and place invites us to attend more closely to the quality of bodily relations with their surrounding milieu. Bringing Simmel's insights into conversation with cultural geographical writing on dwelling and Perec's experimental practices, foregrounding place in exhaustion encourages us to become attentive to bodily exposure. Where Simmel observes how exposure to the sensory bombardment in the city can be exhausting, he closes off the potentials of the multiplicity of urban life through an instrumentalist, utilitarian disposition that is epitomized in the blasé gaze. In contrast, Perec attempts to open up to the multiplicity of the city by experimenting with an attempt to exhaust place itself. However, in attempting to exhaust place, he also seems to exhaust himself. The significance of the concept of exposure that is at the heart of both Simmel's and Perec's accounts is illuminated in cultural geographical work on dwelling that has sought to highlight how the practices of enclosure that constitute dwelling respond to a primary ontological exposure to alterity. The final section of this chapter extends Perec's implicitly nonhuman understanding of exhaustion further by turning to a vein of poststructuralist thought that helps to consider the relationship between exhaustion and possibility.

Exhausting Possibilities

The notion of exhausting possibilities might initially have a familiar ring to it, if we consider this idea from the point of view of working through myriad options to achieve an intended outcome. However, my argument here builds on Gilles Deleuze's (1997) writing on "exhausting the possible" as a way of thinking about how exhaustion might be implicated in processes of transformation that are different from the first two ways of thinking about exhaustion presented in this chapter. Deleuze's argument is concerned with thinking about exhaustion ontologically, in other words, how it changes the nature of what is. To clarify, the preoccupation throughout Deleuze's antifoundationalist philosophy is with the primary impersonal forces that individuate different kinds of bodies, where difference itself materializes through an interplay of forces, rather than being understood as an attribute or an identity. In seeking to develop more dynamic and relational understandings of our traditional geographical objects of analysis such as bodies, place, and space, recent cultural geography has drawn much from Deleuze's process philosophy (see for instance Roberts 2019). Given his interest in the primacy of processes of individuation, rather than fully formed "molar" subjects, Deleuze challenges us to imagine a much more impersonal sense of exhaustion, rather than understanding exhaustion as a characteristic of a specific body that might be more or less exhausted. A Deleuzian understanding of exhaustion might initially sound strange, given that he is a thinker who is ostensibly concerned with creation, joy, and affirmation rather than negation and finitude. However, exhaustion for Deleuze is a necessary part of creation and transformation.

In an essay that is principally concerned with the repetitious and contradictory styles of writing of Samuel Beckett, Deleuze (1997) makes the point that exhaustion is different from tiredness or fatigue of the sort that was discussed in the first part of this chapter. Exhaustion is not about mere incapacity, such as being unable to realize an idea, plan, or intention. In other words, exhaustion is not an outcome of an attempt. To explain this, Deleuze makes an important distinction between what he calls "realizing the possible" and "exhausting the possible." The idea of "realizing the possible," which is the subject of critique in many of his other writings, would be to proceed by selecting from a series of pregiven possibilities, thereby proceeding by limitation and exclusion. However, the idea of "exhausting the possible" is rather different. Revealing something of what he enjoys in

Beckett's unconventional prose, Deleuze writes that exhausting the possible is "to combine the [whole] set of variations of a situation, on the condition that one renounce any order of preference, any organization in relation to a goal, any signification" (1997, 153). In other words, one becomes exhausted by renouncing all instrumental, determinate outcomes.

Where exhaustion in the first part of this chapter was broadly the result of activity, and in the second part, exhaustion was broadly the result of passivity, exhaustion for Deleuze can be understood in terms of both activity *and* passivity, or "the exhaustive *and* the exhausted" (1997, 154), as he writes. Deleuze is fascinated by the way that the repetitious qualities of Beckett's writing indicates that while there is an activity of exhaustion, as in the activity of exhausting a series of possibilities, there is also a passivity of exhaustion, as in a site of exhaustion in the exhausted body (Wasser 2012). But this body, for Deleuze, is not the "molar" body that is implicated in Rabinbach's and Simmel's accounts. Deleuze's "body" is conceived in a much less humanistic way, understood as the preindividual site of passive synthesis, in other words, how experience is passively synthesized and incorporated into the body through the retention of what has happened and expectations of what will come (see Dewsbury and Bissell, 2015).

Appreciating the passive synthesis that folds activity and passivity allows Deleuze to speculate on the pivotal role of exhaustion in the transformation of the present. He says that the present passes only when it is fully exhausted. In this ontological sense, exhaustion, then, is absolutely vital to the ongoingness of experience. Unlike mere tiredness, exhaustion is obtained only "when the forces that constitute the passive self exceed the self's ability to capture them" (Wasser 2012, 132). What is so radical about this understanding of exhaustion, then, is that it is not about lack, of incapacity, but rather it is about fullness. Exhaustion for Deleuze is a threshold, and because it is a change in state, exhaustion is an affect. As Audrey Wasser summarizes, "exhaustion is thus a kind of satiety: not a tendency towards zero, but simultaneously a moment of stasis and a passage to a recursively transformative action" (2012, 132). Exhaustion from this point of view therefore concerns what a body is capable of withstanding before it changes in state.

In this understanding, exhausted bodies are not exhausted because they have run out of energy. Instead, they are exhausted *by what they exhaust*. This is significant because where cultural geographers have drawn succor from the generative, creative ontology that unfolds through his writing, Deleuze's formulation of exhaustion that is immanent to its activity reveals a curious aspect of finitude in his thinking (see also Culp 2016). This is a different kind of finitude than the "absolute" finitude that is more characteristic of cultural geographical work on biopolitics. For instance, in Rose's (2013) development of the relationship between governance and exposure, he argues that governance is much more reactive than has often been theorized, and it is actually our primary and irreducible exposure as bodies that calls for governance. Using Agamben's terms, Rose argues that "we are all *Homo sacer* because we are always already exposed to death" (2013, 220). Important here is the implication of a finitudinal understanding of exposure. The use of hunger and illness as illustrative examples of this condition brings us closer to Rose's conceptualization of the negative, which is predicated on an understanding of exposure that is our own absolute finitude as subjects.

However, to imagine exposure in such absolute finitudinal terms risks underplaying how it is this primary exposure, our vulnerability, that actually gives rise to our vitality, rather than compromising it. To explain this, and to return to exhaustion in this context, what Deleuze's understanding of exhaustion offers us is a more inhuman notion of finitude, or death, to that offered by Agamben. In *Anti-Oedipus* Deleuze and Guattari (1977) contrast death as defined in relation to the bounded organism with the "experience" of death. They write that "the experience of death is the most common of occurrences in the unconscious, precisely because it occurs in life and for life, in every passage or becoming, in every intensity as passage or becoming" (1977, 330). This allows us to go beyond thinking about exposure as potentially traumatic infraction, as it is for Simmel, toward imagining how exposure is the necessary site of passivity to activate a change in state, a modification to a body, an affect; where every threshold of exhaustion, every satiation is a little inhuman death. What this means is that exhaustion becomes part of the very conditions of creation.

Deleuze's conceptual doubling of the concept of exhaustion alerts us to the activity of exhausting and the necessary passivity of a site of exhaustion. He highlights how exhaustion reveals forms of finitude that are less absolute and much more transitional, understood in the sense of a bodily modification. In this regard, even if we were to take exhaustion as a malady, a kind of sickness, in the sense of it being a problem of active affections, Deleuze's writings show how this is not necessarily a condition of closure or decomposition. For instance, in his writing on Nietzsche, he rethinks the conventional hierarchy of active and reactive forces. On one hand, where an active force is "one which goes to the limit of its consequences" (2006, 61), exhaustion could be imagined as a reactive force in the sense of a force that separates a body from what it can do. But Deleuze asks, "Does not this reactive force in its own way, go to the limit of what it can do?" (2006, 61). In other words, he asks whether we could think of this as a reactive force becoming active. He experiments with the idea of illness. But we could substitute illness with exhaustion as an example of a condition dominated by reactive forces in the sense that "it narrows my possibilities and condemns me to a diminished milieu to which I can do no more than adapt myself" (2006, 61). However, he proceeds by suggesting that "in another way, it reveals to me a new capacity, it endows me with a new will that I can make my own, going to the limit of a strange power" (2006, 61). In this sense, exhaustion might "bring us new feelings and teach us new ways of being affected" (2006, 61–62).

Throughout Deleuze's work we see the significance of exposure, of passive affections to activity, or active affections. In *Spinoza: Practical Philosophy* (1988), this is manifested in the passage from passive joy to active joy through the leap from a joyful passion to an action that happens when we comprehend the common relationship shared between the outside body and our body. This passivity—this exposure to "the non-representational voice from an always differentiating and non-relational elsewhere" (Dewsbury 2011, 181)—is central to the learning process where the subject seeks to transform itself. As Brady Heiner suggests, "by seeking to be affected by a maximum of joyful passions, the subject creates the conditions of possibility that allow it to leap into possession of its power to act (its active affections)" (2003, 41). In *Difference and Repetition* (2004), this learning is expressed through the concept of habit, where sensations, or passive affections, become incorporated into a body through repetition, becoming new desires, new active affections. In both of these examples, passive affections are not weaker forms of active affections, but rather they are crucial to the formation of active affections, thereby increasing our power to exist and act.

In short, this understanding of exhaustion moves us in a different direction, beyond imagining exhaustion as either an effect of activity *or* passivity. Through Deleuze's posthumanist process philosophy we can see how the exhaustion of the possible combines both activity and passivity as a way of conceptualizing the transformation of the present. This ontological understanding of exhaustion potentially offers a conceptual resource to think about some very practical geographical problems. For instance, through his ethnographic work with a postindustrial suburb of Cardiff, Julian Brigstocke reflects on the persistent theme of lost futures and temporal inertia that characterized conversations with his project participants. Echoing this Deleuzian view of exhaustion, he speculates that there might be "a curious kind of potentiality that emerges from the saturation of the present and a sterility of time, from the evacuation of possibility" (2016, 93). In short, rather than seeing exhaustion as lack or depletion, this understanding invites us to think of exhaustion more affirmatively as a necessary threshold for a transforming present.

Conclusion

The concept of exhaustion troubles the implicit presence of the maximally aware subject of much social scientific thought whose capacities can be activated at will and are available to be worked on. Emphasizing precisely this point, Crary argues that "most mainstream social theory prescribes that modern individuals live and act, at least intermittently, in states that are emphatically unsleeplike—states of self-awareness in which one has the ability to evaluate events and information as a rational and objective participant in public or civic life" (2013, 23). Exhaustion, by contrast, reminds us that this image of a maximally aware subject is necessarily a modernist fiction. As a state of being in the world that is ostensibly characterized by fragility and vulnerability, exhaustion challenges us to rethink some of our long-held academic habits of thinking about the nature of our bodily being in the world. Acknowledging the significance of exhaustion therefore opens up a patterned terrain of important political and ethical concerns.

However, exhaustion is a complex, multivalent concept that has a changing history. Drawing inspiration from different thinkers who have been captivated by the concept in different ways, this chapter has attempted to demonstrate the historical contingency of exhaustion, as it has been understood differently at different times and through different conceptual lenses. As Rabinbach's historical account reminds us, in the preindustrial era, exhaustion took on a much more benign status and was actually seen as a necessary accompaniment and natural response to work rather than maligned as "spent batteries" (1992, 39), which became the dominant interpretation of the industrial era. Yet this understanding of exhaustion as an effect of bodily activity, explored in the first part of this chapter, is only one avenue of thought. The preceding two parts of this chapter have developed the concept along alternative lines, seeking to think about exhaustion of place, through exposure or passivity, and exhaustion of possibility as satiation of the present. These alternative understandings take us beyond exhaustion as a problem of bodily fatigue toward thinking about exhaustion as a much more ontological problem concerning relations of exposure and enclosure and the transformation of the present.

Perhaps most significantly in the context of this collection on the negative, what we also witness in the progression of ideas in this chapter is an ambiguity about the negation that exhaustion does. Each of the three forms of exhaustion explored in this chapter oscillate between thinking about exhaustion in terms of the *negation* of vitality and thinking about exhaustion as a *condition* of vitality. In the section that explored the exhaustion of bodies, on the one hand exhaustion names a depletion of energy, but on the other hand exhaustion acts as a cue for bodily restoration. In the section that explored the exhaustion of places, on the one hand exhaustion is an effect of being overwhelmed by a place, but on the other hand, exhaustion is a technique for attuning to the multiplicity of place. In the section that explored the exhaustion of possibility, on the one hand exhaustion is the still point of satiation, but on the other hand, exhaustion is the tipping point for the present to pass.

However, rather than concluding by affirmatively recuperating the negative as yet another positive (a romantic gesture indeed), I finish by briefly suggesting how exhaustion might be better approached as a concept that foregrounds liminality rather than potentiality. Where the liminal has predominantly been understood representationally, in terms of marginality when measured against an idealized norm, where difference is referred back to the same, Doel's (1994) reflections on what he calls "liminal materialism" challenges us to think about liminality in terms of nonrepresentational thresholds. Thus, in this regard, exhaustion might be most sensitively approached as a threshold that challenges us to acknowledge the vulnerabilities that are immanent to the vital. Expressing precisely this folding of the vital and the vulnerable, Connor writes that "exhaustion is not the defeat of the will, but the manic, clenched persistence of the will into its very extinction" (2004, 55). As a liminal concept that foregrounds thresholds of potentiality, exhaustion is surely a concept worthy of further geographical enquiry.

Notes

Sincere thanks to Mitch and Paul for their friendship and collegiality over the course of this project. I'm particularly grateful to Mitch and the other contributors in this collection for their helpful comments on a draft shared at the Aberystwyth workshop in 2017. Thanks also to Tim Edensor for reading and providing useful feedback on a previous version.

1. The chapter on Myalgic Encephalomyelitis has been criticized for its suggestion that it is a psychological condition, a diagnosis that is refuted by much contemporary biomedical research.

References

Abrahamsson, Sebastian, and Paul Simpson. 2011. "The Limits of the Body: Boundaries, Capacities, Thresholds." *Social & Cultural Geography* 12 (4): 331–38.

Agnew, John. 1987. *Place and Politics: The Geographical Mediation of State and Society*. London: Allen & Unwin.

Andrews, Hazel, and Les Roberts, eds. 2012. *Liminal Landscapes: Travel, Experience and Spaces In-between*. London: Routledge.

Askins, Kye. 2008. "From Enthusiasm to Exhaustion: A Day in the Life of a Geography Lecturer." *Ephemera* 8 (3): 312–21.

Bale, John. 2011. "Running: Running as Working." In *Geographies of Mobilities: Practices, Spaces, Subjects*, edited by Tim Cresswell and Peter Merriman, 35–50. Aldershot UK: Ashgate.

Berardi, Franco. 2009. *The Soul at Work: From Alienation to Autonomy*. Los Angeles: Semiotext(e).

———. 2010. "Exhaustion and Senile Utopia of the Coming European Insurrection." *e-flux journal* 21 (December): 1–8.

Berlant, Lauren. 2007. "Slow Death (Sovereignty, Obesity, Lateral Agency)." *Critical Inquiry* 33 (4): 754–80.

———. 2008. "Thinking about Feeling Historical." *Emotion, Space and Society* 1 (1): 4–9.

Bissell, David. 2009. "Travelling Vulnerabilities: Mobile Timespaces of Quiescence." *cultural geographies* 16 (4): 427–45.

———. 2015. "Virtual Infrastructures of Habit: The Changing Intensities of Habit through Gracefulness, Restlessness and Clumsiness." *cultural geographies* 22 (1): 127–46.

———. 2018. *Transit Life: How Commuting Is Transforming Our Cities*. Cambridge MA: MIT Press.

Brigstocke, Julian. 2016. "Exhausted Futures." *GeoHumanities* 2 (1): 91–101.

Cockayne, Daniel. 2016. "Entrepreneurial Affect: Attachment to Work Practice in San Francisco's Digital Media Sector." *Environment and Planning D: Society and Space* 34 (3): 456–73.

Connor, Steven. 2004. "Chronic Fatigue." *Performance Research* 9 (4): 54–58.

Crary, Jonathan. 2013. *24/7: Late Capitalism and the Ends of Sleep*. London: Verso.

Cresswell, Tim. 2006. *On the Move: Mobility in the Modern Western World*. London: Routledge.

Culp, Andrew. 2016. *Dark Deleuze*. Minneapolis: University of Minnesota Press.

Deleuze, Gilles. 1988. *Spinoza: Practical Philosophy*. San Francisco: City Lights.

———. 1997. "The Exhausted." In *Essays Critical and Clinical*, by Gilles Deleuze, 152–74. Translated by Michael A. Greco and Daniel W. Smith. Minneapolis: University of Minnesota Press.

———. 2004. *Difference and Repetition*. London: Continuum.

———. 2006. *Nietzsche and Philosophy*. New York: Columbia University Press.

Deleuze, Gilles, and Felix Guattari. 1977. *Anti-Oedipus: Capitalism and Schizophrenia*. Translated by Robert Hurley, Mark Seem, and Helen R. Lane. Minneapolis: University of Minnesota Press.

Dewsbury, John-David. 2011. "The Singularity of the 'Still': 'Never Suspend the Question." In *Stillness in a Mobile World*, edited by David Bissell and Gillian Fuller, 175–91. London: Routledge.

Dewsbury, John-David, and David Bissell. 2015. "Habit Geographies: The Perilous Zones in the Life of the Individual." *cultural geographies* 11 (1): 21–28.

Doel, Marcus. 1994. "Deconstruction on the Move: From Libidinal Economy to Liminal Materialism." *Environment and Planning A* 26 (7): 1041–59.

Goffman, Erving. 1972. *Relations in Public*. London: Penguin.

Gregg, Melissa. 2011. *Work's Intimacy*. Cambridge UK: Polity.

Han, Byung-Chul. 2015. *The Burnout Society*. Stanford CA: Stanford University Press.

Hanson, Susan, and Geraldine Pratt. 1988. "Reconceptualizing the Links between Home and Work in Urban Geography." *Economic Geography* 64 (4): 299–321.

Harrison, Paul. 2007a. "'How Shall I Say It . . . ?': Relating the Nonrelational." *Environment and Planning A* 39 (3): 590–608.

———. 2007b. "The Space between Us: Opening Remarks on the Concept of Dwelling." *Environment and Planning D: Society and Space* 25 (4): 625–47.

———. 2008. "Corporeal Remains: Vulnerability, Proximity, and Living on after the End of the World." *Environment and Planning A* 40 (2): 423–45.

———. 2009. "In the Absence of Practice." *Environment and Planning D: Society and Space* 27 (6): 987–1009.

Heiner, Brady Thomas. 2003. "The Passions of Michel Foucault." *Differences: A Journal of Feminist Cultural Studies* 14 (1): 22–52.

Lefebvre, Henri. 1984. *Everyday Life in the Modern World*. Translated by Sacha Rabinovitch. London: Transaction.

Ley, David, and Marwyn Samuels. 1978. *Humanistic Geography: Prospects and Problems*. London: Routledge.

Mandel, Jennifer L. 2003. "Negotiating Expectations in the Field: Gatekeepers, Research Fatigue and Cultural Biases." *Singapore Journal of Tropical Geography* 24 (2): 198–210.

Massey, Doreen. 2005. *For Space*. London: Sage.

McDowell, Linda. 1993. "Space, Place and Gender Relations: Part I. Feminist Empiricism and the Geography of Social Relations." *Progress in Human Geography* 17 (2): 157–79.

Moss, Pamela. 2014. "Shifting from Nervous to Normal through Love Machines: Battle Exhaustion, Military Psychiatrists and Emotionally Traumatized Soldiers in World War II." *Emotion, Space and Society* 10 (February): 63–70.

Perec, Georges. 2010. *An Attempt at Exhausting a Place in Paris*. Translated by Marc Lowenthal. Cambridge MA: Wakefield.

Rabinbach, Anson. 1992. *The Human Motor: Energy, Fatigue, and the Origins of Modernity*. Berkeley: University of California Press.

Riding, James. 2017. "Writing Place after Conflict: Exhausting a Square in Sarajevo." *GeoHumanities* 3 (2): 431–50.

Roberts, Tom. 2019. "Resituating Post-Phenomenological Geographies: Deleuze, Relations and the Limits of Objects." *Transactions of the Institute of British Geographers* 44 (3): 542–54.

Rose, Mitch. 2012. "Dwelling as Marking and Claiming." *Environment and Planning D: Society and Space* 30 (5): 757–71.

———. 2013. "Negative Governance: Vulnerability, Biopolitics and the Origins of Government." *Transactions of the Institute of British Geographers* 39 (2): 209–23.

Schaffner, Anna. 2016. *Exhaustion: A History*. New York: Columbia University Press.

Simmel, Georg. 2002 "The Metropolis and Mental Life." In *The Blackwell City Reader*, edited by Gary Bridge and Sophie Watson, 11–19. Oxford: Blackwell, 2002.

Skelton, Tracey. 2010. "Taking Young People as Political Actors Seriously: Opening the Borders of Political Geography." *Area* 42 (2): 145–51.

Straughan, Elizabeth, David Bissell, and Andrew Gorman-Murray. 2020. "Exhausting Rhythms: The Intimate Geopolitics of Resource Extraction." *cultural geographies* 27 (2): 201–16.

Thrift, Nigel. 2008. *Non-Representational Theory: Space, Politics, Affect*. London: Routledge.

Thrift, Nigel, and John-David Dewsbury. 2000. "Dead Geographies—and How to Make Them Live." *Environment and Planning D: Society and Space* 18 (4): 411–32.

Wasser, Audrey. 2012. "A Relentless Spinozism: Deleuze's Encounter with Beckett." *SubStance* 41 (1): 124–36.

Whitelegg, Drew. 2005. "Places and Spaces I've Been: Geographies of Female Flight Attendants in the United States." *Gender, Place and Culture* 12 (2): 251–66.

Wilkinson, Eleanor, and Iliana Ortega-Alcázar. 2019. "The Right to Be Weary? Endurance and Exhaustion in Austere Times." *Transactions of the Institute of British Geographers* 44 (1): 155–67.

7 "The Little Murmur of Unconsenting Man"
On Time and the Miracle

Jessica Dubow

The power to say no, this most natural expression of the
continuously changing, renewing, dying, reviving, human
fighting-organism, is something we always have, but not
the courage; all the same while to live is to say no, it follows
that to say no is to say yes.
—Franz Kafka, *Aphorisms*

What, today, is not "theology" (apart from theological
claptrap)?
—Jacob Taubes, *To Carl Schmitt*

The miracle is at first glance an outlandish, unfathomable, inexplicable
thing: either a malfunction in the ordinary course of events (a deviation
from the rules of nature) or something audacious enough to dwarf them (a
testament to an invisible power; the act of a god or the runes and lures of
some numinous diviner).[1] In this, the miracle must have an uneasy claim
on all we include within the sweep of secular reason: the concreteness
of material existence, the recognition of nature's universal conformity
to law, the schemas that measure the world's phenomena by degrees of
probability or grasp them by levels of credibility. On this account, the
miracle is freakish, fraudulent, a mere caprice of the senses. What would
it mean, then, to revalue the miracle? To see in its mendacity the validity
of a philosophical and political event? How might the miracle be released

from the preserves of religion (as from the spells of magic, of demonology) and return us to the actualities and inadequacies of the day to day? In what ways can the very deficiencies of the miracle—that it happens by surprise, only once, and always inconclusively—action a politics, or name the possibility of a politics enjoined to the unbidden, the implausible, or the impossible, as such?

A positioning is in order, from the start. Current and gaining geographic studies have turned to the real and virtual powers of religious faith in its various institutional, embodied, and affective arrangements (Holloway and Valins 2002; Stump 2008; Hopkins, Kong, and Olsen 2012). Where some have provided rich empirical insights into communities of religious ceremony and belief (Kong 1990, 2001, 2010), others have mapped the specifics of its spatial location (Knott 2005). Outside the binds of formalized religion, still others have embraced the esoterica of alternative spiritual practices—the occult, the supernatural, the otherworldly, the extrasensory—insisting on the enchantments secreted in the knowledges of modern social life (Bartolini, MacKian, and Pile 2013, 2019; Pile, 2005, 2006, 2012; Pile, Bartolini, and MacKian, 2019).

In this chapter, the miracle is not the emanation of any metaphysics. Nor, strictly speaking, is it a redescription of the forms and experience of secular modernity: a summoning of ancient ghosts skulking in well-oiled machines, a resurrection of modernity's dusty, disavowed spirits. Rather, in line with recent returns to much older conversations between politics and theology, I focus on the miracle as a temporal act: an occurrence, an occasion, that breaks up and breaks into the midst of things; an opening that usually arises when time is critical but its character most indeterminate. Indeed, my argument will be that such a "miraculous" politics turns on a reconsideration of temporal process itself: stopping its flows, arresting its rhythms, exceeding, or falling short of sequence, series, aim, or end. Corresponding to a specific reading of Judaic theology, what I come to describe as the miracle's *negative temporality* initiates a different sort of worldly commitment: an activity that has no basis in power, might even be impotent, or one whose claimant is not always equal to the demand placed on it. We might see this temporality as a minimal activity—*at once, most essential and least possible*—which refuses to be traded for any calculation, composure, or peace of mind; which carries no remote or final payoff, and asks only that we live in the weakest, most woundable, of presents. As we shall see, it is Judaism's rethinking of the divine miracle that allows us to inhabit the unsteadiness of this experience; only *from* it can we invite new and unpredictable futures, in both temporal and political terms.

In *Welcome to the Desert of the Real*, written in 2002 as a response to the first anniversary of the attacks on the World Trade Center and Pentagon, Slavoj Žižek cites another event in January of the same year: the refusal of fifty-one officers and reservists of the Israel Defense Forces to fight beyond the "Green Line" of Israel's pre-1967 border. While not the first example of selective nonparticipation in the IDF's policy of mandated conscription—in the late 1960s individual Israeli soldiers declined to serve in the occupied Palestinian territories, in 1982 *Yesh-Gvul*² launched its campaign against the Lebanon War and remained active throughout the First Intifada—the event of January 2002, for Žižek, represents the ethical event par excellence. On this account, what the refuseniks accomplished was not only a collapsing of the legal divisions separating citizen from noncitizen; enacting, in their dissent, that borderline or "zone of indifference" which Giorgio Agamben names for the subject both bound and abandoned to the force of the law (Agamben 2005a). More than this, for Žižek, the refuseniks' action amounts to a derailing of secular defenses; instantiating a movement toward that more immaterial, illimitable dimension that we might call the theological. Indeed, in its very exceptionality, the act of defiance delivers the structure of the divine miracle. As Žižek has it:

> It is here, in such acts that—as Saint Paul would have put it—there actually are no longer Jews or Palestinians, full members of the polity and *Homo sacer* . . . We should be unashamedly Platonic here: this "No!" designates the miraculous moment in which eternal Justice momentarily appears in the temporary sphere of empirical reality. . . . Our duty today is to keep track of such acts, of such ethical moments. (Žižek 2002, 116–17)

Invoking the "miraculous moment," Žižek's description clearly participates in those inherited and ongoing debates over whether radical political action is best understood as extraordinary or ordinary, ruptural or decisively ruled, transcendent or immanent—or, more precisely, the Gordian knot that intractably entwines the one within the other. Certainly, too, Žižek's "eternal Justice," like his petitioning of the apostle Paul, registers the peculiar archaicizing of our present age: the sacralization of philosophical questions, the scripturalizing of emancipatory struggles and, in the face of repeated secular deadlock, intuiting the dim, indistinct stirrings of messianic hope (de Vries 1999; de Vries and Sullivan 2006; Blanton and de Vries 2006; Connolly 1999; Taylor 2001; Critchley 2007, 2012; Žižek 2000). In particular, Žižek's reading of the refuseniks' extraordinary act appears to call up Carl Schmitt's early twentieth-century theorization of the theological derivation of political claims. Specifically, it alludes to the assertion in Schmitt's *Political Theology* ([1922] 1985) that just as the miracle waives the given laws of nature, so the earthly sovereign suspends the laws of the state, exceeding the juridical norm without the securities of principle or precedent but declaring the state's absolute right to self-preservation.

"The exception in jurisprudence is analogous to the miracle in theology," is how Schmitt formulates the knot of the paradox; that is, the capacity of sovereign authority to deactivate, disable, and at the same time fulfill the orders of natural or normal lawfulness (Schmitt 1985, 36).[3] For Schmitt, in short, the originary source of juridical regulation—and the space where the orders of law are most vitally in effect—always includes the facility to decide on a state of exception. "Belong[ing] to the very concept of the miracle" (43) in its singular and salvational powers, it is precisely this extra- or illegal inscription *within* the law—the "*outlaw dimension internal to [it]*" (Santner 2006, 22)—that for Schmitt "reveals the essence of State authority most clearly" (Schmitt 1985, 19). Thus, the sovereign decision not only transgresses a normally valid juridical order; it does so in the name of legality, creating a suspended state of affairs to which the law indiscriminately can then apply. "*Being-outside and yet belonging*" (Agamben 2005a, 35). This is the strange and twisting topology that Agamben, in his leading account of Schmitt, gives to the sovereign's "miraculous" violation on which all lawful activity depends. This is why Schmitt can say: "The exception is more interesting than the regular case . . . The exception does not only confirm the rule; the rule as such lives off the exception alone" (Schmitt 1985, 15).

But if Schmitt's miracle is conceived on the side of sovereignty and the violence of its continued survival, in what ways might Žižek's refuseniks reformulate its capacities? How might their "No!"—this exceptional, excessive breach—speak of the impotence, the essential powerlessness, of the ethical act? Can this "miraculous moment" be seen less as any definitive decision than as an unending and *unexceptional*—in Žižek's words, "eternal"—indetermination? Further, insofar as the refuseniks' action—or better, the miracle of their inactivity, the unlikely marvel of their non-action—is directed against the sovereign state, how does it relate to the exception at all?

My answer will be that although the miracle of Žižek's description alludes to Schmitt's transfer of theological into political categories, it pertains to a related but far less familiar figure and line of inquiry. I refer to Franz Rosenzweig (1886–1929), the German-Jewish philosopher and theologian who, although contemporary with the early years of Schmitt's (soon-to-be-lapsed) Catholic conservativism, offers us a very different account of the miracle and the meaning of the miraculous suspension. Although not as frequently cited as Schmitt in recent literatures that seek to renew a theological or messianic potential to radical secular action, Rosenzweig offers an important counterpoint (Dubow 2016, 2020). What emerges with him, I hope to show, is a twofold alternative: a theology no longer analogous to a juridical order and, accordingly, a miracle that suspends those very state-securities that the Schmittian exception seeks to vouchsafe. From this perspective, the instant of the refuseniks' "No!" diverges from Schmitt's model in working against anything resembling the force of an ultimate or executive decision. It is a "No!" that is as unpredictable as it is incomplete, as anguished as it is unwilled. Its pressure isn't the heroic rapture of change— and much less its juridical capture—but the precipitation of crisis; the initiation of a struggle. Above all, it is a "No!" that we can call miraculous precisely because *it takes exception to the very idea of the exception*: demoting sovereign power, untying the miracle from the ligatures of the law/nonlaw, overturning what is taken as the miracle's decisive state and giving it over to the excesses and obliquities of the ethical act (Weber 1992; Santner 2005; Honig 2007).

Crucially, as we shall see, all of this turns on Rosenzweig's particular conception of time in which a specifically Judaic account of the miracle possesses the tension of what I term a *negative temporality*. What I intend by this is not a time that cancels or retracts the processes of historical time; the negative is less an abandonment of history than an interruption that brings to light its hidden structure. This also means that while it is distinguished from the (sovereign) flows of persistence or perseverance, a "negative temporality" is not quite equivalent to the inactivity of prolepsis, postdating, or other forms of awaiting that seem to ready the future and square it quietly away. Indeed, one of its strains is that another, concealed time and another, concealed action makes itself present in the instant of *this* time and *this* action. As such, while my formulation of the negative relates to recent work in cultural geography that revalues passivity, even privation, as a corrective to the positivities of time (Harrison 2009), at issue here is less a reversal of action and actuality than the task of redeeming— which is also to say, *refusing*—them differently.[4] In short, it is a time that proposes nothing, projects nothing, carries no content, and yet brings the distant, the far side, into the extremity and facticity of a *now*. Its negativity consists not in the suspension of time but in the present and ungraspable surplus of it. In this present, the past is unbound from its immobility—*it is a past able to appear and justly claim its incompletions*—and the future faintly imaged but never brought to fulfillment. Indeed, contra Schmitt, we may see it as a temporality that is nonsovereign yet deserves to be called miraculous insofar as it intervenes on behalf of the indigent, the unpreserved, the *unexcepted*. In the end, we might not need to see Rosenzweig's theology of time and the miracle in religious or messianic terms. Like the refuseniks' "No!" the quality of its negativity is not the expression of despair: neither the cry of an exhausted, disheartened world nor a vision of a (political and temporal) state before or beyond it. Weaker than the ambitions of a promise but perhaps strong enough to be released from the captivity of the "what-is" or the "already-known," it is a time immersed in the openness of the present and a miracle that makes space for itself in the midst of the impossible.

Published a year before Schmitt's *Political Theology*, Rosenzweig's magnum opus, *The Star of Redemption* (1921), can be taken as its prescient critique. Although contextualized by the same Weimar-era crises around the legitimacy of liberal democracy and the limits of the constitutional state, Rosenzweig travels a very different route through the coexisting insides and outsides of religion and philosophy alike. Part of what enables this is not just contemporary debates over the relative attributes of Christian and Judaic tradition in an era of post-Enlightenment secularity. It is also initiated, as I've suggested, by the ways in which Rosenzweig implicitly undoes the Schmittian miracle by substituting the question of a "negative temporality" for the question of sovereign efficiency. That is to say, seeing the miracle as it occurs *in* and *as time* and so perforating, or awakening us to the possible perforations of, what is taken to be a full, completed or, in Schmitt's sense, *decisionist* state.

On this account, the miracle emerges as a sudden and eccentric event, a temporary moment cut into the relentless succession and consumption of moments. It is a *this-wordly* irruption that in-completes or un-fulfills time, that saves a moment but without sublating or preserving it. Moreover, such a time requires us to invert the usual metaphorics of the "miraculous moment" and insist on the darkened, weakened—negative—qualities of its illumination. For in taking the instant as its object, Rosenzweig's miracle not only lights up a present; it must grapple with the obscurities that shroud and shadow it—not to end or outshine the chiaroscuros of the lived moment but to intensify, quicken, and rouse us to them. Here, the very inability to dispel a (dense, darkened, disconsolate) present no longer infers the mistrust of political cynicism or the sober gloom of pragmatic rationality. It is the sole form that hope is allowed to retain.[5] Since it lacks the bliss of absolving salvation, here, too, the miracle is always only doubtful. It transpires in the proximity of possibility and the implausible, expectation and disappointment, preparation and misadventure. And it must fail to fully discharge; the requirement of its negativity is to remain negative. The miracle, in Gershom Scholem's words, "possesses a tension that never finds true release" (Scholem 1971, 35). Indeed, that the light it emits shows the recesses of the world to be finite, defenseless, insufficient, entangled, is not only the most tenable of revelations; it is the most emphatic one. "Revelation," Rosenzweig writes in "The *Urzelle*" to *The Star of Redemption*, "pushes itself into the world as a wedge; the This struggles against the This" (Rosenzweig 2000, 65).[6] It is a divine incursion angled in relation to, not set apart from, the empirical limits of the everyday; it kindles the precarities found there.

Put another way, if the exception analogizes the miracle, but in Rosenzweig's rather than Schmitt's version, then it does not attempt to compose the differences between the actual and ideal, the human and divine; it isn't the juridical conjoining of "an omnipotent God and an omnipotent lawgiver" (Schmitt 1985, 36). What it irradiates is neither an exception that might normatively be sustained nor the lineation of a dedicated path: a stage along the way, a future cleared ahead of time, and in advance of its experience. Instead, we might see Rosenzweig's miracle as an exegesis of the present, as an exposition of a particular dimension of time. It exposes at and within any moment a certain excess, an excitation, and its consequence depends on the subject's readiness to respond—and correspond—to the anxieties it discloses.[7] In short, this theology of the miracle refuses sovereign interdiction as it simultaneously entreats us to risk the unexpected, "gracing" apparent necessity with an alternative temporality that can intrude and undo it. With Rosenzweig, as Bonnie Honig puts it, "we are invited to think about how sovereignty postulates not just power or imposition or governance but also, subtly, receptivity, openness and a future" (Honig 2007, 80).

Perhaps this is the postsecular miracle that Žižek's refuseniks represent. A rigorous "No!" that might turn into a reversible "Yes," a sudden exhortation uncoupled from repetition and duration: not the reply to an obligatory command but the weight and exertion of a startling solicitation. Thus even as the force of the refuseniks' negation is anticipatory—the miraculous glimpse of a future, of a "better world or with the world that has to be 'bettered'" (Levinas 1992, 21)—it can never be final. For an exorbitance has been unplugged, a singularity stands out, an uncontainable break has occurred. Indeed, it is a miracle only because it arises when it is no longer possible, or fundamentally impossible, to cleave to (secular, juridical) fantasies of consistency and completeness. What matters, then, is not mastering the miracle's interruption. It is the singular way in which the refuseniks apprehend their "impossible," even impotent, politics together. Or we may say, theirs is a strange sort of miracle, realized in response to a kind of double negativity: both the negativity of present—discontinuous, in-determining—time, and the negativity of refusing any sovereign solution.

"On the Possibility of Experiencing Miracle" introduces part 2 of *The Star of Redemption*, the vast philosophical-theological treatise that Rosenzweig began while serving in the Balkan campaign in World War I and completed in the ruins of that catastrophe. At a time when Central European political structures had definitively failed and a once-solid (German) Idealist version of faith had culminated in the death of Europe's millions—a faith abandoned in a "front-line trench, very weakly manned, risking surrender at the first assault" (Rosenzweig 2005, 103)—the concept of the miracle counted among the casualties of the war. Theology, as Rosenzweig writes, "saw itself forced to carry out, higher up, the evacuation of the line it had held for thousands of years and to take refuge in a new position in further retreat" (103–4). But while 1914–18 confirmed the crises of theology, the decline of the miracle has its origin in the longer story of what Rosenzweig calls the "historical Enlightenment." By this he means the Hegelian (and implicitly, Christian-izing) attempt to find God in history; a mission that takes as its object of faith "the objective, thinkable All and the thinking of this objectivity" (115).

In Hegel, then in Marx, history is certainly the medium that ultimately determines the meaning of events. Endowed with an unequivocal judgment and a clearly intelligible signification, it is history that assesses which event is adequate to the unfolding commands of Reason.[8] So conceived, the miracle is plainly incompatible with modernity. Its very fabric—its nonobjectivity, its errancy, its impermanence—renders it unthinkable: neither real nor possible. What had once been "theology's strongest and surest companion" (103) is now its most awkward opponent.

> If the miracle really is the favourite child of faith, then, at least for some time, faith has seriously been neglecting its parental duties. For at least a century, the child has been only a source of embarrassment for the wet nurse dispatched by its parent, theology: she would have gladly have got rid of it somehow or other, if only—yes, if only—a certain consideration for the parent had not held her back while the child was alive. But time brings counsel. The old parent cannot live forever. And the wet nurse [theology] will know what to do with her poor worm [miracle], incapable as it is of living or dying on its own. She has, moreover, already begun making the preparations. (103)[9]

With *The Star of Redemption*, Rosenzweig, acting as wet nurse, was also preparing to reconstruct the miracle, venturing less to establish its explanatory content than to rethink the structure of its experience in modernity. But on what could a faith in miracles now depend? In its singularity and subjectivism, how might the miracle reenter a world dominated by the objectivist epic or the idealists' maximal "All"? Conversely, how to support the miraculous without forfeiting the merits of modernity or rejecting reason as the ground of philosophical meaning? Such questions form part of what Rosenzweig called "The New Thinking" (*Das neue Denken*), a novel methodological synthesis of religious faith and secular reason able to counter Enlightenment's deadening, and deadly, rationalisms and so engage more directly with the facticity of lived, circumstantial existence.[10] Thus, against a Hegelian and Christianizing logic of dialectic ascent—the historicist idea of temporal progress itself a secular eschatology, a profane argument of divine necessity—"The New Thinking" annuls the movement toward all uttermost or endmost things. A "redemption-in-the-world" (Gordon 2005, 192), a combination of belief *and* knowledge (*Glauben und Wissen*), or the materialist intrigues of what Rosenzweig calls an "absolute empiricism" (Rosenzweig 1999, 101)—the world exploded by the war demanded both.

Philosophy today requires, in order to be free of its aphorisms, and hence precisely for its scientific character, that "theologians" do philosophy. But theologians in a different sense, of course. For . . . the theologian whom philosophy requires for the sake of its scientific character is himself a theologian who requires philosophy—for the sake of his integrity. What was a demand in the interests of objectivity for philosophy will turn out to be a demand in the interests of subjectivity for theology. They complete each other, and together they bring about a new type of philosopher or theologian, situated between theology and philosophy. (Rosenzweig 2005, 116)

If theology and philosophy belong together, then one of Rosenzweig's boldest efforts is to locate the miracle *temporally*: removing it from the jurisdiction of sovereign execution and returning it to existential experience; to all that cannot be known independently of time. In this the miracle becomes something more and wholly other than the arbitrary or unconcrete. It not only means replacing the linearizing flows of historical progress with the facticities of the present. It also abridges the broad spans that separate the present from a defeated past and a deferred future; that is, from those extreme distances that allow time to distend into the paradoxical clarities of myth. Against this, only in the radical syncopation of past, present, and future can the unexpected and as-yet-unknown be realized or what is known reformed and rendered anew. Far from stepping outside or beyond time—either in the guise of speculative abstraction or its supposed opposite, "irrationality"— Rosenzweig's miracle appears in the midst of the intricate, unclosed net of time: sticking to the tensions, the incongruent *tensings*, of the world, to "the fact that here not everything is *assemblabe*" (Levinas 1992, 19). Finally, this is a conception of the miracle freed from a theology (and idolatry) of exception and announced to the actuality—which is the real *historicity*—of history.

It is not possible to explicate—or even gloss—the key themes that make up Rosenzweig's monumental *Star of Redemption*. My more limited aim is to consider the miracle as the disclosure of a particular Judaic, and negative, model of time. In the manner of Žižek's refuseniks, we might see it as a kind of unwilled, uncommanded, or even *prejuridical* miracle: as an "unexceptional" present by which we are somehow summoned and to which we must somehow respond *eventfully*; that is, respond "at the right point of time" (Rosenzweig 2005, 83).[11] If this sort of miracle makes no claim to an assignable cause, if its singularity can never contract to a warranty, it also need not disqualify or eclipse its phenomenal reality. It is not enchantment or demonology. Its meaning neither resides in any wonderous inexplicability nor in a divergence from the observable patterns of natural law. On the contrary. Rosenzweig's Judaic miracle might be a frail and faltering potential, but it is also liberated from the powers of rationalist explanation as from the feints of magical thinking. Indeed, uncoupled from the temporal traps of historicism, it consists precisely in the "taking of time seriously" (Rosenzweig 1999, 87). Even the book of Exodus, Rosenzweig reminds us in his notes on the medieval Spanish poet, Judah-ha-Levi, "explains the miracle of [the parting] of the Red Sea *post eventum* as something 'natural'":

> Every miracle can be explained—after the event. Not because the miracle is no miracle, but because explanation is explanation . . . *In fact nothing is miraculous about the miracle except that it comes when it does.* The east wind had probably swept bare the ford in the Red Sea hundreds of times, and will do so again hundreds of times. But that it did this at a moment when the people in their distress set foot in the sea—that is the miracle. *What only a moment before was coveted future, becomes present and actual.* (Rosenzweig 1953, 289–90, emphases added)

Here we are very far from relations of time as they signify indifferently—we may say, *intemporally*—in a system sanctioned by a divine, otherwordly, or politically sovereign source. For Rosenzweig's miracle "[does] not have to be proven like a universal proposition" or attest to the durability, and ultimate defensiveness, of the "once and for all" (Rosenzweig 2005, 174). As a present event, it comes about only with an inversion of such temporal accomplishments. Holding open the space of that inversion, paying attention to its "ever renewed presentness" (2005, 121), is what it means to hold true to the "star of redemption." The labor of doing so is already a mode of miracle; an enactment—of faith, of fidelity—that is the immanent *other* or *extra* of lawful, sovereign time. Indeed, even if nothing happens or "comes to pass"—achieved in weakness, realized without power, the miracle appears only along with the danger of disappearing unrecognized, unnoticed, overlooked—the imperative is to arrive, and to constantly rearrive, at this presently indeterminate point. "We are instructed to do the negative," as Franz Kafka puts it in his own assumption of this task. "The positive is already within us" (Kafka 2015, 27).

In part 3, book 1 of *The Star of Redemption*—the only section that deals exclusively with Judaism—Rosenzweig focuses explicitly on the relation between a historical and liturgical community to argue the ways that *Judensein* (Jewish-being) transpires in just such an alternative (negative, nonsovereign) temporality. *Judensein* he writes,

purchases its eternity at the price of temporal life. For it, time is not its time, not a field it cultivates and a share in its inheritance. For it, the moment is solidified and remains fixed between an augmentable past and motionless future, so the moment ceases to fly away . . . Past and future become two interchangeable measures; and in so becoming they cease to be past and future and, thus solidified, become likewise an unchangeable present . . . Since the teaching of the Holy Law—for the appellation of Torah comprises the two in one, teaching and law in one—therefore lifts the people out of all temporality and historical relevance of life, it also removes its power over time. *The Jewish people does not calculate the years of its chronology. Neither the memory of its history nor the official times of its lawgivers can become its measure of time; for historical memory is a fixed point in the past that becomes more past every year by one year, but a memory always equally near, really not at all past, but eternally present.* (Rosenzweig 2005, 322–23, emphases added)

To the forgettings and forgings ahead of chronology, Rosenzweig poses an eternal time. Such an eternity, however, leaves no place for anything resembling a calculus: of the past as something that has been and the future conceived as an indefinite extension, a discrete "once" ferried across into a sequence of repetitive, reproductive "once mores." The eternal, in contrast, pours into time. It saturates the present. It "fills the moment" (Rosenzweig 2005, 322). In it is compacted an always undone, always unfinished, past—a past able to momentarily emerge from absence and demand justice—and a future capable of being hastened or expected at any time. Perhaps right now? Perhaps "in the next moment" (322)? Perhaps "as early as today" (306)? Thus the eternal of Judaism radically abbreviates time—not in order to reduce or positively measure it, but to make its excesses tangible, material, graspable. In this, the eternal also fundamentally differs from the "bad infinity" famously condemned by Hegel but which, for Rosenzweig, the progressivist wastes of a Hegelian history still commend: "a past drawn out to an infinite length, a past projected forward"; precisely, not an eternity "but something that interminably crawls along the long strategic roadway of time" (244).

Against this, Rosenzweig's eternal pivots on the experience of its own insufficiency. We can see it as the experience of a lack, or even of a desire, that simultaneously points up what is lacking, what is *wanting*. In its folds lodge the splinters, the sparks, of unanswered pasts that in the sphere of the actual still await redemption and a future able to name itself as that instant. Neither passage nor mere persistence, the eternal thus wagers an inversion at the heart of time. Or rather, it speaks of an immanent redemption "valid at all times" and is therefore "without time" (323). Like the weakness of the uncommanded miracle, it asks us to keep alive the strains of the world or to "[turn] things into something other than they are" (Rosenzweig 1999, 77). With the spirit of its (eternal) negativity, it calls us to take the resolute, or the apparently ruled, as something yielding, wavering, unguarded. And, conversely, it brings the unlikely near-to-hand or places the impossible within the reach of possible action. What the sovereignty of knowledge and historical time mandates, Rosenzweig's miracle can now modify: "What was mute becomes audible, the secret manifest, what was closed opens up, that which as thought had been complete inverts . . . as new beginning" (2005, 119).[12]

Thus the miracle, whatever else it is, is novel, inaugural. Eternally making time happen, it marks the entrance of a rebeginning, the occurrence of a (nonjuridical) just event or the incitement to its ever-renewed efforts. With this argument, Rosenzweig not only rejects the terms of historical necessity, enriching the present with what might newly be brought into the world—but alarmingly, unpreparedly, inconclusively so.[13] He also introduces time as a term in the disclosures of ethical life.[14] As he writes in "The New Thinking": "To need time means: not to be able to presuppose anything, to have to wait for everything, to be dependent on the other for what is ours" (1999, 87).

When a beginning is no longer predicative and there is no end or abstraction to assess it, time ceases to be speculative and arises only as a present contingency. And to be present and contingent is to be weak: vulnerable to the risk of relations, susceptible to the anguish and anxieties of *being-in-relation*. This is why some of Rosenzweig's most remarkable suggestions about the miracle turn on the experience of language; or what following the (converted) Christian theologian and social historian, Eugen Rosenstock-Huessy, he calls "speech-thinking" (*Sprachdenken*) as it enacts the relational conditions of time itself. "The word," as Rosenzweig reminds us, "is only a beginning until it reaches the ear that re-ceives it and the mouth that responds to it" (1999, 87).

Like the structures of faith and hope, in other words, that which we speak and hear is nothing other than an undertaking of the discontinuities of time: the enunciation of a present instant turned consciously toward an externality, a stranger, a neighbor; an exchange between subjects bound to the temporality of its transmission. Indeed, unlike what Rosenzweig describes as the "mute essence" (2005, 174) of conceptual—that is, timeless and therefore incommunicative—thought, what is miraculous about a word, a name, a call, an address is that it does not posit or command anything. It cannot assume knowledge or postulate an explanation. Rather, the word—

immersed in time, nourished by it—lives only as a *sign*, a *symbol*; it is a semiotic form whose meaning is produced only in the temporal event or surprise of its being recognized.[15] And misunderstanding, disappointment, incomprehension is the sign's necessary component. Failure is always a threat, and the content of what is said does not yet imply evidence in a corresponding reality. In this sense the "miracle" of human speech or human dialogue is no less miraculous—both *momentary* and *momentous*—than is the word received from a divine source. Both set in motion an orientation other than a (sovereign) predicate, a signifying order, a *juris-diction*. Both constellate an ethical relation in which neither side—speaker and respondent, mouth and ear, an "I" that seeks a "you"—rests on the stability of self-enclosure. And both transpire only "in the non-permanent, in the moment" (Rosenzweig 2005, 176). Thus, language takes on the character of an authentic miracle insofar as in it insufficiency, agitation, incompletion do not so much disappear as change their significance. They invite the experience of an *eventful* encounter: a mutual exposure beyond the self, a revealing or revelation for whomever utters or receives it.

"Slanting through words there come vestiges of light," writes Kafka (1973, 287). Weakened and muddied though it is, what is illuminated in Rosenzweig's miracle—and in the muted light of our enunciations—is nothing but this sudden relational risk. The way in which a subject speaks or fails to speak, hears or fails to hear, is thus more than a matter of linguistic communication. In taking time, in *making time*, it also ties language to its present in-determinations, or to what it means to be *in-determined* by the presence of others.

And perhaps, this is what happens in religious experience. For if, as miracle, language and speech are inseparable from relations of time, then prayer and liturgy might be taken as the ultimate deepening of that profane imperfection. For Rosenzweig, this is sounded out every time the successions of secularized history are disrupted by the rhythms of Judaic ritual life. Here, in the daily-weekly-yearly cycles of prayer, as in the periodic return of a commemoration, ceremony, or observance, time saturates the everyday, swells within it, and so the "moment ceases to fly away" (Rosenzweig 2005,

322). Here, too, a memory reactivated, rebegun in the moment, makes the past contemporary, "really not at all past" (323) and, if we respond, hurries the future "into the very nearest thing, into the today" (307). Thus, for example, when the Hebrew bible tells the story of Exodus, as when the ritual of Passover requires that we annually retell it—"every individual is supposed to regard the Exodus out of Egypt as if he himself has also gone out" (323)—at issue is neither the precedent of origin nor its temporal commitment to repetition, reiteration, preservation. It is an unplugging of the past as it lays a critical claim on the present—a past that takes place as "ever new 'in the moment'" (173)—and the "not yet" (*noch nicht*) of a future that is always already here. Likewise, even those theological-political verdicts usually set into the end of times, the Jewish Day of Atonement and the Day of Judgment, are handed over to the inversions of the event. Here, where "no waiting counts, no hiding behind history" (344), there is neither redemptive deliverance nor wrathful damnation. There is only the intensifying of an ordinary, incalculable, accounting. Here, where what "yearly returns [is only] this the 'latest' judgement" (344), what arises is neither time redeemed nor time revoked. There is only the unfulfillable facticity of time spent, time lived. If these are moments of the most profound attestation, they are testimonies to unending, ever-present, incompletions. As Kafka puts it in his own practice of this Judaic point: "Only our concept of Time makes it possible for us to speak of the Day of Judgment by that name; in reality it is a summary court in perpetual session" (Kafka 2006).

To be sure, in all religious experience the practices of ritual and liturgy oppose the flow of the historical, inserting enclaves of eternity into the line of additive time. Judaism has no monopoly in this. To some extent, as Stéphane Mosès reminds us, the civil calendars of the secular world also include privileged moments—holidays, memorializations, celebrations— whose function is to "tell the same story, repeat the same scenario" (Mosès 2009, 58) in ways that simultaneously contract and accelerate time or, at least, put a brake on its mere passing. Rosenzweig's originality does not lie here. More crucial, for my purposes, is a certain shrouded or "inverted theology" (Adorno 1983, 245–71) in which time is returned to indeterminacy.[16]

Alternatively, we may see it as a time in which the singular instant comes to suspend sovereignty, and the event of the miracle is what sits in judgment of history. From this perspective, what progressivism negates becomes the unlikely site of possibility in the present: the useless and inoperative turn into the counterpoints of power, "eternity" vouches for that which is urgent or emergent, and hope breaks through precisely where the temporal governance of history is interrupted. "What for dialectical [non-inverted] theology is light and shadow is reversed," as Theodor Adorno writes of the Jewish messianism of Kafka (1983, 269). Henceforth, faith gives over to the disjointedness of time and "the moribund becomes harbinger of Sabbath rest" (270). Once again, the question is not any Schmittian (or sabbatical) exceptionality. It is a matter of living the break of the event emphatically: directing ourselves to "the demands of the day" (*die Forderung des Tages*) and taking away from this intensity a way of thinking and doing otherwise. Present impossibility, in short, is the very ordeal in which the miracle is located; it is not a barrier to its realization or the last word. If no historical or empirical situation can promise an approaching redemption, none excludes the dare that now, *this time*, something else, something other—unwilled, unbidden, ill-advised—might happen.

Where do these reflections leave us? What does it mean to abandon all positive predications, to give up strong assertions and admit only the (minimal but maybe also miraculous) presentness of time? A tentative, and paradoxical, answer might be that only a theology conceived in a mode of negativity—finite, contingent, out-of-joint—leads us back to a form of life able to think of hope, of redemption. And that the temporality of the miracle takes us back to the fragmentariness of this experience. Another answer, also paradoxical, might be that such a miracle shows us that it is secularity, and not theology, by which we are ensnared: that chronology itself is what magically captivates and transcends, transfixing us in the bright light of its sovereignties. In this, Rosenzweig's miracle not only works against our compliance in existing organizations and the emptied repetitions of individual and social life. It also offers a way out of the (Schmittian) state's extraordinary powers and asks that we suspend sovereignty's own suspensions. It allows us to see, in Eric Santner's words, the reversal at the heart of the matter: "that it is really secular thought that is most deeply invested in fantasies of exception, in other words, of being "excepted" [that is, 'saved'] from the lot . . . of finite human existence" (2005, 133). Indeed, insofar as it is geared to terrestrial time, we may see the Judaic miracle as a divine event announced for the sake of secularity; for the surprise of its unguarded, "uncommanded" openings, languages, inaugurations, incompletions. And we might add, on the side of a suddenly eternal—that is, both a timely and untimely—justice.[17] In a world where all odds are against it, the miracle makes it possible to breach a *chronic* (even reasoned, reasonable) despair over what is broken, dispirited, defeated. One can have no faith, be beyond belief, and yet, if the moment arises, recognize and respond to a rent in the unjust continuum of secular time (Critchley 2012).

Žižek's example of the refuseniks is *this* anachrony, *this* rent. In the instant of their "No!"—their miraculous refusal or in-completing of time—we might find occasional hints, echoes, moments, anticipations, of another politics. It is a "No!" that contains the little murmur of a little "yes": not as an affirmation that enshrines all that had been said but which generates the very indeterminacy it would seem to decide. It is also a "No!"—and a shaky "yes?"—that asserts nothing, fulfills nothing, but still lives for what might be gleamed in the obscurities of the present. In this, what I have proposed as a "negative temporality" not only graces time with an alternative perception—call it a miracle—but returns us to the communicative core of all ethics: "The power to refuse cannot come from us, nor in our name alone, but from a very poor beginning that belongs first to those who cannot speak" (Blanchot 1997, 112).

Notes

1. I take the first part of my title from a phrase in Samuel Beckett's 1953 novel, *The Unnamable*.
2. Literally translated as "there is a limit" or "there is a border."
3. Schmitt uses the analogy of the miracle on at least two other occasions: in a 1934 revised edition of the *Political Theology* published after he had joined the National

Socialist German Workers' Party and in his final work, *Political Theology II: The Myth of the Closure of Any Political Theology* (1970), his polemical self-exculpation from Nazi allegiance.

4. Among other geographical writings, I have in mind Paul Harrison's wonderful account of sleep as it works against the signifying priorities given to doings, actions, and energies in social scientific, and specifically geographic, accounts of practice and embodiment. Framed in part by Agamben's ideas of impotentiality as the potentiality "to not-be," Harrison's argument has various similarities to my own, except that my task is to show how "impotentiality" might testify to the ongoing importance of theological thinking.

5. The structure of this perception is by no means unique to Rosenzweig. Together with the apophatic speculations of much anti- or post-Hegelian thought, it speaks to a specifically German-Jewish tradition that understands the messianic as contained in the most seemingly diminished, devalued states. To this belongs the "darkness of the lived moment" which Ernst Bloch elaborates in *Spirit of Utopia* (1918); the "weak messianic force" of Walter Benjamin's "now-time" (*Jetztzeit*) in "Theses on the Philosophy of History" (1940); the "inverse" or "other theology" that Theodor Adorno elaborates in his "Notes on Kafka," and the "negative political theology" of Jacob Taubes's *The Political Theology of Paul* (1993), who reclaims the founding father of the Christian Church as a radical Jew. In their different vocabularies and directions, Emmanuel Levinas, Jacques Derrida, Giorgio Agamben, Alain Badiou, and Slavoj Žižek are the contemporary inheritors of this German-Jewish intellectual history.

6. The "*Urzelle*" ("Cell") refers to Rosenzweig's 1917 letter to Rudolf Ehrenberg in which he first formulates his philosophical system central to *The Star of Redemption*.

7. For a brilliant psychoanalytic reading of the miracle as an "ex-citation" of the subject's "creaturely" energies, see Santner, "Miracles Happen," 76–133.

8. To be sure, Schmitt's miracle is also the expression of a fundamental anti-Hegelianism and, like Rosenzweig's, it is premised on Hegel's metaphorical death. In Schmitt's case, however, it is Hegel as a philosopher of (bourgeois) normalcy and legal-bureaucratic rationality that forms the basis of his attack and, accordingly, of his arguments in favor of authoritarian decisionism. The famous words with which Schmitt greeted Hitler's accession to power—"[on this day, January 30, 1933] one can say that 'Hegel died'"—has been understood in just this sense; namely, the triumph of Nazism as the surpassing of Hegel's *Rechtsphilosophie* as a way of life based on universal principles and norms. The fundamental distinction between Schmitt's conservative, revolutionary anti-Hegelianism and Rosenzweig's Judaic variant is just one of the many ways in which their conceptions of the miracle differ.

9. Rosenzweig's extended metaphor, here, alludes to part 1 of Goethe's *Faust*. In response to a choir of angels singing the Easter message of Christ's resurrection, Faust declares,

"I hear your message, my faith it is that lags behind; and miracle is the favourite child of belief."

10. On the striking and complex resemblances between Rosenzweig's "New Thinking" and similar departures made by Martin Heidegger (evident especially in Heidegger's 1964 essay "The End of Philosophy and the Task of Thought"), see Peter Eli Gordon's major study, *Rosenzweig and Heidegger: Between Judaism and German Philosophy*. For the first account (1942) of the possible parallels and differences between Rosenzweig's and Heidegger's understanding of temporal existence, see Löwith, "M. Heidegger and F. Rosenzweig."

11. On the idea of a "precreedal, prejuridical experience of faith," as it links to Agamben's reading of St. Paul, see Critchley, "You Are Not On Your Own," 226–28.

12. As in many other things, Rosenzweig's understanding of Judaic time parallels Agamben's advocacy of Paul as he reads it through Walter Benjamin's messianism. "Here, the past (the complete) rediscovers actuality and becomes unfulfilled, and the present (the incomplete) acquires a kind of fulfilment." See Agamben, *The Time That Remains*, 75. One of Benjamin's own versions of this runs as follows: "[Remembrance] can make the incomplete (happiness) into something complete, and the complete (suffering) into something incomplete. That is theology." In Benjamin, *The Arcades Project*, 471.

13. As initiative, Rosenzweig's present time corresponds in interesting ways with Hannah Arendt's theme of natality or "birth-as-action" which she posits as a uniquely human and political faculty. See Arendt, *The Human Condition*, 175–81.

14. While it is difficult to see Rosenzweig as an ethical theorist or a theorist of alterity, in the manner of a later Emmanuel Levinas, the structuring of relationality *as* temporality suggests this possibility. On the clear distinctions between Rosenzweig and Levinas, whose *Totality and Infinity* (1961) acknowledges its debt to *The Star*, see Gordon, *Rosenzweig and Heidegger*, 200–201. For full-length studies of the affinities between Rosenzweig and Levinas in relation to their contributions to modern Judaism and philosophy, see Gibbs, *Correlations in Rosenzweig and Levinas* and Cohen, *Elevations*.

15. For an extended discussion of the miracle as a "sign-event" or as an "event of meaning" see Santner, "Miracles Happen," 83–86. On Rosenzweig's conception of speech in relation to the cognate categories of the written word and silence, see Glazer, "The Concept of Language," 172–84.

16. First used by Adorno in a 1937 letter to Benjamin with reference to Kafka, the concept of an "inverse theology" is elaborated in Adorno's later writing on Kafka. There it refers to Kafka's collapsing of the qualitative distinctions between the theological and the profane and the related dualisms they impose. "In Kafka . . . ambiguity and obscurity are attributed not exclusively to the Other as such but to human beings, and to the conditions in which they live" (Adorno 1983, 259). My reading of Rosenzweig's temporal model echoes something of this inversion.

17. For a related exploration of justice as a "disjointure" of time see Derrida, *Spectres of Marx*.

References

Adorno, Theodor. 1983. *Prisms*. Translated by Samuel and Shierry Weber. Cambridge MA: MIT Press.

Agamben, Giorgio. 2005a. *State of Exception*. Translated by Kevin Attell. Chicago: University of Chicago Press.

———. 2005b. *The Time That Remains: A Commentary on the Letter to the Romans*. Translated by Patricia Dailey. Stanford CA: Stanford University Press.

Arendt, Hannah. 1998. *The Human Condition*. Chicago: University of Chicago Press.

Bartolini, Nadia, Sara MacKian, and Steve Pile. 2013. "Psychics, Crystals, Candles and Cauldrons: Alternative Spiritualities and the Question of Their Esoteric Economies." *Social & Cultural Geography* 14 (4): 376–88.

———. 2019. "Spirit Knows: Materiality, Memory and the Recovery of Spiritualist Places and Practices in Stoke-on-Trent." *Social & Cultural Geography* 20 (8): 1114–37.

Beckett, Samuel. 1958. *Three Novels: Molloy, Malone Dies, The Unnamable*. New York: Grove.

Benjamin, Walter. 1999. *The Arcades Project*. Translated by Howard Eiland and Kevin McLaughlin. Cambridge MA: Belknap.

Blanchot, Maurice. 1997. *Friendship*. Translated by Elizabeth Rottenberg. Stanford CA: Stanford University Press.

Blanton, Ward, and Hent de Vries, eds. 2013. *St. Paul and the Philosophers*. New York: Fordham University Press.

Cohen, Richard A. 1994. *Elevations: The Height of the Good in Rosenzweig and Levinas*. Chicago: University of Chicago Press.

Critchley, Simon. 2007. *Infinitely Demanding*. London: Verso.

———. 2012. *The Faith of the Faithless: Experiments in Political Theology*. London: Verso.

———. 2013. "You Are Not on Your Own: On the Nature of Faith." In Blanton and de Vries 2013, 226–28.

Connolly, William. 1999. *Why I Am Not a Secularist*. Minneapolis: University of Minnesota Press.

Derrida, Jacques. 1994. *Spectres of Marx*. Translated by Peggy Kamuf. London: Routledge.

de Vries, Hent. 1999. *Philosophy and the Turn to Religion*. Baltimore MD: Johns Hopkins University Press.

de Vries, H., and Lawrence E. Sullivan, eds. 2006. *Political Theologies: Public Religions in a Post-secular World*. New York: Fordham University Press.

Dubow, Jessica. 2016. "Judaism's Other Geographies: Franz Rosenzweig and the State of Exile." *Environment and Planning D: Society and Space* 34 (3): 528–44.

———. 2020. *In Exile: Philosophy, Geography and Judaic Thought*. London: Bloomsbury.

Gibbs, Robert. 1992. *Correlations in Rosenzweig and Levinas*. Princeton NJ: Princeton University Press.

Glazer, Nahum N. 1988. "The Concept of Language in the Thought of Franz Rosenzweig." In Mendes-Flohr 1988, 172–84.

Gordon, Peter Eli. 2005. *Rosenzweig and Heidegger: Between Judaism and German Philosophy*. Berkeley: University of California Press.

Harrison, Paul. 2009. "The Absence of Practice." *Environment and Planning D: Society and Space* 27 (6): 987–1009.

Holloway, Julian, and Oliver Valins. 2002. "Editorial: Placing Religion and Spirituality in Geography." *Social & Cultural Geography* 3 (1): 5–9.

Honig, Bonnie. 2007. "The Miracle of Metaphor: Rethinking the State of Exception with Rosenzweig and Schmitt." *diacritics* 37 (2–3): 78–102.

Hopkins, Peter, Lily Kong, and Elizabeth Olsen, eds. 2012. *Religion and Place: Landscape, Politics and Piety*. Dortrecht: Springer.

Kafka, Franz. 1973. *Wedding Preparations in the Country and Other Posthumous Prose Writings*. Translated by Ernst Kaiser and Eithne Wilkins. London: Secker & Warburg.

———. 2006. *The Zürau Aphorisms*. Edited by Roberto Calasso. Translated by Michael Hofmann. New York: Schocken.

———. 2015. *The Aphorisms*. Translated by Willa and Edwin Muir and Michael Hofmann. New York: Schocken.

Knott, Kim. 2005. *The Location of Religion: A Spatial Analysis*. London: Equinox.

Kong, Lily. 1990. "Geography and Religion: Trends and Prospects." *Progress in Human Geography* 14 (3): 355–71.

———. 2001. "Mapping 'New' Geographies of Religion: Politics and Poetics in Modernity." *Progress in Human Geography* 25 (2): 211–33.

———. 2010. "Global Shifts, Theoretical Shifts: Changing Geographies of Religion." *Progress in Human Geography* 34 (6): 755–76.

Levinas, Emmanuel. 1992. "Foreword." In Mosès 1992, 13–23.

Löwith, Karl. 1942. "M. Heidegger and F. Rosenzweig, or, Temporality and Eternity." *Philosophy and Phenomenological Research* 3 (1): 53-77.

Mendes-Flohr, Paul, ed. 1988. *The Philosophy of Franz Rosenzweig*. Hanover NH: University Press of New England.

Mosès, Stéphane.1992. *System and Revelation: The Philosophy of Franz Rosenzweig*. Translated by Catherine Tihanyi. Detroit: Wayne State University Press.

———. 2009. *The Angel of History: Rosenzweig, Benjamin, Scholem*. Translated by Barbara Harshav. Stanford CA: Stanford University Press.

Pile, Steve. 2005. "Spectral Cities: Where the Repressed Returns and Other Short Stories." In *Habitus: A Sense of Place*, edited by Jean Hillier and Emma Rooksby, 235–57. London: Routledge.

———. 2006. "The Strange Case of Western Cities: Occult Globalisations and the Making of Urban Modernity." *Urban Studies* 43 (2): 305–18.

———. 2012. "Distant Feelings: Telepathy and the Problem of Affect Transfer over Distance." *Transactions of the Institute of British Geographers* 37 (1): 44–59.

Pile, Steve, Nadia Bartolini, and Sara MacKian. 2019. "Creating a World for Spirit: Affectual Infrastructures and the Production of a Place for Affect." *Emotion, Space and Society* 30:1–8.

Rosenzweig, Franz. 1953. *Franz Rosenzweig: His Life and Thought*. Edited by Nahum N. Glazer. New York: Schocken.

———. 1999. *Franz Rosenzweig's New Thinking*. Edited by A. Udoff and B. E. Galli. Syracuse: Syracuse University Press.

———. 2000. *Franz Rosenzweig: Philosophical and Theological Writings*. Translated by Paul W. Franks and Michael L. Morgan. Indianapolis: Hackett.

———. 2005. *The Star of Redemption*. Translated by Barbara Galli. Madison: University of Wisconsin Press.

Santner, Eric L. 2005. "Miracles Happen: Benjamin, Rosenzweig, Freud, and the Matter of the Neighbor." In *The Neighbor: Three Inquiries in Political Theology*, edited by Slavoj Žižek, Eric L. Santner, and Kenneth Reinhard, 102–3. Chicago: University of Chicago Press.

———. 2006. *On Creaturely Life: Rilke, Benjamin, Sebald*. Chicago: University of Chicago Press.

Schmitt, Carl. (1922) 1985. *Political Theology: Four Chapters on the Concept of Sovereignty*. Translated by George Schwab. Chicago: University of Chicago Press.

Scholem, Gershom. 1971. *The Messianic Idea in Judaism and Other Essays on Jewish Spirituality*. New York: Schocken.

Stump, Roger W. 2008. *The Geography of Religion: Faith, Place and Space*. Lanham MD: Rowman & Littlefield.

Taylor, Charles. 2007. *A Secular Age*. Cambridge MA: Harvard University Press.

Weber, Samuel. 1992. "Taking Exception to Decision: Walter Benjamin and Carl Schmitt." *diacritics* 22 (3–4): 5–19.

Žižek, Slavoj. 2000. *The Fragile Absolute: Or, Why Is the Christian Legacy Worth Fighting For?* London: Verso.

———. 2002. *Welcome to the Desert of the Real! Five Essays on September 11 and Related Dates*. London: Verso.

8   Dislocation: Disorientation: Disappearance: Distance

John Wylie

Dislocation:

Sometimes I think that I saw it happen directly; sometimes that it was only out of the corner of my eye. A glimpse and a flicker, in stuttering motion, like when an old film is slowed down to the point where you can see the joins of the frames. It could even be that I didn't actually see it happen at all; I only saw the aftermath, the consequences. Perhaps my ongoing remembrance of the event has filled things in for me retrospectively, so that I seem to see (though really to *feel* as much as see) the exact moment when she lost her footing as she ran, slipped, and tumbled onto the rocks.

A bad fall. We were up on Dartmoor, a high moorland in the southwest of England. The landscape there is studded with stark rocky outcrops, locally called Tors. By virtue of their relative hardness, these rocks have resisted erosion and so have come to stand exposed to the elements—wind, rain, and frost. Over the ages, therefore, the Tors have weathered, cracked, and splintered, so that today they appear almost like ruinous, ancient hilltop temples or tombs, with their spires, columns, and slabs of rock ringed by wider circles of boulders and smaller debris.

The Tors of Dartmoor are magnets for rock climbers and for walkers, clamberers, and day-trippers such as us, who drive up to the high moor at the weekend from the surrounding region. On the day I am speaking of here, we were at one of the best-known Tors—Hound Tor, famous for its connection to the Sherlock Holmes mystery, *Hound of the Baskervilles*. I can't remember why she started to try to run when the ground we were crossing, just below the peaks of the Tor, was so steep and uneven, requiring your care and attention with every step. She was only seven at the time though—my elder daughter.

I think my wife was a few feet closer and reached her first. I was only a second or two behind though, and I remember that my first feeling at that scene was relief. She hadn't hit her head, she was sitting up, dazed but clearly awake, there were no obvious cuts or bleeding. It was actually a bystander, an older woman who happened to be passing nearby, who said that there seemed to be something wrong with her arm. And one thing I do recall now is that she wasn't sobbing or frantically upset in the shocked and gulping way young children who've fallen or hurt themselves can often be.

Her arm—yes. It's odd to recollect how it did take us a minute or two to properly understand she had hurt it badly. That she couldn't really move it, that she didn't know what was wrong with it. That we had to get down off this hillside and back to the car as quickly as we could. Everyone must find themselves in moments like these, at some point in their life. The landscape splinters, becomes profoundly inhospitable in an instant. We huddled together and stumbled down the slopes to the car park. She couldn't be carried, and by now she was starting to cry with fright.

Once we had her coat off and she was sitting in the car, our fraught trek down from the Tor finally complete, I was able to take a closer look. Her arm—her left arm—was clearly all wrong in some way, that was obvious even under her jumper. It looked twisted and lifeless, as if withered from birth. And I think that it was at that point that I began to focus on a specific word I'd never had cause to pay attention to before: *dislocation*. We managed to get her seatbelt on and drove down off the moor and back onto the main roads, straight to the hospital.

This all happened nearly ten years ago. And the story could easily end there too—a shocking and upsetting event, but also in a sense a humdrum one. At the hospital, diagnosis was swift—elbow *dislocation*: not that common an injury but hardly unknown either, especially in younger children with flexible and hyperextendable joints. We moved through X-ray, through a (for me) stomach-churning relocation procedure under local anesthetic, and finally on to plaster. We kept our appointments in the weeks that followed, and when the plaster came off, all seemed well.

Except that then it kept happening, again and again, in the months and years that followed. Eight times in total the joint dislocated. We discussed surgery with the doctors, but they made sense when they said it was best to let time take its course—because any ligament-tightening while she was still a child could lead to arthritic problems in the joint in later adult life. But sometimes it seemed to take only the smallest impact—on one occasion, for example, from jumping feet-first into a swimming pool. A frantic few moments as I scrambled to reach her, struggling in the water. And, as the years went by, so the dominant feeling become one of *dismay* and *disappointment*. Her arm—always the same arm—would be encased in plaster for several weeks at a time and nursed in a sling for more weeks after that. She couldn't safely take part in any kind of contact sport. An aura of fragility emerged. Her overall physical confidence diminished and has stayed lower than it should be to this day. She has never jumped into a pool since.

Nor has she ever been back to Hound Tor. My wife and I have, though, at least two or three times on our own. Once, I remember, we tried to locate the exact spot where it had first happened. But we couldn't—we *disagreed*, and not just on precisely where she had first fallen, but on the sequence of subsequent events, who had done and said what. It was clear, clambering once again over the broken ground around the base of the Tor, that it was not just one body that had suffered here. Time, memory, and even in a way the landscape itself had been *dislocated*.

This is a truism of shocking and traumatic events, of course. They show how thin the crust of any seemingly secure and settled order really is. Our misplaced faith in location. The fatal error of our geographies.

Dis-Geographies:

The prefix *dis-* is widely used and understood in the English language. Most commonly its use carries a negative connotation, as for example in words such as *disrespect*, *dislike*, or *discomfort*. In such cases, there is also a sense of a positive and, perhaps, primary or regular state that is being negated or qualified. In this way, words that begin with *dis-* can often seem to signify decidedly secondary phenomena, in comparison to an *original* that they are defined against. And this may be true of some key geographical or spatial terms of this ilk. *Place* and *location* could be viewed, for example, as indicating primary and original states of affairs—to be in place, to be located, as a kind of natural or given order—whereas *displacement* and *dislocation* are aberrations, deviations, indications that something has gone wrong. There cannot be many things more unnatural-looking than a *dislocated* joint.

In the context of this book, this chapter began as an embryonic but rather grandiose set of ideas about words beginning with *dis-* and the prospects they offered, alongside words beginning with *de-*, *un-*, and *mis-*, for formulating a wider "negative geography." Following the haunted logics introduced by Derrida (1994), such a geography would proceed from the observation that, far from being a secondary and separate phenomenon, a word such as *displacement* was always already inside place, insidiously at work within it; in truth defining and constituting it. I imagined a wholesale revisioning of key concepts and received nostrums, such that attention would refocus upon a series of phenomena hitherto somewhat hidden behind their supposed originals. What would a geography look like, for instance, that assumed that *displacement* was primary, that *displacement* was in fact the *precondition* of anything we might call "place"?

But my ambitions in this kind of direction quickly faltered in the face of not just the scale of the idea, but also the complexity and nuance. Many *dis-* words in English are not negations or qualifications at all, as I will *discuss* a little further below. There are also, importantly, many instances of course where the purportedly original term is lost to common usage, and the prefixed version now stands alone, so to speak. For example: *disguise, distinguish, distort, disparage.*

What I offer in this chapter is therefore a more circumspect and focused set of reflections, organized around four *dis-* words that I have found persistently intriguing—or perhaps *disturbing, distinctive.* I have already spoken about *dislocation*. The other three are *disorientation, disappearance,* and lastly *distance*. A *disquieting* affective quality threads through all four words; they all describe occurrences and states of affairs where a supposedly secure and sure-footed sense of place and belonging is in various ways queried and *disrupted*.

In the rest of this section, though, I will offer a wider and more speculative initial thematizing of the geographies of *dis-*. I make no claims to specialist linguistic or etymological expertise here, and nor is my listing intended to be exhaustive or definitive. I aim instead to offer a provisional but hopefully critical and reflective layout of the generation of complex geographical meanings and experiences in this family of words. As will hopefully be clear, this involves accentuating the negative first, but beyond that also considering some further types of *dis-* terms that suggest other formations of knowledge, spatiality, and subjectivity.

1. Negativity

As noted above, perhaps more frequently and directly than any other meaning or usage, the geographies of *dis-* imply negative thoughts and actions, whether directed toward others or objects. See for example: *disable, dislike, disavow, disown, disparage, disregard, disrespect.*

2. Harmful transformations

As a variant or subcategory of point 1 above, the geographies of *dis-* can often imply deliberately harmful impacts and effects, notably in respect of bodies. See for example: *disfigure, dishonor, distort, disembody.*

3. Unhappiness and spiritual or emotional loss

One further negative category of terms sees the affective geographies of *dis-* involve diversely negative or challenging feelings, either experienced in oneself or being inculcated in others. See for example: *disappoint, disgruntle, disenchant, dishearten, dismay, disquiet, disillusion.*

4. Purification and expulsion

It is sometimes the case that the geographies of *dis-* involve attempts to attain a more "pure" or singular state of being, or state of affairs, through the deliberate expulsion or exclusion of particular elements. See for example: *disgorge, disinfect, dismiss.*

5. Lost, astray

The geographies of *dis-* frequently invoke a sense of having lost one's ground or of being unsure and uncertain of one's place in the world. A *disaster* is the loss of one's guiding star, one's pathway in life. This may also involve a loss of bodily propriety. See for example: *disaster, disorient, disruption, disinherit, disarray, disheveled.*

6. A specific pathway to follow

Alternately, however, the geographies of *dis-* may involve becoming a follower of a particular pathway or committing to a specific journey through life. See for example: *disciple, discipline.*

7. Spatial spread, reach, and intensity

Perhaps the most obvious "geography" at work here. The geographies of *dis-* often pertain to spatial patterns and processes, consciously programmed, mapped, or measured. See for example: *distribute, disseminate, dissolve, dispense, disease.*

8. Spatial and temporal incoherence

But the clear corollary to the point above is that the spatialities of *dis-* are just as commonly about a loss of spatial and temporal coherence. See for example: *disintegrate, discontinue, disorder, dissipate, disperse.*

9. Singularize and pinpoint

A third clearly spatial element of the geographies of *dis-*, and one linked to my fourth point above regarding purification, involves the need to single out specific features, objects, or people for the purposes of visibility, or measurement, or admiration, or approbation. See for example: *distinguish, discriminate, discrete, distill.*

10. Visibility and invisibility

The geographies of *dis-* are sometimes characterized by a stress upon questions of visibility and invisibility. They involve both showing and concealing, hiding away and bringing to light. See for example: *discover, disappear, disclose, dispel, display.*

11. A sense of apartness

The geographies of *dis-* may at times invoke a set of actions or dispositions that invoke or act to shape a more isolated and remote state of being, sometimes with connotations of apathy, withdrawal, and indifference. See for example: *disconnect, disengage, distance, disinterest.*

12. A sense of objectivity

Lastly, occasionally and variably, the geographies of *dis-* also characterize an approach or an attitude that is "apart" and *distant* in a rational, scrutinizing sense. See for example: *dispassionate, disinterested, discern.*

What can we take from this provisional *discussion* and *dissection* of the varied geographies of *dis-*? I hope in part that this is where my chapter can contribute to the wider themes and propositions of this collection. Negatives, nons-, and absences are difficult to work with in terms of phenomenological and affective experiences, as the editors discuss in their introduction, precisely because any action, description, or reference that brings them into light, into visibility, itself negates their particularity, their specific manner of not-being. Just as it is frequently impossible to prove a negative—to prove you do not possess something or have not done something—so it is difficult to frame the negative without lapsing into positivity and presence. Another choice is to portray the negative as a kind of vital vacuum, an inaccessible and indescribable void or exteriority that nonetheless produces forms of life by way of imperative response (see Rose 2014). But the varied geographies of *dis-* I have mentioned allow us to at least partially sidestep these stark options. For me, their differences and specificities offer us forms of *negative resourcefulness* in attempting to rewrite geographies of presence, identity, and settled order.

Disorientation:

Like many people currently resident in the United Kingdom, I experienced the events of June 23, 2016, and their aftermath as a profound *disorientation.* To be *disoriented* is commonly also to be nauseated, and I woke the day after the Brexit referendum already feeling sick and anxious after an uncertain night of fitful sleep. I happened to be away, external examining, and my first confirmation of the *disaster* that had befallen Britain was a text from home at about 6 a.m. In an unfamiliar bedroom, I scrambled for the TV remote.

On occasions such as this, whether they be geopolitical traumas or events such as significant family births and deaths, I often feel a *distance* come alive within me, a kind of self-conscious watchfulness, such that there is part of me that always feels like an accidental bystander, caught up in the event but also in a sense uninvolved. I think this sometimes comes across to others as an inappropriate flippancy and excessive sarcasm in my response to events. On the afternoon of June 24, the day after the decision in favor of Brexit, I had to take a long train journey back home across Britain, and this did not help me at all. The Wi-Fi was infuriatingly intermittent and slow. The countryside we curved through, at least on the first part of the journey, was abundant and vivid, basking complacently in the midsummer sunlight, and seeming more than ever like the smuggest of falsehoods. The lie of the land, more evident than ever before as I sat oscillating between unassuaged anger and detached *disbelief.*

I wonder now who they all were, the hundreds of different people I shared a carriage with on three separate trains that day. I'll confess that I drank a succession of cans of beer, a habitually poor choice that further darkened my mood. Through all the hours of the journey, I don't recall anyone saying anything out loud about the referendum vote, positive or negative. But I don't believe that I was imagining the rather tense and brittle atmosphere on these trains, with passengers hunched even more tightly than usual around their screens, watching it all unfold. And I succumbed that day to another bad habit I have since at times struggled to shake off—that of mentally assigning all the strangers I pass and encounter in everyday life to the two Manichaean categories of "leaver" or "remainer." By the time the train finally reached my home station I was already feeling a little sickened by myself, my newly *disoriented* self.

In their essay on "Everyday Brexits," Ben Anderson and Helen Wilson (2018) *discuss* the different ways in which the referendum result and (at the time of writing, for both them and me) its ongoing fallout is felt. They note its time-out-of-joint quality: Brexit has somehow both already happened and is still yet to happen. Noting further that the predictions and analyses of economic geographers and regional scientists are themselves part and parcel of this febrile and *dissonant* atmosphere, they also argue for a need to move beyond "the dramatic sense of event that marked the period immediately after the referendum result" (292). Instead, in acknowledging the myriad affective dimensions and innumerable minor choices and itineraries that current circumstances involve "a geography of Brexit might start by mapping how Brexit surfaces and becomes with everyday life and in everyday spaces, as it shifts from a dramatic *disruption* to something that touches people and becomes personal as it oscillates between the foreground and background of their lives—occasionally intensifying in moments of contestation and *dissensus*" (292).

Dissensus, in the terms employed by Jacques Rancière (2015), seems an uncannily apt word in the context of Brexit, insofar as it indicates, beyond a sense of a negated or broken political consensus, a more basic rupturing of taken-for-granted stances and perceptions. Did I ever really believe that a majority would vote to leave the EU? Do I even believe it now? The personal geographies of Brexit, and specifically the implications of the electoral verdict, surface in experience first of all as a *loss of confidence* in my judgment and perception, almost to the point of being a matter of shame and embarrassment. I no longer know how things *stand* in the UK or how the land lies; the landscape has lost its cardinal directions and way-markings.

This is why it seems appropriate to speak here about *disorientation*. In *Queer Phenomenology*, Sarah Ahmed (2006) offers a series of lucid observations about the phenomenologies of orientation and *disorientation*. If the former denotes a relatively secure and settled world of assured locations and directions—at least for those whose bodies are straight, white, and comfortably fed—then the latter can be understood as a certain *loss* of worldly certainty, whether momentarily or more persistently. In this way "*disorientation* as a bodily feeling can be unsettling, and it can shatter one's sense of confidence in the ground or one's belief that the ground on which we reside can support the actions that make a life feel liveable. Such a feeling of shattering, or of being shattered, might persist and become a crisis" (2006, 157).

As Ahmed goes on to elucidate, *disorientation* is as much quotidian as "shattering." It might inhere, for example, in the irritation we experience when our concentration upon a particular object or task is interrupted.

More widely, however, *disorientation* speaks to the lived experiences of those who find themselves either oblique to or more visibly excluded from orientated spaces—for example from landscapes and lifelines as they are heteronormatively orientated. Ahmed's argument, though, is not that experiences of *disorientation* should be fetishized or viewed as having some inherently transformative potential. As she writes, the aim is to "think about how queer politics might involve *disorientation*, without legislating *disorientation* as a politics. It is not that *disorientation* is always radical. Bodies that experience *disorientation* can be defensive" (2006, 158).

This last sentence almost sounds like a common explanation for why so many in the UK voted to leave the EU in 2016, and also for the subsequent reaction of many who voted to remain. Ahmed's focus in her work is not specifically upon national identity or nationalism, but I hope I can adopt her insights in this context. Anderson and Wilson (2018, 294) note that "the event of Brexit continues to (re)produce and (re)animate relations of power, to *(dis)orientate*, and give rise to new forms of collective and bodily life that shape, unravel or enliven everyday practice and experience in often incoherent and fragmented ways." This will still be true even if you are reading these lines many years from now. I doubt if I will have reoriented myself to life in England no matter how much time passes. Born in Northern Ireland, I am entitled to both British and Irish citizenship—a highly privileged position. Before Brexit I was happy to inhabit the ambiguity that this situation supplies. In particular, I was happy to endorse the double negative implied: the latitude to be neither British nor Irish, to sidestep any insistence that your identity had to be pure and singular. The *disorientation* of Brexit, as it unfolds over time, is mostly, but not only, about finding myself suddenly an outsider, an other in the landscape I'd dwelt in for over twenty years. When, in October 2016, a few months after the referendum, the then-UK prime minister, Theresa May, stated in a speech that "if you believe you are a citizen of the world, you're a citizen of nowhere," the situation clarified further for me. In this new actuality, to be a legitimate person at all now involved, it seemed, a necessary commitment to somewhere—to place, ground, blood. I started the process of applying for an Irish passport. I felt the *disorientation* of finding yourself *obliged* to be orientated, one way or another.

Disappearance:

"How to Disappear Completely" is the title of a track on the British band Radiohead's 2000 album, *Kid A*. For much of the track, a straightforward guitar-strumming pattern oscillates between E minor and G major. Above this, the lead singer croons in a long-drawn-out falsetto, and more lush orchestral string arrangements swell and fade. These layers of sound run through several cycles and also gradually build in intensity as the track progresses. But the song is perhaps best known for its distinctive ending: instead of a straightforward crescendo, the voices and strings collapse into a swooning, *discordant* fugue. The effect makes for a few moments of uneasy listening. And then, from within the heart of this *dissonance*, a high-pitched, crystal-clear voice emerges, carrying the central three-note refrain of the song onward and upward, into an aerial, sonically purified space.

The listener is thus left with a complex but satisfying sense of resolution and renewal. The overall tone of "How to Disappear Completely" is intensely elegiac, if not doleful. But by the end, the song's title seems like a misnomer. We could perhaps understand the song's soaraway finale as indicating one sort of *disappearance*—thought of as a kind of escaping or breaking free. Or, given its ethereality, as a sublimation, a turning-into-air. But the song's crescendo can also be heard, I think, as a keen sense of presence and thereness reasserted. Just at the precise point where order and progression seem to have utterly *dissolved*, a singular voice reappears, insistently placing itself at the center of the listener's perception.

The lesson is that it is impossible to *disappear* completely. Just as it's impossible to somehow begin all over again, as if there had ever been some unshadowed instant of beginning in the first place. This doesn't stop people from trying to, however, or at least from advising others on how to best go about *disappearing*. This is something I learned when, in the course of working on this chapter, I first typed "how to disappear completely" into my chosen internet search engine. I was hoping of course to find out more about the track by Radiohead, but many of the suggested pages were, in fact, step-by-step guides to vanishing. Or let me put this more precisely: they were guides to how to *disappear* if you were a male American or British citizen with credit cards and social media accounts and a paranoid sense of being under surveillance by governments and corporations.

These rather pathetic fantasies, with their unacknowledged but clearly visible senses of entitlement and their juvenile, masculinist vision of what freedom might be, stand in stark contrast to the trauma and heartbreak of actual *disappearance*, both in terms of those people who go missing and those, so to speak, left behind. Across their rich and varied analyses of the geographies of missing people in the UK, Hester Parr and Olivia Stevenson's (2015) *discussion*, "No News Today," is *distinctive* for me because of its focus upon the difficulties of *witnessing* people who have gone missing. The specific issue at stake here concerns the *disjuncture* experienced by families between their acute sense of the individuality and uniqueness of the missing person and formal police approaches, which tend toward more impersonal categorizations of motivation and character. Thus, while the fact of *disappearance* is acknowledged, the status of bearing witness to *disappearance* is questioned. The ongoing presencing of the absent person is thereby rendered difficult, almost in some cases suspect and uncertain, and the emotional trauma of the situation is redoubled. For most of those who are known to have died, Parr and Stevenson argue, processes of remembering and narrating may achieve a stable absent-presence, one that ensures the ongoing salience of both loss and recognition. So, in respect of those who have disappeared, they suggest the need for

> the creation of new spaces of characterful witness. If renewed attention could be directed to ways of discussing and gathering and retaining character witness not only as a function of police work, but also as an important form of cultural work, then a version of durable biographies for missing people may be possible. In part this is about trying to create an adequate narrative space of recognition for the missing. (308)

They further describe characterful witnessing as "an active process whereby the biography of the missing is held open, as continuing, and as related to their new possible geographies" (309). What is envisaged is therefore somewhat akin to a mourning process, but crucially one that does not seek some closure or resolution—or even some reciprocal dialogue. Instead, the open contingency of *disappearance*, the breaking-up of the world that it involves, is recast as a sequence of potential reappearances, invisible in one sense, but plotted out nonetheless as an apparitional life-course.

It thus remains impossible to *disappear* completely. Those who like to dream and plan of doing so are merely fantasists, because they mistakenly assume their own singularity and coherence. As if their lives were theirs alone, as if their subjectivity really were some sealed and self-sufficient ipseity. Just as no pure moment of presence is ever within reach, so you could never hope to vanish without a trace. Even your attempts to erase yourself will register and echo, and like a ghost that tries to hide away you'll be glimpsed and not forgotten.

Distance:

Out of all the different words that could be considered here, *distance* is perhaps the most proverbially spatial. It is also the term with the most significant geographical pedigree, having served time as both object of and frame for analysis, for writers and researchers across paradigms of inquiry. At some points in the past, especially during the quantification of geographical analysis in the 1960s, it could even be claimed that geography *was* the study of *distances*, especially distances as conceived metrically, in the objective sense, as the measured space separating two distinct entities, whether bodies, cities, or planets. This kind of *distance* is not simply amenable to measurement, it *is* measure, and so comes to serve as the yardstick by which a multiplicity of geographical patterns, processes, and relationships can be mapped, modeled, and visualized. In this way, just as much as *points* (see Doel 1999), *distances* come to have ontological weight within the quantitative geographies that emerged in the era of spatial science. Thus we eventually arrive at Tobler's (1970) "first law of geography":

"everything is related to everything else, but near things are more related than *distant* things."

But *distance* is also an example of something I mentioned earlier in this chapter—a *dis-* prefixed word where the link to a root word is commonly severed in usage. *Dis-stance*. With some such words, the root has dropped from regular usage (*disparage, distinguish*). *Stance* remains an everyday word, of course, but I do not think that *stance* and *distance* would be routinely paired or considered together. With this in mind, what might the latent presence of *stance* within *distance* have to tell us about the nature of *distances*?

First of all, stance is an intriguing word because, in a manner similar to words such as perspective or outlook, it has come to denote a person's attitudes, values, and opinions. It signifies *you*, in other words. Your stance on a topic is, fairly frequently, an indication of *who you are*, what kind of person you are, culturally, politically, and so on. In this sense, *distance* might therefore readily connote a sense of otherness and difference, insofar as it is by definition the negation or *disturbance* of your stance.

A second point to make regarding stance is that it is, of course, very much a bodily word, a word that involves a particular bodily *posture*. If words like perspective or outlook define personhood in primarily visual terms, as a gaze upon the world, stance by contrast offers us a figure who is *upstanding*. You are not sitting or lying down, you are not reclining or slouching—instead you are standing up. Stance in this way has a decidedly active signification. The person who is standing up is, so to speak, ready to act, clearly possessed of agency and capacity. And as is likely already obvious, these associations also come with *distinctively* moral overtones. The *upstanding* person is a figure of moral probity, even righteousness. Secure in their standing within their society, they signify correct behavior, they are trustworthy and reliable. The upstanding person is someone whose stance is firm and secure, someone who can be depended upon. Within all this, however, there are also clearly conservative, starchy undertones. An upstanding pillar of the community is an upholder of the status quo and a figure, at least potentially, of *disapproval* and negative judgment.

Equally, the upstanding person may be exposed as a hypocrite or fraud; their supposed propriety in fact but a mask for poor or illegal behaviors.

If *distance* was straightforwardly the negative of all that is implied by stance, then we would arrive quite quickly at some apparently definitive conclusions. *Distance* would equate with difference and otherness, as noted above. It would be not-me and not-here, and in fact it would take its difference *from* an originary stance. The further away from this upstanding figure you went, the greater the degree of difference would be apparent. *Distance* would equally carry not just a sense of strangeness and foreignness, it would have a *disreputable* connotation. Simply by virtue of not being *stance*, distance would appear not just different but suspicious and doubtful too. Or perhaps, to turn this around, the *distant* would seem latently rebellious, dangerous, or threatening.

Alternately, however, it could be argued that, rather than being the negation or opposite of stance, in a manner akin to self and other, distance instead must be understood as a particular kind of relation to stance—to the upstanding subject. In this way, these formulations, and in particular a vision of a world epicentered by stance, begin to echo a classical phenomenological account of *distance*. If, as Merleau-Ponty (1962) argues in the *Phenomenology of Perception*, spatiality begins with and proceeds from the body—implicitly a standing body, we could argue—then *distance* and closeness, the near and the far, would necessarily have to be reckoned from the stance of the body. Here, and also, as Harrison (2007) argues, in the writings of Martin Heidegger, *distance* does not straightforwardly signify difference or threat. Instead the *distant* is domesticated and familiarized through its relation to stance. Proceeding from the given perspective of the subject the *distances* of the world are orderly and even graceful. The near and the far array themselves in such a fashion that everything is in its right place, in a composed, ordered, and reassuring landscape organized around the subject. The distant is, so to speak, assimilated by stance (see Harrison 2007).

But as I write these words and review this chapter in late June 2020, a new and distinctive sense of *distance* has emerged. With the advent of COVID-19, human populations across the world have been instructed, and sometimes compelled, to *keep distant* from one another. This has meant absorbing an insight that will have been familiar to those working in health and medicine but novel in practice for others—that in order to *take care* (of yourself and others) you must *keep your distance.* For those with the resources to practice and patrol it, a new kind of bodily propriety has emerged, upending longstanding cultural norms regarding personal space and everyday interaction. The limits and boundaries of the body-as-ordinarily-conceived have been extended, as if every body were now haloed by a coronal nimbus, an imperceptible dome of tiny droplets and particles. To see others as potential threats, to see your own body in terms of vulnerability—this is something close to a normalized *disposition* for some. But to practice care via *distancing*—via face masks, via stay-home orders, via a sudden infrastructure of new signage—runs against the grain of all that associates care with closeness, empathy, tactility.

Thus, in many countries where restrictions on movement, contact, and interaction have been imposed in attempts to contain the spread of the virus, it is also the case that a specific kind of *distance* has been lost, for now: *touching distance.* Other human bodies—at least beyond the household, an important consideration—have become untouchable, ringed by a private cordon sanitaire as if we were all now in some way holy or regal, untouchable, and thus placed above and beyond the mundane press and packaging of life.

But in saying this, I think it is crucial to note that the response to the pandemic clarifies one thing above all: the relation between *distance* and *privilege.* Distance, especially in the sense of a "spaciousness" surrounding a particular subject or group, has always been a matter of privileges and inequalities. In the context of 2020, when presented with a plea to sanctify, at least in theory, everybody, the inability of many to *distance* themselves induces terror, shame, and outrage. *Disproportionately,* those who succumb to the virus are those who must travel to work and must work closely with others, those whose accommodation is cramped and confined—in a way, if I may be permitted this phrasing, those whose *standing* in the world is lowered and compromised. If your standing is relatively high, by virtue of wealth or advantage, then you are better able to *distance* yourself. You might have the funds to be remote and secluded, or even to flee, hide, or withdraw from view—in other words, you have the stance required to array a more secure set of *distances* around yourself.

A fuller and more systematic analysis of the multiple geographies produced by the coronavirus pandemic will of course itself require greater *distance*, time, and perspective. But across all of the terms I have considered in this chapter—*dislocation, disorientation, disappearance, distance*—my consistent if oblique theme has been to query complacent geographies of location, order, settlement, and identity. These geographies are simultaneously fragile—open to shocks and ruptures—but also highly durable, as we have seen. But for me at least the promise of a more negative geographical imagination lies in its potential to think otherwise, the negative resources of *disturbance* and *disruption*. No location without *dislocation*, then. No place without *displacement*. And no stance without *distance*.

Notes

To Lola, who said yes, I could go ahead. And to Mitch, David, and Paul for patience and support.

References

Ahmed, Sara. 2006. *Queer Phenomenology: Orientations, Objects, Others*. Durham NC: Duke University Press.

Anderson, Ben, and Helen Wilson. 2018. "Everyday Brexits." *Area* 50 (2): 291–95.

Derrida, Jacques, 1994. *Spectres of Marx: the State of the Debt, the Work of Mourning and the New International*. London: Routledge.

Doel, Marcus. 1999. *Poststructuralist Geographies: The Diabolical Art of Spatial Science*. Edinburgh: Edinburgh University Press.

Harrison, Paul. 2007. "The Space between Us: Opening Remarks on the Concept of Dwelling." *Environment and Planning D: Society and Space* 25 (2): 625–47.

Merleau-Ponty, Maurice. 1962. *Phenomenology of Perception*. London: Routledge.

Parr, Hester, and Olivia Stevenson. 2015. "'No News Today': Talk of Witnessing with Families of Missing People." *cultural geographies* 22 (2): 297–315.

Rancière, Jacques. 2015 *Dissensus: On Politics and Aesthetics*. London: Bloomsbury.

Rose, Mitch. 2014. "Negative Governance: Vulnerability, Biopolitics and the Origins of Government." *Transactions of the Institute of British Geographers* 39 (2): 209–23.

Tobler, Waldo. 1970. "A Computer Movie Simulating Urban Growth in the Detroit Region." *Economic Geography* 46 (June): 234–40.

9   To Wound Life, to Prevent Its Recovery

Enforcing Vulnerability in Gaza

Mikko Joronen

> In concrete terms, starting in the seventeenth century, this power over life evolved in two basic forms. . . . The second focused on . . . the body imbued with the mechanics of life and serving as the basis of the biological processes: propagation, births and mortality, the level of health, life expectancy and longevity, with all the conditions that can cause these to vary. Their supervision was effected through an entire series of interventions and *regulatory controls: a biopolitics of the population.*
>
> —Michel Foucault, *History of Sexuality*

> How *can a power such as this kill,* if it is true that its basic function is to improve life, to prolong its duration, to improve its chances, to avoid accidents, and to compensate for failings?
>
> —Michel Foucault, *Society Must Be Defended* (emphasis added)

These words Michel Foucault made in the introductory part of the *History of Sexuality* (1976) and the lecture course *Society Must Be Defended*, held during the same time period (1975–76), provide an example of Foucault's first takes on biopolitics. During the decade, Foucault's discussion of biopolitics expanded into a cavalcade of writings and lectures, eventually merging with analyses of governmentality in *Security, Territory, Population* (1977–78), even to such extent that the concept of biopolitics practically disappeared in the following lecture course named, paradoxically, the *Birth of Biopolitics* (1978–79) (Foucault 2007; Foucault 2000, 403–17; see also Elden 2016; Legg 2016). Since Foucault's writings, the productive regulatory techniques and the vitalizing aspect of biopower—regulating life by making rather than taking it—have been discussed by many inside and outside geography (Agamben 1998, 2005; Barnett 2015; Crampton and Elden 2007; Esposito 2008; Rose and Abi-Rached 2013). Within geography there has been an abiding interest in tracing the shifts within Foucault's own thinking (e.g., Elden 2016; Legg 2016, 2019), while others have opened up new avenues for thinking biopolitics, for instance, as (meta)colonial political ontology (Jan 2019). Albeit helpful in understanding more complex ways through which power and governing operate in contemporary political, social, and spatial setups, critical voices have increasingly questioned the theoretical and practical autonomy of biopower. A crucial part of this are contributions relocating their foci to *thanatopolitical* forms and techniques of governing (Clough and Willse 2011; Joronen 2016; Mbembe 2003; Murray 2008), while others have elaborated the connection between Foucault's analysis of biopolitics and neoliberalism (Oksala 2013; Joronen 2013). Within the literature on Israel/Palestine, the discussion of biopolitics has been centered on scrutinizing Israel's control of the occupied population (and territories) through the fostering techniques vitalizing different realms of Palestinian life, from education, reproduction, and health care to those of sanitation, labor, and agriculture (e.g., Gordon 2008; Parsons and Salter 2008; Griffiths and Repo 2018). Yet here, too, a growing body of authors have argued that a step beyond the biopolitical schema in explaining Israel's colonial project is needed, emphasizing instead the role of thanato-/necropolitics, the Agambenian logics of exception, abandonment, and inclusive exclusion, or the ever-present messiness of governing (e.g., Hammami 2016; Ghanim 2009; Joronen 2019; Lentin 2016; Weizman 2011a).

Although joining these critical voices, my aim here is not to simply abandon the field opened up by the discussions of bio- and thanatopower; rather, it is my aim to *problematize the division* drawn between different positive (capacitating/affirmative) and negative (repressive/harming) forms of power, politics, and modes of governing. Certainly, some doubts have already been raised about the particularities of such projects (Ojakangas 2005), but as Sergei Prozorov (2013) has shown, numerous studies exemplify how biopolitics, as a theory and practice, tends to become constantly entwined around its opposite—the thanato-/necropolitics of annihilation, calculated killing, destruction, and abandonment (Butler 2015a; Margaroni 2005; Puar 2009). Foucault also recognized this connection in his work on modern racism when paying attention to the tendency of racism to purify a supposedly "superior race" through the annihilation and exclusion of the "inferior" ones (Foucault 1978, 149–50; Foucault 2003, 255–60). Yet, more thorough explication of the connection between bio- and thanatopolitics had to wait until the writings of authors like Giorgio Agamben, Roberto Esposito, and the joint works of Michael Hardt and Antonio Negri (Agamben 1998, 2005; Espositio 2008; Hardt and Negri 2005). Although these authors, each in their own way, were able to show how the connection to thanatopolitics was intrinsic rather than coincidental to biopolitics, my argument proceeds in a different direction.

In what follows, my aim is to show how the life-fostering and -protecting forms of power and the thanatopolitical techniques of politicizing death remain both rooted to the *vulnerability and fragility of life*, even to such extent that the line of division between the two forms of power collapses. Such rethinking, I show, can be as much theoretically coherent as helpful in understanding the complexities in existing ways of governing, colonization, political violence, and counterinsurgency that states, such as Israel, are practicing today. In particular, this chapter shows how different techniques are used to constitute a way of governing that, on the one hand, is premised on the ability to wound life without killing, while on the other hand maintains life without letting it to recover. It is important to underline, however, that such problematization of wounding and preserving functions of power is not done merely for the sake of locating a new foundation for how power works today in Palestine (i.e., Gordon 2008), but rather to show how governing becomes possible precisely due to a lack of such foundations. Such *ontological negativity*, I suggest in this chapter, denotes a life that is haunted by its own intrinsic precariousness—its frailty, vulnerability, and finitude—to the extent that such life, always prone to precarization, can become a target or a tool of governing. By developing the notion of vulnerability as ontological negativity, I distance myself particularly from the affirmative takes on biopolitics, which some have suggested could carry biopolitics beyond the neoliberal, fascist, and other violent takes that frame it as a "power that creates life" (*biopotere*) rather than a "life that creates power" (*biopotenza*) (see Casarino and Negri 2004; Coleman and Grove 2009; Espositio 2008). By doing so, I wish to complicate some of the geographical readings that view politics as the vital capacity to rear-range and affirm force differentiations (see Anderson and Harrison 2006; McCormack 2007; Thrift 2008). Instead, I address the problems related to ways of framing power as a capacity and of overcoming what I refer to as the "ontological negativity" with specified meta-ontological configurations.

I begin by showing the fundamental entanglement of bio- and thana-topolitics in several Israeli acts of occupation and war in the Gaza Strip. I focus on two cases where biopolitical logics of regulation operate simultane-ously as thanatopolitical means of governing the space and the population of Gaza. In the first case, I scrutinize Israel Defense Forces' (IDF) use of preemptive warning techniques during its fifty-one-day military invasion of Gaza in 2014 (named Operation Protective Edge by IDF). These tech-niques, I show, mobilized Gazan civilians, not as passive targets of killing, but as self-preserving bodies made responsible for saving their own lives. In the second case, I discuss the role of Israel's calculation of food import calories in establishing the ongoing siege of the Gaza Strip after Hamas's electoral victory in 2006. Here, I show how equilibrium was created between the minimum aid and the prevention of total collapse of the region. By importing the minimum "humanitarian necessity" and so keeping Gazan bodies on the "verge of hunger," such cruel biopolitics maintained Gazan lives as wholly vulnerable and dependent. In both instances death is not just a sovereign decision of the state (of Israel) to "take life or let live" (Fou-cault 2003, 241) but part of a complex entanglement of different elements of power that aim to govern life through its precariousness, fragility, and finitude—that is, through the ability *to wound life* and *prevent its recovery*. Thus, I argue that the governing of Gazan lives should not be considered on the grounds of affirmation versus violent subjugation of the vital capacities of life. Instead, I show how governing in the two cases operates by enforcing the *vulnerability of living*. Crucial for this, the chapter concludes, is to separate the wounding and caring functions of governing from the ontological negativity of fragile and vulnerable life—a life that, I conclude, makes certain ontologies of power possible and finite at the same time.

Warned Bodies: Thanatopolitics of Responsibilization

On June 8, 2014, Israel launched a massive military operation named Operation Protective Edge in the Gaza Strip. Though accompanied by the usual military jargon of weeding out Hamas terrorism, the conditions behind the 2014 war were somewhat different from the preceding ones. During the first half of the year, Hamas and Fatah, the main Palestinian political parties, had made a preliminary agreement to restart negotiations on the joint management in Palestinian territories. The rapprochement of the parties and the final formation of the Palestinian State it ultimately pointed to posed a problem for the Netanyahu-run government. Diplomatic contravention would have stood against Israel's official, mainly rhetorical (and strategic), commitment to UN peace efforts and the two-state solution. Acts of war due to the Palestinian peace efforts were also out of the question, particularly as the United States and European Union (EU) had given their wait-and-see support to the Palestinian negotiations (Finkelstein 2014). Suddenly Hamas—which had emaciated under the Israeli blockade, losing some of its support (most notably from Egypt)—was aligning with Mahmoud Abbas, the leader of Fatah, who as the voice of the Palestinian State was declaring its support for peace negotiations, including the preconditions set by the EU and United States. Netanyahu's main excuse, underlining the necessity to root out Hamas terrorism before making any final agreements with the Palestinian Authority, had quickly vanished. Netanyahu reacted, stating almost immediately that he would *never* tolerate a fully sovereign Palestinian state in the West Bank (Horowitz 2014).

June 2014 offered a new chance to deal with the situation as three settler youths had gone missing in the West Bank. Under the wings of a rescue operation half a dozen Palestinians were killed, houses destroyed, villages put under curfew, and several hundred people arrested in the West Bank (Liddell 2014). Israel held that a Hamas West Bank "terror cell" was responsible for the kidnapping and killing of the settler youths, whose bodies were found dead near the West Bank city of Hebron. Hamas's leadership, which had just made a significant political turn by opening up at least a hypothetical possibility that the Palestinian Authority could take power in Gaza, denied they had had any role in coordinating the events (Finkelstein 2014; Zavadski 2014). Other militant factions in Gaza, however, reacted to the provocations of Netanyahu with (mainly self-made) rockets. Israel replied quickly, doubling the size of the no-go buffer zone within Gaza Strip, hence forcing the civilian population further to a small center area, which the IDF then hammered with 6,000 airstrikes, around 35,000 artillery shells, and 14,500 tank shells fueled by the United States (OCHA 2015; UNHRC 2015). With these operations—conducted in the densely populated civilian areas, which according to Israeli claims operated as Hamas's cells, command centers, rocket stocks, launch areas, and so on—the IDF wiped out entire civilian neighborhoods (such as Shuja'iya) with massive shelling it referred to, somewhat paradoxically, as the "pinpoint strikes." The damage to the civilian population was vast: in addition to almost 2,300 Gazan victims, approximately 70 percent of them civilians (551 children), basic infrastructure in Gaza—including schools (some operating as UN civil shelters), medical facilities, 75,000 homes, one-third of Gaza's mosques, 360 factories, and the only power plant in Gaza—were almost completely destroyed (Joronen 2016, 339). The kidnapping and killing of three settler teenagers in the West Bank had quickly turned into an aggressive military operation with massive shelling of several densely populated civilian areas in Gaza. As several investigations—conducted by organizations from the United Nations Human Rights Council (UNHRC) to the Russell Tribunal— concluded, evidence of war crimes, including crimes against humanity (murder, extermination, persecution) and incitement to genocide were the result of Israel's attack against the surrounded (practically defenseless) Gazan civilian population (e.g., Russell Tribunal 2014; Breaking the Silence 2014; Taylor 2014; UNHRC 2015).

During (and after) the war, Israel tried to legitimize the rising civilian death toll by several means, ranging from videos of canceled air strikes to propaganda campaigns, assuring much was done to prevent harm to civilians (IDF 2014). One of these means was the use of preemptive *warning techniques* that Israel boosted with noticeable media, internet, and propaganda campaigns circulated via blogs, newspapers, Twitter, and embassy internet pages (Joronen 2016; Perugini and Gordon 2017). By widely reporting the IDF's use of cautionary SMS-messages, phone calls, air-dropped leaflets, loudspeaker announcements, radio messages, and what Israel called "roof knocking" (a dropping of light explosives to the rooftops of targeted buildings before the actual strike), Israel aimed to create an image of a legal and ethically sound military operation, where everything was done to avoid harming the Gazan civilian population. Indeed, international humanitarian law (ICRC 1977, article 57[2]) requires that effective warning needs to be given before conducting military operations in civilian areas. Yet warnings themselves do not give a legal free ride to wipe out entire civilian neighborhoods: accountability always remains on the side of the attacker. Israel, however, took an opposite interpretation. Instead of taking responsibility for the rising death toll of Gazan civilians, it used warnings techniques to claim that responsibility for the civilian deaths was *on the civilians themselves.*

Such thanatopolitical responsibilization—that is, the activation of targeted bodies to save themselves from forthcoming death and destruction (Joronen 2016)—raises several concerns. For instance, warnings were given selectively—and on many occasions (especially in roof-knocking cases) only a very short period of time was allowed for civilians to move out of the warned areas (Amnesty International 2015; Forensic Architecture 2014). This is not to say longer fleeing times would have solved the issue, as more time cannot guarantee that the civilians have the capacity to move out of the warned area—this being evident in the case of young children (alone at home), the elderly, and people with disabilities and sicknesses.

As the testimony of an IDF lieutenant serving during the Protective Edge underlined:

> The whole "roof knocking" thing was understood [by Hamas] very quickly. Hamas forces are very light, really, and for them—in contrast to the general [Gazan] population, and this is the great tragedy—"roof knocking" gave them enough time to go down into some burrow, or to run between the houses and vanish from the area. But for a family with a grandmother who's sitting in the living room, it's a bit harder. (Breaking the Silence 2014)

It is also the case that often more than several rounds of missiles were fired after a warning, or the blast radius of rockets was much wider than the warned targets required, these making the escape from the targeted premises practically impossible, even with longer getaway times. On a general level, the ethical and legal considerations one can spot from the IDF propaganda videos, news, posters, infographs, etc. thus seemed to be in sharp contrast to the testimonies from the field—many given by the Israeli soldiers themselves (OCHA 2014; UNHRC 2015; Breaking the Silence 2014).

As the number of civilian victims kept rising, Israel started to accuse Hamas of using civilians as *human shields*. Though at least some of the released evidence turned out to be completely fabricated (e.g., Porter 2014), in general such a claim operates by equating an unarmed population with a weapon ("a shield"). Such juxtaposing blurs the distinction between civilian and combatant fundamental to international law, hence transforming Gazan civilians into figures that can be killed without committing a war crime (Bargu 2016; Perugini and Gordon 2017). In fact, as Laleh Khalili writes, quasi-legalizations like this have become an obsession for contemporary states to justify their dubious practices of conducting deadly military operations in civilian areas. Whether the war on terror, counterinsurgencies, or war as a means to govern occupied areas, this "obsession" has turned international law into another weapon in governments' arsenals. Here war is no more a Clausewitzian "continuation of politics," but a form of lawfare, where politics and law operate as a "continuation of war" (Khalili 2013).

What I want to argue here is that both the preemptive warnings and human-shield arguments function as *strategic devices* for justifying the targeting of civilians. In both cases, the distinction between the civilian and the combatant—which the international humanitarian law fundamentally relies on—has become a target of politicization, which, by blurring the distinction, aims to turn civilian areas into legitimate combat zones and justify the civilian deaths as collateral damage.

When seen as strategic devices, we can start to paint a different picture of the use of warning techniques. Rather than simply protecting civilian lives, warnings create a gap between the conditions set by the Israeli military apparatus (i.e., the marking of civilian spaces as battlefields) and the field of possible acts so granted for those in the targeted areas. Certainly, there are calculations involved in the military actions, as the pros and cons of attacking civilian premises need evaluation (Butler 2015b). Civilians alike need to wager whether the IDF is willing to commit war crimes (by killing bodies clearly identifiable as civilians) or whether risking one's life to thwart a military assault of civilian homes and neighborhoods is worth doing. What the warnings create, however, is not merely a sum between the calculations of the military and the calculations of the targeted. Rather they produce *a momentary suspension of the ontological status* of the targeted, creating a *precarious* situation where the targeted themselves *become responsible* for saving their own lives. In this regard warning techniques are thanatopolitical devices that lean on the responsible self-government of the targeted and thus make targeted bodies accountable for producing themselves as illegitimate targets: they either remain in or vitalize themselves to leave the civilian spaces IDF has appointed as combat zones. Combatants are hence not defined on the grounds of visible symbols, such as military outfit or guerilla actions, but on the basis of how (Palestinian) bodies *act in appointed spaces*. In other words, the ontological setup fabricates a delimited space with a certain configuration of possible acts, which implementation resolves the status of the targeted on the grounds of their movement, and while doing so, moves the responsibility for the civilian deaths upon the "warned" bodies.

Considering their obvious thanatopolitical character (i.e., the imposition of the threat of death), it is curious that the warning techniques also seem to contain several life-preserving and -vitalizing functions: one, they steer the movement of bodies in space; two, they activate and make targeted bodies accountable for protecting and preserving themselves; and three, by doing so, they enable the ethical "polishing" of military violence. As the first function indicates, in the moment of warning, a *governmental space* is set up. It is the targeted sites and the surrounding spaces that are marked as combat zones through warnings. Targeted bodies, in turn, are moved into a gray area, where they need to reclaim their ontological status (as civilians) through their movement in the warned and targeted sites. In other words, the warning of civilians constitutes a space of revealing for the governmental process of responsibilization to emerge.

This leads to the second function: the transition of responsibility, and the concern for civilian well-being, to the targeted bodies. Ultimately, bodies in the warned sites are called to protect themselves by acting responsibly. If they indeed are civilians (according to the logic of warning), they need to confirm this by leaving the warned areas. Such *responsibilization* operates through the self-vitalizing and -governing subjects, empowering them to save themselves in the midst of war. It is here where we arrive at the third function: the justification of *military aggression as less harmful* and the *careful* conduct of ethical warfare. By responsibly leaving warned areas, and so reclaiming their civilian status (or by not leaving and so becoming "legitimate" military targets, i.e., combatants and human shields), it is the acts of responsible bodies that ensure fewer civilian casualties emerge. The targeted bodies are hence set accountable, not only for saving themselves, but also for assuring the ethicality of the military conduct itself. By positioning Palestinian bodies with certain spatial and ontological conditions, warning techniques thus mobilize, activate, and control Gazan civilians, not as passive targets of destruction, but as active bearers of conditions, distinctions, moralities, concerns, and legalities machinated by the military apparatuses.

As the three functions discussed above underline, warning techniques operate as strategic devices that not only turn death into a matter of calculation, but also set bodies within preset positions that support the functions of the military apparatus (see Esposito 2015; Heidegger 1977; Joronen 2016). While fleeing helps Israel to justify its military aggressions as a less fatal war conduct, decisions to stay in the warned areas allow the IDF to legitimize its thanatopolitical violence not only as something directed to combatants and human shields alone, but as care and concern toward the civilian population. Warning techniques thus compose a twofold thanatopolitical strategy. On the one hand, they position bodies in relation to marked battlespaces—bodies that are empowered (via threat of death) to enact their equivalence with legitimate or illegitimate military targets (combatants or human shields vs. fleeing civilians). On the other hand, warning techniques legitimize military aggression within densely populated civilian areas as ethically and legally sound operations which subtly care for their consequences. In other words, warnings bracket military *killings* with a protection and *care for* civilian life. Such care channels the responsibility for civilian deaths to civilians themselves, therefore becoming defined against the possible death of the body, and thus, the finitude of life. In this regard, thanatopolitical positioning is not merely about calculating death; it is about *regulating life by using the care for the civilians as a strategic asset of killing.*

Kept Alive: "Red Line" of Humanitarian Calculations

Despite the widespread civilian suffering associated with Israeli military operations in Gaza, it would be misleading to assume that Gaza remains affected only by calculated violence, suffering, and death during times of aggressive military invasions. The ongoing blockade of Gaza, which Israel set after Hamas's electoral victory in 2006, has significantly hampered everyday life, making Gaza one of the most aid-dependent places in the world (World Bank 2018). The closure policy set by the Israeli Security Cabinet in September 2007 has consisted of harsh restrictions on the movement of goods, supplies, and people to and from Gaza, particularly during its early phase between 2007 and 2010 (Gisha 2012; Israel Ministry of Foreign Affairs 2010). As Israel's own documentation shows (Gisha 2009), the restrictions were set to weaken the Hamas regime with "economic warfare" that aimed to shut down Gaza's economy. Such restrictions created severe shortages of basic goods and materials and also led to high unemployment and rising poverty (Gisha 2012; OCHA 2010).

One of the most striking policies in this regard has been Israel's calculation of the minimum number of calories needed to contain Gaza without triggering a massive humanitarian crisis (COGAT 2008a, 2009; Gisha 2012; Weizman 2011b). Dov Weissglas, the main advisor to the Israeli prime minister at that time, suggested in 2006 in a public discussion with the IDF chief of staff, head of the Shin Beth, and the foreign minister Tzipi Livni, that Hamas's electoral victory should be responded to with cuts to the food supply. "It's like an appointment with a dietician," Weissglas said and continued, "Palestinians will get a lot thinner, but won't die" (Levy 2006). Reference to a "diet" may have been frivolous when presented by Weissglas but, as is often the case, it did refer to an emerging state of affairs. It was not until 2012, however, that this trajectory was fully revealed, when the Israeli food policy document, *Food Consumption in the Gaza Strip—Red Lines* (from here, *Red Lines*), was finally released to the public after a three-and-a-half-year-long legal battle put forward by several human rights organizations.

As the *Red Lines* document (and several other publications related to it) revealed, the Israeli Ministry of Defense had calibrated, together with the Israeli Ministry of Health, a minimum diet that would be able to cause a desirable economic effect in Gaza without causing a humanitarian crisis among its civilian population (COGAT 2008a, b). The *Red Lines* document measured the daily need of calories and the size of a "food basket required by the [Gazan] population," turning these calculations into a model of exporting 106 truckloads of imports from Israel to Gaza every weekday (COGAT 2008a). The number of truckloads, however, was significantly below the minimum "red line" of 106 loads, especially at the beginning of closure (2007–8), when on average 65 trucks entered Gaza on each scheduled day (Gisha 2012, 6–8). On many occasions the imported food supplies reflected the interests of Israeli producers and their lobbying rather than the Palestinian needs. This caused a temporary shortage of vital goods such as drugs, medical supplies, and baby formula. Luxury products—which curiously included everyday items such as hummus and sesame paste—were not imported to Gaza at all. The calculations did not pay attention to special needs either, or to rising consumption during Muslim holidays. In fact, the Israeli Ministry of Defense held that their policy did not allow quantities to exceed the minimum calculated "necessity," as the restriction policy was steered only by the "real need for direct consumption of the production" as defined by the occupying force (Gisha 2012, 6).

Restrictions to food imports caused several direct and indirect consequences. Firstly, they created competition within the Gazan economy over scarce resources. In fact, calorie-calculation documents did not mention the distribution inside the Gaza Strip at all, naively assuming that distribution would result in an equal share of food supplies among the Gazan population. Accordingly, food regulations inflicted the most distress on those already in the most vulnerable position rather than on the Hamas leaders. Simultaneously Israel complicated several local food production chains in Gaza: it unilaterally expanded the no-go zones on which most of the Gazan farming lands were located, while at the same time intensifying aerial fumigations of farmland and harassments of Gazan farmers and fishers (Al-Haq 2011; Farming Under Fire 2016). This created, secondly, what Smith and Isleem (2017) call the "metabolic rift"—an attempt to prevent independent nutrition production through isolation of the Gazan population to crowded urban centers and refugee camps (see also Smith 2016). A food survey that the United Nations Relief and Works Agency for Palestine Refugees in the Near East (UNRWA), World Food Programme, and Food and Agriculture Organization of the United Nations conducted after a year of tight restriction policy showed health repercussions among the Gazan population. The number of Gazan residents receiving humanitarian aid, for instance, increased from 63 percent in 2006 to 80 percent in 2007 (UNRWA 2008). Altogether the humanitarian calculation of imported calories blurred the violence of the blockage from which the most vulnerable suffered the most. Gaza was never merely sealed and cut off from the world; instead, the everyday civilian life under the siege was made wholly dependent on the strategies, restrictions, and policies of the occupying force.

Like the thanatopolitical responsibilization of warning techniques, the food restriction policies were composed of elements and functions originating in different logics, modalities, and mobilizations of power. On the one hand, truckloads operated as a form of humanitarian biopolitics: they offered calculations of the health and average nutritional need of a population, thus showing *concern* about the well-being of Gazan civilians (particularly, in their claim to prevent full-scale humanitarian crisis). On the other hand, these techniques were part of the closure policy meant to seriously *wound* and hamper life in Gaza. It is revealing that the straightforward calculations paid hardly any attention to the actual scarcity and need in the region, where significant parts of the population suffered from the multiplying coeffects of the economic and mobility restrictions. In fact one may ask whether, in the light of rising food insecurity (56 percent of the Gazan population not having proper and nutritious food in 2008), increasing reliance on humanitarian aid, restrictions reducing fishing areas to less rich coastal waters, extensions of military buffer zones (to cover over 35 percent more of Gaza's agricultural land), a complete lack of fertilizers and pesticides (due to import restrictions), a lack of irrigation in 70 percent of spring crops (due to the lack of fuel available for the pumps), and the constant harassment of farmers in near-border arable lands (some already badly contaminated), food calculation policies appear nothing more than the strategic inducing of squalor, or what I refer to as the preservation of vulnerability (Al-Haq 2011; OCHA 2010; UNRWA 2008; UNCTAD 2012). The minimum standards of one vital condition of life—the need for nutrition—may have been calculated, but in a manner that installed scarcity and precarious living conditions while making the Gazan civilian population deeply dependent on the acts of the occupying force. Calorie calculations were, after all, part of a blockade, where the main function was to impair living conditions in Gaza and so to further prevent Gaza from recovering from precarities induced by the earlier military invasions.

Considering the above, the calorie calculation policy should be understood as an integral part of the wounding and harming functions of power. Such precarization engendered an "art of governing" which aimed at keeping Gazan life on the "verge of hunger" through the techniques discussed above. The *Red Lines* policy may have been wrapped up into humanitarian biopolitics, but nevertheless engendered spaces of suffering and scarcity that prevented life from recovering from its wounds. Restrictions on civilian goods and the calculated suffering they caused, especially to the most vulnerable portion of the Gazan population, thus lay bare how the precarious living conditions under the siege were strategically orchestrated, calibrated, and maintained under the humanitarian means of biopolitical governing.

Politics in between Life and Death: Vulnerability

Whether taking the form of belligerent military violence or the slow violence and scarcity of a blockade, Israel's control of Gaza seems to operate in between two modes: the one orchestrating and maintaining spaces of scarcity, suffering, and death and the other entwined around the humanitarian protection and care for the civilian population. Here the caring and threatening, vitalizing and wounding logics can emerge together in compositions containing different, even seemingly opposite elements of control. The claim I wish to put forward in this section is that such compositions should not be simply seen as outcomes of always overlapping modalities of power, where these modalities merge into messy spatial relations and complex practices of government. Rather, the examples force us to question the nature and the origin of governing itself; namely, the ontological negativity and the inexhaustibility of how vulnerability operates as an ungrounding source of governing.

I start below by first showing how different forms of power operated in the two cases discussed above as different means of mobilizing *vulnerabilities* in Gaza. Instead of merely approaching them as set hybrid forms of power, which indicates a mixture of originally separate modalities—joint emergence of sovereign, bio-, and thanatopower, for instance (Foucault 1981, 239)—my aim is rather to question the theoretical autonomy of different ontologies of power by showing how their key elements are each time connected to the different ways of distributing vulnerability. The question of what exactly is governed when life is regulated through its simultaneous caring and harming is thus raised in the second subsection, particularly as one needs to explain how different, even opposing elements can operate together in (ontologically inexhaustible) compositions of governing. Accordingly, I conclude by separating *negative functions* of governing from the *ontological negativity* of (groundless) life, thus arguing that it is the latter that conditions the former, so offering a negative origin for different forms of governing to emerge.

WOUNDING BIOPOLITICS: PRECARITY AS GOVERNING

As shown above, warning techniques and food calculations both contain elements one could identify with the forms of power discussed at beginning of this chapter. What defines roof knocking, for instance, is a combination of thanatopolitical mobilization of bodies (based on the threat of death) and the active and vitalizing responsibilization (empowering the warned bodies to govern their own spatial actions). In the case of responsibilization, the biopolitical element seems quite apparent, particularly as it relies not only on a claim to preserve (civilian) life but on the activation and self-government and hence on a logic of power Foucault scrutinized in his works on governmentality and neoliberal subjectification (Foucault 2008; see also Joronen 2013; Lemke 2013; Oksala 2013). And yet, it is the threat of death which the responsibilization leans on. Considering these two elements—thanatopolitical and biopolitical—warning techniques can thus be said to operate as calculative-strategic devices, which pass the responsibility for preserving civilian lives for the civilians themselves—to their own active *concern* to save themselves. Not only are the elements of activation, vitalization, and self-protection operative here; the dynamics between threat (of *death*) and care (for one's own *life*) are also central for how warnings function.

A similar unity of opposing elements characterizes the *Red Lines* calorie regulation policies. Here calculations aim to regulate the well-being of a population and, in this regard, operate as biopolitical-humanitarian devices to ensure that the minimum living conditions among the Gazan population are maintained. And yet they do not function as simple efforts to improve and make life better, but as calculated aims to maintain vulnerability and suffering within the Strip. Of course, as Agier (2002) reminds us, humanitarianism has long been linked to wars and military violence, not only as a response to catastrophes and exoduses that wars provoke, but as an act of gaining tactical support with food kits and medical supplies air-dropped for the enemy civilian population. What makes the food regulation policy in Gaza different, however, is Israel's use of humanitarianism as a tool for maintaining Gaza in a vulnerable and wholly dependent situation. The situation in Gaza shows that, far from being a humanitarian alternative to war, the siege has worked in concert with war as to further injure and prevent the recovery of the Gazan population. With an aim to harm Gaza not only by means of scarce sanctions but also by hampering the food-production chains within the Strip, humanitarian-biopolitical calibrations have thus operated in parallel with the general aim to keep the Gazan population precarious—alive, but on the verge of hunger, and ultimately, death.

Considering the efforts to cause suffering and squalor, any humanitarian element attached to Israeli food-regulation policies in Gaza needs to be seen in connection to thanatopolitical means of calculating death and its probability (Ghanim 2009; Joronen 2016; Mbembe 2003). If not a direct calculation of maximum or strategic death rates, nor a way of using the threat of death as a military strategy, in such regulation death comes to the fore as a twofold figure. On the one hand, the filling of minimum requirements of life may keep death away or at least within such a scope where scarcity doesn't flick into genocide, while on the other hand, it is ultimately death that is so kept in view. Life is not directly abandoned here, nor simply left without rights and crucial care of the others (cf. Agamben 1998; Margaroni 2005). Rather, life's dependence on nutrition is used to control Gaza by *keeping life in the region at constant state of precarity*. The calibration of what exactly is required to maintain squalor, suffering, and poverty—or more broadly precarity—is thus ultimately about calculating the probability of death: about keeping death at a proper distance and thus a target of strategic calculation. The biopolitical prevention of humanitarian catastrophe, we should thus conclude, is part of the thanatopolitical art of governing where calibrations of "humanitarian necessities" function between humanitarian care and calculated closeness of death, hence engendering highly vulnerable spaces for Gazan civilians to dwell in.

What seems to characterize the merging of these, to some extent contrary elements of governing, is in both cases the way they constitute, maintain, and mobilize *precarities* among the Gazan population. In the case of roof knocking, death may be prevented and warned about (and hence life protected with warnings) but without removing the threat or the possibility of death itself: warned bodies are bodies exposed to spaces of life-threatening vulnerabilities and violence. Likewise, humanitarian practices in general may operate to alleviate precarities, but together with the control of food chains of besieged Gaza they offer a tool for maintaining strategic levels of shortage and suffering. One food ration per day may be more than zero, but still keeps life vulnerable, inasmuch as preemptive warnings do not remove, but indicate inducing of highly vulnerable, life-threatening conditions among the civilian population. Their biopolitics is wounding; something maintaining vulnerable spaces in Gaza.

Vulnerability, as it characterizes both military and humanitarian violence, hence seems to remain somewhat *in between the regulation of life and death.* Humanitarian calibrations that do not remove precarities; warnings that do not prevent but justify the killing of civilians: in both cases the power of governing originates in the manifold politics of positioning the always-already vulnerable, fragile, and finite bodies.

PRECARIOUSNESS: THE ORIGIN OF GOVERNING

In his article on "negative governance," Mitch Rose locates the origin of governing precisely in this vulnerability of life—in the "primordially negative condition that is the condition of being exposed" to the facticity of "being in the midst of *life itself*" (Rose 2014, 215; my emphasis). Rose builds his argument by showing, through his study conducted in Egypt, how the strategic decisions not to govern operate as a way of governing that leaves life at the mercy of its own precariousness. It is the absence of governing that hence reveals the inherent precariousness and frailty of living, as according to Rose it is the precariousness of "life itself" that is so mobilized as means of governing. A somewhat similar argument has been put forward more recently by Adam Ramadan and Sara Fregonese, who, in the context of Palestinian refugee camps in Lebanon, show how the *absence of the state* has produced a space for what they refer to as the "sovereign absence" eventually filled with "partial, hybrid, and overlapping sovereignties" (Ramadan and Fregonese 2017).

To some extent, my argument here differs from both of these elaborations. While Rose helpfully points out how the inherent vulnerability of the human condition—the always-present negativity of life as precarious, finite, and indebted to the care of others—can be mobilized as a modality of governing that *governs by not governing*, as I have shown herein such condition can be also used to actively *promote* various forms of state violence that use the precariousness of life to maintain, enforce, and engender strategic and calculated levels of precarity (see also Joronen 2017). It is precisely the state that has so strategically induced, not a complete abandonment of the Gazan population, but vulnerable spaces of scarcity, suffering, threat, and death. Vulnerabilities in Gaza are hence not inflicted simply by leaving life at the mercy of its own precariousness; life's inherent vulnerability is rather mobilized to maintaining and engendering strategic levels of precarity.

Whether vulnerabilities are imposed via absence of governing (Rose 2014), through absence of state (Ramadan and Fregonese 2017), by continuously prolonging precarious conditions through the slow functions of state bodies (Joronen 2017), or by making decisions that enforce strategic levels of precarity (as seems to hold true in the cases under scrutiny here), it is the fundamental precariousness of life that is used as a source of governing. The origin for different ways of mobilizing particular situated *precarities* is thus the *precariousness* of life itself—the frailty, vulnerability, and perishability inherent in being a living being. In this regard, as Judith Butler aptly writes, "precarity designates that politically induced condition in which certain populations suffer from failing social and economic networks of support more than others, and become differentially exposed to injury, violence and death" (Butler 2015a, 33). *Precarity*, she adds, consist of the "differential distribution of *precariousness*" (emphasis added), where populations are differently "exposed to state violence," but also to elements that are not enacted by the state, but which state's juridical instruments fail to "provide sufficient protection or redress." Vulnerability of living, as the quotes show, is always also a political condition; these political conditions, in turn, have their capacity to affect because life remains inherently wounded and so exposed and receptive to uses of (political) power. It is vulnerability that hence enables power to remain powerful: it denotes a condition that different modes of power mobilize and lean on as their source of governing (Joronen and Rose 2020).

As the discussion above shows, vulnerability of living—its precariousness; its woundedness—can be used to promote differing means that each employ precarity for their purpose of governing. This is not to favor wounding and harming *forms* of power over the capacitating and caring ones, but to recognize the fundamental lack in life—its ontological finiteness, frailty, and precariousness—as a negating and groundless origin of governing. Vulnerability, in spite of being distributed through the practices of the state, never resides in the hands of the sovereign, but within the life itself. No "immunizing" technique of the state can thus fully remove this inherent precariousness of living, despite the fact that these techniques are equally capable of harming and wounding life, even to end it (Esposito 2008, 192–94; Hardt and Negri 2005, 20). Caring and threatening, vitalizing and weakening, life-improving and death-calculating elements can thus emerge together in various compositions, not only forcing life (in Gaza and elsewhere) under precarious conditions and situations, but above all, by using the inherent vulnerability of life as their source of governing. In this regard, governing is not grounded in vital powers capable of organizing force differentiations, but in the fundamental vulnerability, receptivity, and exposure of life to manifold ways of organizing its woundedness. Power is not merely a capacity, less an affective force, but epiphenomenal to vulnerability and the space of reception it enforces. Ontological negativity, which I turn to next, names precisely this receptivity, exposure, and woundedness at the heart of all acting, doing, and living.

Conclusion: On Ontological Negativity

Politics of death and care, life-threatening thanatopolitics and life-preserving biopolitics, vitalization and suffocation, subjugation and capacitation may all operate against one another as general logics of power, yet emerge side by side in techniques used to forge and maintain the bodies under precarious conditions. Typically, racist eugenics (Foucault 2003), "ticking bomb" arguments (Hannah 2006), or arguments underlining the "proportional killing" as a necessary "lesser evil" (Weizman 2011b) have used such logics as a means of protecting the life of a "valuable" (portion of) population from those seen as threatening and ungrievable, even disposable. However, the events I have discussed in this chapter are somewhat different in nature. They show how the biopolitics of preemptive warnings and humanitarian aid, seemingly concerned with the well-being, protection, and vitalization of Gazan civilians, merge into thanatopolitical logics of using hunger, scarcity, and the threat of death as strategic means to govern. Care can be a care imposed in front of impending death, as the use of warning techniques exemplify; alternatively, care can function as a care that prevents mass starvation, but simultaneously keeps death at calibrated distance, as the food restriction calculations highlight. Targeted bodies made responsible for reducing civilian casualties—to care for their own lives—but also calculations of minimum humanitarian needs, both thus use the protection, care, and vitalization of life in the service of bringing additional death and suffering—*to wound life, and to prevent its recovery.*

To understand such unity between diverse, to some extent even contrary elements and functions of power, not only as they come together in existing ways of governing but also without creating an insurmountable theoretical schism, I want to conclude by proposing "ontological negativity" as a key for approaching the relationship vulnerability has to various formations of power and formations of governing. This does not mean a call for more subtle elaboration of novel ontologies (of vulnerability, power, force, capacity, etc.), but rather of giving each ontological configuration of power the attention its own singularity deserves. If positive and vitalizing capacities of life are alone celebrated, attempts to understand subtle ways of control, violence, and governing may be thwarted beforehand with path dependencies growing from the ontological one-sidedness of an academic discourse (Joronen and Häkli 2017; Rose 2014). Life, however, is never a mere rejoicing of vitalist forces, but is constantly faced with its own negativity—that is, with its own frailty, impossibility, finitude, and precariousness; its *woundedness*. Such negativity should not be paralleled with the negative functions of power—the hampering, damaging, debilitating, and subjugation of life; its wounding and *precarization*. Such ontological negativity rather signifies the *im*possibility to lay down a final ontological stance about what life *is* and what forms it takes, instead underlining what life may lose, including life itself. Ontological negativity, in other words, denotes a fundamental lack of final substance—a life always *haunted* by its own intrinsic negativity; its incapacity to be no more than a vulnerable, incomplete, and fragile happening. Precariousness, in this regard, does not define what life *is*; precariousness rather denotes the way in which life remains defined by what undefines, exposes, and incapacitates it (see Joronen and Rose 2020). We are not bound to precariousness, because it offers a foundation for a life; we are bound to precariousness because it presents, as Butler aptly writes, "the joint of our nonfoundation" (Butler 2015a, 129)—a condition that makes all foundations and ontological forms fragile, incomplete, finite, and so incapable of prevailing in the fangs of time (on how this is related to political action, see Athanasiou 2016; Joronen 2019). Such lack of foundations—the ontological negativity—means life is always already exposed and so inherently insecure, wounded, and prone to failure. It is this fundamental woundedness of living that different politicizations and forms of power ultimately lean on.

References

Agamben, Giorgio. 1998. *Homo Sacer: Sovereign Power and Bare Life*. Stanford CA: Stanford University Press.

――――. 2005. *State of Exception*. Chicago: University of Chicago Press.

Agier, Michel. 2002. "Between War and City: Towards an Urban Anthropology of Refugee Camps." *Ethnography* 3, no. 3 (September): 317–41.

Al-Haq. 2011. *Shifting Paradigms: Israel's Enforcement of the Buffer Zone in the Gaza Strip*. Ramallah: Al-Haq.

Amnesty International. 2015. "The Gaza Platform: An Interactive Map of Israeli Attacks during the 2014 Gaza Conflict." Amnesty International and Forensic Architecture. http://gazaplatform.amnesty.org/.

Anderson, Ben, and Paul Harrison. 2006. "Questioning Affect and Emotion." *Area* 38 (September): 333–35.

Athanasiou, Athena. 2016. "Nonsovereign Agonism (or, beyond the Affirmation versus Subjugation)." In *Vulnerability in Resistance*, edited by Judith Butler, Zeynet Gambetti, and Leticia Sabsay, 256–77. Durham NC: Duke University Press.

Bargu, Banu. 2016. "Bodies against War: Voluntary Human Shielding as a Practice of Resistance." *American Journal of International Law* 110 (January): 299–304.

Barnett, Clive. 2015. "On Problematization: Elaborations on a Theme in Late Foucault." *Nonsite.org*, June 22, 2015. https://nonsite.org/article/on-problematization.

Breaking the Silence. 2014. *This Is How We Fought in Gaza: Soldier's Testimonies and Photographs from Operation "Protective Edge."* Breaking the Silence. https://www.breakingthesilence.org.il/pdf/ProtectiveEdge.pdf.

Butler, Judith. 2015a. *Notes towards the Performative Theory of Assemblage*. Cambridge MA: Harvard University Press.

――――. 2015b. "Human Shields." *London Review of International Law* 3, no. 2 (September): 223–43.

Casarino, Cesare, and Antonio Negri. 2004. "It's a Powerful Life: A Conversation on Contemporary Philosophy." *Cultural Critique* 57 (Spring): 151–83.

Clough, Craig, and Patricia Willse. 2011. "Beyond Biopolitics: The Governance of Life and Death." In *Beyond Biopolitics*, edited by Craig Clough and Patricia Willse, 1–18. Durham NC: Duke University Press.

COGAT (Coordinator of Government Activities in the Territories). 2008a. *Food Consumption in the Gaza Strip—Red Lines*. Israeli Ministry of Defense: Coordinator of Government Activities in Territories.

――――. 2008b. *Procedure for Monitoring and Assessing Inventories in the Gaza Strip*. COGAT, State Response on September 18, 2008. http://www.gisha.org/userfiles/file/publications/redlines/footnotes/state_response18.9.08.pdf.

――――. 2009. "Procedure for Monitoring and Assessing Inventories in the Gaza Strip." *Standing Orders Corpus Instructions and Procedures, Order no. 605*. Tel Aviv: Coordinator of Government Activities in the Territories, Economic Branch.

Coleman, Mathew, and Kevin Grove. 2009. "Biopolitics, Biopower, and the Return of Sovereignty." *Environment and Planning D: Society and Space* 27 (January): 489–507.

Crampton, Jeremy, and Stuart Elden, eds. 2007. *Space, Knowledge and Power: Foucault and Geography*. Aldershot UK: Ashgate.

Elden, Stuart. 2016. *Foucault's Last Decade*. Cambridge UK: Polity.

Esposito, Roberto. 2008. *Bios: Biopolitics and Philosophy*. Minneapolis: University of Minnesota Press.

———. 2015. *Persons and Things: From the Body's Point of View*. Cambridge UK: Polity.

Farming under Fire. 2016. "Palestinian Farmers and Workers Attacked by Israeli Soldiers Near the Green Line, inside Gaza Strip." *Farming under Fire* (blog). http://farmingunderfire.blogspot.fi/.

Finkelstein, Norman G. 2014. *Method and Madness: The Hidden Story of Israel's Assaults on Gaza*. New York: OR Books.

Forensic Architecture. 2014. *Bombing of Rafah*. Centre for Research Architecture, the Department of Visual Cultures, Goldsmiths, University of London. http://www.forensic -architecture.org/case/rafah-black-friday/#toggle-id-2.

Foucault, Michel. 1978. *History of Sexuality. Volume I: An Introduction*. New York: Pantheon.

———. 1981. "'Omnes et Singulatim': Towards a Criticism of Political Reason." In *The Tanner Lectures on Human Values: Vol. 2*, edited by Sterling M. McMurrin, 223–54. Salt Lake City: University of Utah Press, 1981.

———. 2000. "The Political Technology of Individuals." In *Power: Essential Works of Foucault 1954–1984*, edited by James D. Faubion, 403–17. New York: New Press.

———. 2003. *Society Must Be Defended: Lectures at the Collège de France 1975–1976*. New York: Picador.

———. 2007. *Security, Territory, Population: Lectures at the Collège de France 1977–1978*. New York: Picador.

———. 2008. *Birth of Biopolitics: Lectures at the Collège de France, 1978–1979*. New York: Palgrave Macmillan.

Ghanim, Honaida. 2009. "Thanatopolitics: The Case of the Colonial Occupation in Palestine." In *Thinking Palestine*, edited by Ronit Lentin, 65–81. New York: Zed.

Gisha. 2009. *Israel Uses the Closure as Economic Warfare. HCJ 9132/07 Al-Bassiouni v. the Prime Minister. Paragraphs 43, 44 in the State's Response from 1.11.2007*. Gisha—Legal Center for Freedom of Movement. www.spg.org.il/docs_html/eng/Eng_traders/legal /doc%20full_eng%20trader_legal_01.pdf.

———. 2012. "Reader: 'Food Consumption in the Gaza Strip—Red Lines.'" *Position Paper*. Gisha—Legal Center for Freedom of Movement. https://right2info.org/resources /publications/case-pdfs/isreal_gisha-v.-ministry-of-defense/israel_gisha-v.-ministry -of-defense_more-info.

Gordon, Neve. 2008. *Israel's Occupation*. Berkeley: University of California Press.

Griffiths, Mark, and Jemima Repo. 2018. "Biopolitics and Checkpoint 300 in Occupied Palestine: Bodies, Affect, Discipline." *Political Geography* 65 (July): 17–25.

Hammami, Rema. 2016. "Precarious Politics: The Activism of 'Bodies That Count' (Aligning with Those That Don't) in Palestine's Colonial Frontier." In *Vulnerability in Resistance*, edited by Judith Butler, Zeynet Gambetti, and Leticia Sabsay, 167–90. Durham NC: Duke University Press.

Hannah, Matthew. 2006. "Torture and the Ticking Bomb: The War on Terrorism as a Geographical Imagination of Power/Knowledge." *Annals of the Association of American Geographers* 96, no. 3 (January): 622–40.

Hardt, Michael, and Antonio Negri. 2005. *Multitude: War and Democracy in the Age of Empire*. London: Penguin.

Heidegger, Martin. 1977. *The Question concerning Technology, and Other Essays*. New York: Harper & Row.

Horowitz, David. 2014. "Netanyahu Finally Speaks His Mind." *Times of Israel*, July 13, 2014.

ICRC (International Committee of the Red Cross). 1977. *Protocol Additional to the Geneva Conventions of 12 August 1949, and Relating to the Protection of Victims of International Armed Conflicts (Protocol I)—Article 57: Precautions in Attack*. Geneva: International Committee of the Red Cross.

IDF (Israel Defense Forces). 2014. "How Is the IDF Minimizing Harm to Civilians in Gaza?" Israel Defense Forces Blog, July 16, 2014. http://www.idfblog.com/blog/2014/07/16/idf-done-minimize-harm-civilians-gaza/.

Israel Ministry of Foreign Affairs. 2010. "Prime Minister's Office Statement following the Israeli Security Cabinet Meeting. Israel Ministry of Foreign Affairs, June 20, 2010." http://www.mfa.gov.il/mfa/pressroom/2010/pages/prime_minister_office_statement_20-jun-2010.aspx.

Jan, Najeeb. 2019. *The Metacolonial State: Pakistan, Critical Ontology and the Biopolitical Horizons of Political Islam*. Oxford: Wiley & Sons.

Joronen, Mikko. 2013. "Conceptualizing New Modes of State Governmentality: Power, Violence and the Ontological Mono-Politics of Neoliberalism." *Geopolitics* 18, no. 2 (March): 356–70.

———. 2016. "Death Comes Knocking on the Roof: Thanatopolitics of Ethical Killing during Operation Protective Edge in Gaza." *Antipode* 48, no. 2 (March): 336–54.

———. 2017. "Spaces of Waiting: Politics of Precarious Recognition in the Occupied West Bank." *Environment and Planning D: Society and Space* 35, no. 6 (December): 994–1011.

———. 2019. "Negotiating Colonial Violence: Spaces of Precarisation in Palestine." *Antipode* 51, no. 3 (June): 838–57.

Joronen, Mikko, and Jouni Häkli. 2017. "Politicizing Ontology." *Progress in Human Geography* 41, no. 5 (June): 561–79.

Joronen, Mikko, and Mitch Rose. 2020. "Vulnerability and its politics: Precarity and the Woundedness of Power." *Progress in Human Geography* (November). https://doi.org/10.1177/0309132520973444.

Khalili, Laleh. 2013. *Time in the Shadows: Confinements in Counterinsurgencies*. Stanford CA: Stanford University Press.

Legg, Stephen. 2016. "Subject to Truth: Before and after Governmentality in Foucault's 1970s." *Environment and Planning D: Society and Space* 34, no. 5 (February): 858–76.

——. 2019. "Subjects of Truth: Resisting Governmentality in Foucault's 1980s." *Environment and Planning D: Society and Space* 37, no. 1 (September): 27–45.

Lemke, Thomas. 2013. "Foucault, Biopolitics, Failure." In *Foucault, Biopolitics and Governmentality*, edited by Jakob Nilsson and Sven-Olov Wallenstein, 35–52. Huddinge: Södertörn Philosophical Studies.

Lentin, Ronit. 2016. "Israel/Palestine: State of Exception and Acts of Resistance." In *Resisting Biopolitics: Philosophical, Political and Performative Strategies*, edited by S. E. Wilmer and Audrone Zukauskaite, 271–86. New York: Routledge.

Levy, Gideon. 2006. "As the Hamas Team Laughs." *Haaretz*, February 18, 2006. http://www.haaretz.com/as-the-hamas-team-laughs-1.180500.

Liddell, Graham. 2014. "Protective Edge Has Nothing to Do with Protection." *Mondoweiss*, July 12, 2014.

Margaroni, Maria. 2005. "Care and Abandonment: A Response to Mika Ojakangas' 'Impossible Dialogue on Bio-Power: Agamben and Foucault.'" *Foucault Studies* 2 (May): 29–36.

Mbembe, Achille. 2003. "Necropolitics." *Public Culture* 15 (January): 11–40.

McCormack, Derek. 2007. "Molecular Affects in Human Geographies." *Environment and Planning A* 39 (February): 359–77.

Murray, Stuart J. 2008. "Thanatopolitics: Reading in Agamben a Rejoinder to Biopolitical Life." *Communication and Critical/Cultural Studies* 5, no. 2 (June): 203–7.

OCHA (United Nations Office for the Coordination of Humanitarian Affairs). 2010. *Between the Fence and a Hard Place: The Humanitarian Impact of Israeli Imposed Restrictions on Access to Land and Sea in the Gaza Strip*. East Jerusalem: United Nations Office for the Coordination of Humanitarian Affairs, Occupied Palestinian Territory and World Food Programme.

——. 2014. *Gaza Crisis Atlas*. East Jerusalem: United Nations Office for the Coordination of the Humanitarian Affairs, Occupied Palestinian Territory.

——. 2015. "Data Featured in the Report of the Independent Commission of Inquiry on the 2014 Gaza Conflict: Key Figures on the 2014 Hostilities." United Nations Office for the Coordination of Humanitarian Affairs, Occupied Palestinian Territory. Posted June 23, 2015. https://www.ochaopt.org/content/key-figures-2014-hostilities.

Ojakangas, Mika. 2005. "Impossible Dialogue on Bio-Power: Agamben and Foucault." *Foucault Studies* 2 (May): 5–28.

Oksala, Johanna. 2013. "Neoliberalism and Biopolitical Governmentality." In *Foucault, Biopolitics and Governmentality*, edited by Jakob Nilsson and Sven-Olov Wallenstein, 53–72. Huddinge: Södertörn Philosophical Studies.

Parsons, Nigel, and Mark B. Salter. 2008. "Israeli Biopolitics: Closure, Territorialisation and Governmentality in the Occupied Palestinian Territories." *Geopolitics* 13 (December): 701–23.

Perugini, Nicola, and Neve Gordon. 2017. "Distinction and the Ethics of Violence: On the Legal Construction of Liminal Subjects and Spaces." *Antipode* 49, no. 5 (November): 1385–405.

Porter, Gareth. 2009. "Exclusive: Israel's Video Justifying Destruction of a Gaza Hospital Was from 2009." *Truthout*, September 6, 2014. https://truthout.org/articles/israels -video-justifying-destruction-of-a-hospital-was-from-2009/.

Prozorov, Sergei. 2013. "Powers of Life and Death: Biopolitics beyond Foucault." *Alternatives: Global, Local, Political* 38 (August): 191–93.

Puar, Jasbir K. 2009. "Prognosis Time: Towards a Geopolitics of Affect, Debility and Capacity." *Women & Performance: A Journal of Feminist Theory* 19, no. 2 (October): 161–72.

Ramadan, Adam, and Sara Fregonese. 2017. "Hybrid Sovereignty and the State of Exception in the Palestinian Refugee Camps in Lebanon." *Annals of the American Association of Geographers* 107, no. 4 (October): 949–63.

Rose, Mitch. 2014. "Negative Governance: Vulnerability, Biopolitics and the Origins of Government." *Transactions of the Institute of British Geographers* 39, no. 2 (July): 209–23.

Rose, Nicholas, and Joelle M. Abi-Rached. 2013. *Neuro*. Princeton NJ: Princeton University Press.

Russell Tribunal. 2014. *Emergency Session on Gaza*. Brussels, September 24, 2014. http:// www.russelltribunalonpalestine.com/en/wp-content/uploads/2014/09/TRP-Concl. -Gaza-EN.pdf.

Smith, Ron. 2016. "Isolation through Humanitarianism: Subaltern Geopolitics of the Siege on Gaza." *Antipode* 48, no. 3 (June): 750–69.

Smith, Ron, and Martin Isleem. 2017. "Farming the Front Line: Gaza's Activist Farmers in the No Go Zone." *City* 21, nos. 3–4 (June): 448–65.

Taylor, Adam. 2014. "What Happened When Palestinian Children Were Killed in Front of a Hotel Full of Journalists?" *Washington Post*, July 16, 2014.

Thrift, Nigel. 2008. *Non-Representational Theory: Space, Politics, Affect*. London: Routledge.

UNCTAD (United Nations Conference on Trade and Development). 2012. "Report on UNCTAD Assistance to the Palestinian People: Developments in the Economy of the Occupied Palestinian Territory." United Nations, United Nations Conference on Trade and Development. July 13, 2012.

UNHRC (United Nations Human Rights Council). 2015. *Report of the Detailed Findings of the Independent Commission of Inquiry Established Pursuant to Human Rights Council Resolution S-21/1: Human Rights Situation in Palestine and Other Occupied Arab Territories*. A/HRC/29/CRP.4.

UNRWA (United Nations, Relief and Works Agency for Palestinian Refugees in the Near East). 2008. *Joint Rapid Food Security Survey in the Occupied Palestinian Territory*. https://unispal.un.org/pdfs/RapidAssessmentReport_May08.pdf.

————. 2014. "Statement by the UNRWA Commissioner-General Pierre Krähenbühl." United Nations, Relief and Works Agency for Palestinian Refugees. July 24, 2014. http://www.unrwa.org/newsroom/official-statements/statement-unrwa-commissioner-general-pierre-kr%C3%A4henb%C3%BChl.

Weizman, Eyal. 2011a. "Thanato-tactics." In Clough and Willse 2011, 177–212.

————. 2011b. *The Least of All Possible Evils: Humanitarian Violence from Arendt to Gaza.* London: Verso.

World Bank. 2018. "Net ODA Received per Capita (US$)—West Bank and Gaza." https://data.worldbank.org/indicator/DT.ODA.ODAT.PC.ZS?end=2018&locations=PS&most_recent_value_desc=true&start=1993&view=chart.

Zavadski, Katie. 2014. "It Turns Out Hamas May Not Have Kidnapped and Killed the Three Israeli Teens After All." *New York,* July 25, 2014.

10 Come and See
Witnessing and Negation in the Mobile Killing Units of Nazi Germany

Richard Carter-White

Introduction

In Holocaust historiography, the mass murders committed by the *Einsatzgruppen*—ss paramilitary death squads—are often considered a first step toward the eventual emergence of extermination camps as a means of genocide (Rhodes 2003; Stone 1999). Working alongside police battalions and supported by the German army, from June 1941 the *Einsatzgruppen* followed the military advance into the Soviet Union with the mission of murdering groups including Jews, Communist Party leaders, and suspected partisans (Beorn and Knowles 2014; Friedländer 2008). Often supported by local collaborators (Arad 1999; Burds 2013), the *Einsatzgruppen* killings typically functioned by rounding up Jewish communities in towns and villages, taking them to nearby locations, and shooting individuals at close range. Approximately 1.4 million Jews across Eastern Europe were killed in this manner (Hilberg 2003). Yet despite its "success," the problems associated with this method of killing were among the factors leading to the development of centralized sites of industrial murder, in the form of the camp. The inefficiency of shooting as a means of mass violence exacerbated the practical obstacles of secrecy and labor presented by the necessity of traveling to dispersed locations for each killing operation (Arad 1999). These logistical issues were resolved by the centralized logic of the camp, but equally prominent in historical narratives of this period is the relief offered by systems of quasi-factorial killing for the psychological burden of face-to-face murderers. Two prominent authorities on the Nazi death camps, Yitzhak Arad and Raul Hilberg, refer to the Auschwitz commander Rudolf Höss in making this point:

> Eichmann came to Auschwitz and disclosed to me the plans for the operations as they affected the various countries concerned. We discussed ways and means of carrying out the extermination. It could be done only by gassing, as it would have been absolutely impossible to dispose, by shooting, of the large numbers of people that were expected, and it would have placed too heavy a burden on the ss men who had to carry it out, especially because of the women and children among the victims. (Höss 1961, quoted in Arad 1999, 8–9)

> Höss observed the corpses and listened to the explanations of the camp physician. The victims [of gas], he was assured, had not suffered in agony. He concluded that death from the gas was bloodless and that its use would spare his men a great psychological burden. (Hilberg 2003, 941)

The history of the *Einsatzgruppen* therefore helps place the evolution of the camps into sites of mass murder in historical context, by demonstrating that the genocidal ambitions of the Third Reich were perceived as resting upon the development of an alternative method of mass killing to one that required the proximity of killers to their victims, as offered by the camp system's routinized division of labor (Bauman 2000). While in full agreement with the interpretation of such historians as Arad, for whom the story of the death camps begins with the drawbacks of open-air shooting (1999), in this chapter I examine in detail the problematic proximity of mobile killing units to their victims. Specifically, drawing on key works of Holocaust history and perpetrator testimony, I suggest that this proximity was imbued with a complex dynamic of witnessing and negativity, which enabled the construction of what historian Christopher Browning calls the "political planet" within which this technically inefficient and psychologically damaging process could nonetheless succeed in murdering so many people (2001, 72).

The phrase "political planet" evokes the contribution geographers have made to the study of genocide and the function of the negative therein. A consistent theme throughout this work is how the forms of deterritorialization that constitute genocide—including such negative spatial practices as *destroying* everyday lived spaces, *depopulating* urban spaces, *erasing* political spatialities, and *emptying* social space through dehumanizing spectacles of violence (Barnes and Minca 2013; Lunstrum 2009; Tyner 2009, 2012)—are perceived by perpetrators as a necessary and legitimate "territorial cleansing" that enables the construction of new and idealized political forms (Egbert et al. 2016). From the spatial imaginations of Nazi Germany to the Khmer Rouge's vision of a pure communist society, the project of utopian reterritorialization provides genocide with a political context that justifies violence as "an effective—and legitimate—strategy of state-building" (Tyner 2012, 25). James Tyner's biopolitical analysis of genocide, population, and the state identifies how such justification relies on an imaginative geography of inclusion and exclusion, whereby the differential valuation of life can not only impose a necessary degree of moral distance between killer and victim, but can even recompose the act of killing as one that secures the well-being of the population as a whole (Tyner 2009, 2012; see also Cooper 2009). Thus, a distinct political planet is created, in which murder is recategorized as necessary and good.

Elizabeth Lunstrum has introduced witnessing as a concept relevant to genocidal world-building, insofar as forcing victims to watch acts of extreme violence helps spread fear and deterritorialize lived spaces into "landscapes of terror and insecurity" (2009, 889). Here I want to extend this idea by turning attention to the perpetrators' own witnessing of the violence they inflicted. The open-air shootings conducted by the Nazi mobile killing units were organized events of violence entailing multiple intersecting acts of witnessing and performance, which were vital for individuals negotiating their place within the perpetrator community. Yet as elaborated in cultural geographical writings, witnessing is fundamentally characterized by a paradoxical spatiality of proximity and distance, presence and absence, which can lend even physically proximate witnesses to an event a contrary sense of dislocation and disorientation (see Carter-White 2009, 2012, 2016; Harrison 2007, 2010). Drawing on the biopolitical philosophy of Roberto Esposito, I seek to demonstrate the political implications of this ambivalent spatiality by arguing that the close-range witnessing of the mobile killing units to their own acts of violence provided a scene for the "immunization" of this community of killers (Esposito 2015): a relation of unspeakably violent proximity that both required and enabled the negation of the perpetrators' moral obligation to those outside their community, with the embodied experience of negation itself strengthening the communal ties of those within and reinforcing the ideological grounds of their genocidal actions.

This argument speaks to central debates within geographical discussions of violence. Springer and Le Billon herald the capacity of geographical perspectives to move beyond the binary interpretation of violence as either *direct* or *structural* in nature, emphasizing instead the relational unfolding of violence "within the wider assemblage of space" (2016, 2). This notion of violence as a *process* is evident in geographical research that has attended to embodied experiences of violence not simply as the outcome of malevolent individual agency or overarching structural inequality, but as a meaningful practice in itself that is both shaped by broader social relations (Little 2017; Tyner and Inwood 2014) but that also fundamentally reconstitutes the social space through which regimes of power operate (Doel 2017; Philo 2017). The latter point is crucial to this chapter's argument, because the violence described in the sections that follow did not occur simply because its perpetrators acted upon a sense of legitimacy that they had received from the ideological structures of Nazism; the implementation of violence, in all its sickening horror, was itself crucial to the communication and legitimation of this ideological worldview.

Accordingly, after an initial discussion of the multiple types of witnessing that took place during killing operations, I argue that sites of proximate killing were structured by a distinctive spatiality of witnessing emergent from two seemingly contradictory forms of negation: absolution, whereby Nazi authorities worked to manage, erase, or otherwise lessen the effects and repercussions of killing in close quarters, and degradation, whereby the visibly horrific violence inflicted upon the victims acted to dramatize the separation of the perpetrator group from existing moral systems and thus strengthen the bonds of its members. In addition, I argue that these two opposing forms of perpetrator negation acted to reinforce one another in an aporetic "immunitary" structure that allowed killers to lessen their sense of guilt and invest themselves in a Nazi community of violence. The description of proximate forms of killing as being characterized by negativity is not intended to mitigate the perpetrators' responsibility on the basis that they were not "really there," but rather to widen the meaning of complicity and participation to incorporate acts that might seem to place perpetrators at an (absolving) "distance"; an analysis which is therefore equally of relevance to the camps and the attempt to invent a form of perpetrator-less murder in those institutions.

Intersections of Witnessing

As was typical of the Nazi apparatus of destruction, the mobile killing operations exhibited significant evolution and improvisation. This is illustrated by Hilberg's (2003) division between two stages in the killings: a first "sweep" from the invasion of the Soviet Union in June 1941 until the end of the year, and another over the course of 1942. The first sweep was characterized by rapidity, as the *Einsatzgruppen* kept pace with the military front, and according to Beorn and Knowles this stage can be broken down into periods defined by the targets for murder: an initial focus on "communist functionaries, Jewish leadership, and Jewish men of military age," until the scope was expanded to include all Jews in late summer 1941 (2014, 99). These shifting goals meant that the *Einsatzgruppen* often returned to the same communities numerous times (Hilberg 2003). By contrast the second sweep was oriented toward the "complete annihilation of the remaining Soviet Jews" (Hilberg 2003, 383), with an increased use of Order Police and auxiliary police units entailing a greater death toll from fewer operations (Beorn and Knowles 2014). Although police units were more prominent in the second sweep, from the beginning the *Einsatzgruppen* was assisted in its task by a range of other groups, including the military (both German and collaborating forces), local militia, and civilians (Hilberg 2003).

Despite such complexity, Hilberg outlines a standardized murder procedure that was used to maximize speed and efficiency:

> In every city the same procedure was followed with minor variations. The site of the shooting was usually outside of town, at a grave. Some of the graves were deepened antitank ditches or shell craters, others were specially dug. The Jews were taken in batches (men first) from the collecting point to the ditch. The killing site was supposed to be closed off to all outsiders, but this was not always possible. . . . Before their death the victims handed their valuables to the leader of the killing party. In the winter they removed their overcoats; in warm weather they had to take off all outer garments and, in some cases, underwear as well. (Hilberg 2003, 327–28)

The degree of standardization should not be overemphasized, due to variations in local specificities and unit commander preferences. With such a range of participants and the growing frenzy of violence as the scope of victims widened, many methods and scenes of killing emerged, with varying degrees of organization, spontaneity, and sadism (Fritzsche 2009; Klee, Dressen, and Riess 1991; Stone 1999). But the basic procedure described above is sufficient to indicate a scene of highly charged and intersecting witnessing, incorporating victims, perpetrators, and various types of "outsider."

Of greatest concern to the perpetrators was the presence of outsider witnesses. Attempts were made to hide the killings from local residents, including "chasing away" spectators (Browning 2001, 108) and organizing detours to divert traffic from the site (Hilberg 2003) in order to avoid unrest among populations themselves accorded a lowly position on the Nazis' racial hierarchy. Harder to control was the witnessing of parties assisting with the operation but deemed "outside" the core unit of killers, particularly the military. Hilberg refers to "indignation" among troops upon witnessing the work for which they had been enlisted, but equally problematic was the enthusiasm among troops for whom the shootings had become a sensational spectacle: "They watched, took pictures, wrote letters, and talked" (2003, 332; see also Fritzsche 2009), causing the news to spread into Germany and ensuing embarrassment for military commanders. Another concern was that soldiers' witnessing of mass murder was translating into voluntary and "excessive" violence, leading one military unit to issue an order strictly regulating army participation in *Einsatzgruppen* killings, including banning spectatorship of shootings (Hilberg 2003, 335–36). Finally, toward the end of the second sweep in summer 1942, fear among the ss of future witnesses to their crimes prompted Himmler to form a Kommando dedicated to the destruction of mass graves (Hilberg 2003, 406). Although this project failed, it indicates both that the presence of absent witnesses may have been felt by the perpetrators as they carried out killing operations, and that the perpetrators perceived these "operations" as indeed constituting crimes that exceeded the boundaries of conventional warfare.

Apart from the public nature of the atrocities, one obstacle to regulating the presence of outsider groups at the killing sites was the variety of non-visual witnessing that accompanied mass murder by shooting. The sound of gunfire was particularly apt to create "involuntary witnesses":

[Major] Rösler commanded the 528th Infantry Regiment in Zhitomir. One day while he was sitting in his headquarters . . . he suddenly heard rifle volleys followed by pistol shots. Accompanied by two officers, he decided to find out what was happening. . . . The three were not alone. From all directions, soldiers and civilians were running toward a railroad embankment. Rösler, too, climbed the embankment. What he saw there was "so brutally base that those who approached unprepared were shaken and nauseated." (Hilberg 2003, 333)

Little attention is given in Hilberg's account to the witnessing of victims at the killing sites. However, the killing procedure that he describes—the separation of groups into smaller batches at the collecting point which were then taken to the murder site, with men going first—suggests that the victims' perception of events was a concern for the perpetrators, to be managed by dividing the victims at a distance from the site and pre-

CARTER-WHITE

emptively killing those most able to potentially resist first. This concern is explicitly evident in Christopher Browning's influential study of Reserve Police Battalion 101 and the involvement of a group of "ordinary men" in the open-air killings. Recalling the battalion's "initiation" as mass murderers at the village of Józefów, where in a single day they killed a minimum of 1,500 Jews (Browning 2001, 225), Browning describes how the operation was organized around the "pendulum traffic" of two firing squads operating in a forest outside the village, with one squad leading a group of victims from an unloading point on the edge of the forest to an execution site within the woods while the other squad returned to collect a newly arrived group of victims (Browning 2001, 61). One captain was responsible for selecting execution sites throughout the day, with these sites spaced out "so that the next batch of victims would not see the corpses from the earlier execution" (Browning 2001, 61; see also Arad, Gutman, and Margaliot 1999, 400). Such efforts were again made more difficult by aural witnessing, as with a massacre in Lublin when music from loudspeakers was used in vain to disguise the sound of gunfire (Browning 2001, 138). While in these cases the witnessing of victims was treated as something to be managed and suppressed, on other occasions killings were performed in a deliberately public manner that capitalized on the witnessing of local populations as a means of terrorizing possible future victims (Hilberg 2003, 334).

If the intersection of witnessing by "outsider" and victim groups posed a series of problems for the organization of mobile mass shootings, it was the psychological fallout from the field of perpetrator witnessing that prompted innovations in mass murder (Klee, Dressen, and Riess 1991). As Hilberg notes, the diverse personnel recruited into the murders were not necessarily trained killers; most *Einsatzgruppen* officers were professionals in their thirties (2003, 291), a large proportion of whom held doctoral degrees (Beorn and Knowles 2014), and while highly motivated, indoctrinated, and specially selected for the task these were "bureaucrats—men who were accustomed to desk work" (Hilberg 2003, 337) and "in no sense hoodlums, delinquents, common criminals, or sex maniacs" (Hilberg 2003, 291; see also Browning 2001; Fritzsche 2009). Yet when it came to the killing sites, "everybody had to watch shootings" (Hilberg 2003, 337), including these would-be desk killers. This was partly for enforced complicity, to ensure that all those with knowledge of the killings "would have to share the fate of those who did this work" (Hilberg 2003, 337), but also to supervise the killing sites and conduct of the shooters and to learn from demonstrations of murder strategies by other units (Browning 2001). But additionally, and crucially, while the officers were watching the killings they, in turn, were watched by the rank and file of the military, paramilitary, and police units responsible for the killings. These individuals had typically been incorporated into shooting operations because they were unsuitable for conventional military duty; they were, as Browning describes Police Battalion 101, the "'dregs' of the manpower pool available at that stage of the war" (2001, 165), and despite ideological training and the virulently anti-Semitic context (Friedländer 1998) "had not volunteered to shoot Jews" (Hilberg 2003, 341). Unit leaders were thus "in a position to set the tone for the behavior expected and encouraged from the men" (Browning 2001, 87), through scrutiny of their own conduct, speeches (Hilberg 2003, 343), and demonstrations of murderous practice (Angrick 2008). Aside from the mutual witnessing between officers and rank and file, the killing sites became a scene of witnessing between the shooters themselves, as individuals established reputations among the unit as more- or less-enthusiastic, efficient, sadistic, or reluctant members of a genocidal community (Kühne 2010).

At the intersection of these multiple lines of perception dwelt the individual murderer's witnessing of his[1] own actions. Hilberg describes the disturbing dreams, physical sickness, and psychological breakdowns experienced by killers as they relived the bloodbaths they had conducted (Hilberg 2003, 337–43; see also MacNair 2002). Such witnessing again exceeded the visual, with the stench of burning bodies witnessed in the bodily testimony of illness and vomiting among perpetrators (Browning 2001, 141), while the visual outlasted the temporal duration of the killing event, through the inscription of blood and gore upon terrain, clothes, and the killers themselves (Browning 2001, 64–65). According to Hilberg it was Himmler's witnessing of the gruesomeness of close-range shooting, and the visible effect it had on the perpetrators, that prompted his request for "other killing methods more humane than shooting" (2003, 344), a request eventually culminating in the gas van, itself a precursor to the gas chambers (Arad 1999).

The multisensorial perception of victims, perpetrators, and "outsiders" was an essential component of the mobile killings, a force to be managed and manipulated but that also spilled beyond the control of the planners of mass murder. This highly charged and unpredictable intersection of witnessing was a consequence of deploying such a proximate form of killing, and the inward effect it had on the killers was as much a threat to the project of genocidal de/reterritorialization (Lunstrum 2009) as the outward leaking of photographs and stories of atrocity to Germany and beyond. In the next section I examine how, prior to the institution of camps designed to address this problem, the scene of open-air killing was deliberately striated with negations that would obscure the proximity of killers to their victims.

Negation of Witnessing

Despite the apparent psychological burden experienced by the shooters, "there was no breakdown in the operations as a whole" (Hilberg 2003, 346). The mobile shootings succeeded in killing over one million people. Again drawing on Browning's unique study of the transformation of Police Battalion 101 from the dregs of German manpower to a weapon of genocide, in this section I suggest that various types of negation were incorporated into the operations to absolve the killers of their sense of responsibility while enabling the violence to continue.

Browning's study of Battalion 101 is invaluable for this analysis because of its emphasis on the possibility of negotiation. Before their initiation as a killing squad, any individuals among this group of "ordinary men" who felt unable to participate were explicitly given the option by their commander to withdraw (Browning 2001), and even beyond this particular unit no formal punishment was ever imposed upon a member of German forces for refusing to participate in killing operations (Klee, Dressen, and Riess 1991). Yet despite this option to refuse, only a small number did, with the majority of this unexceptional group of people eventually becoming hardened killers (Browning 2001, xviii). Instead, what emerges from perpetrator testimonies is a community of violence punctuated by a series of substitutable negations that allowed those who struggled with their consciences to distance themselves from the victims and effectively void themselves as perpetrator-subjects.

The most obvious manner in which perpetrators sought to negate a form of killing characterized by physical proximity was by inserting physical distance between themselves and the act of killing. Outright refusing to kill and requesting alternative duties (Browning 2001, 62, 113), such as escorting victims from the collection point or guarding the border of the killing site (Beorn and Knowles 2014), was only the most direct way of doing this. In larger-scale operations, it was possible for those unwilling to publicly display their unease to evade in more subtle ways, by laboring other tasks until the shooting was over or finding "legitimate" reasons to remain in residential areas, away from forest massacres (Browning 2001, 62–63). Sometimes evasion would occur midmassacre, as with this member of a point-blank range firing squad:

> The shooting of the men was so repugnant to me that I missed the fourth man. . . . It was not that I could no longer aim accurately, rather that the fourth time I intentionally missed. I then ran into the woods, vomited, and sat down against a tree. To make sure that no one was nearby, I called loudly into the woods, because I wanted to be alone. . . . I think that I remained alone in the woods for some two to three hours. (Browning 2001, 67–68)

It was considered beneficial to the unit when such individuals relieved themselves, since inaccurate shooting would lead to more bloody and disturbing wounds (Browning 2001, 68).

According to Beorn and Knowles, the imposition of physical distance genuinely helped to relieve the perpetrators' consciences. Referring to the testimony of German soldiers, they note the construction of a "moral (or immoral) landscape" (2014, 112) whereby individuals associated particular places—such as the killing site—with evil and moral culpability, and by contrast used their own spatial separation from the victims as evidence of moral absolution. These soldiers "viewed their actions in preventing the escape of the victims as distinct and separate from murder," despite the necessity of this role for the success of the operation (2014, 112).

Over time these attitudinal dispositions became formalized into a spatial division of labor, whereby those known to be enthusiastic killers assumed the most proximate roles, while those who had established their reluctance to kill would be automatically assigned other tasks (Browning 2001). The degree of labor specialization is illustrated by the testimony of a driver in the vicinity of the Babi Yar ravine in Kiev, where 33,771 Jews were murdered over two days in September 1941:

> There were only two marksmen carrying out the execution. One of them was working at one end of the ravine, the other at the other end. I saw these marksmen stand on the layers of corpses and shoot one after the other. The moment one Jew had been killed, the marksman would walk across the bodies of the executed Jews to the next Jew, who had meanwhile lain down, and shoot him. It went on in this way uninterruptedly, with no distinction being made between men, women and children. . . . In addition to the two marksmen there was a "packer" at either entrance to the ravine. These "packers" were Schutzpolizisten [uniformed police], whose job it was to lay the victim on top of the other corpses so that all the marksman had to do as he passed was fire a shot. (Klee, Dressen, and Riess 1991, 65–66)

The witness goes on to emphasize the relentless pace of the killing and the sensory assault of its aftermath (Klee, Dressen, and Riess 1991, 66). While the obscured sense of participation that accompanied spatial separation from such nightmarish sites would have likely relieved the moral discomfort of killers, the clarification of roles and negotiated negation of proximity therein also made for a more organized, efficient, and routinized killing process (Browning 2001). Physical distancing reinforced the sense of moral absolution derived from the hierarchical structure of the killing operations, with Nazi leaders declaring in speeches that the leadership accepted responsibility for the genocidal initiative itself, implying that the practitioners of mass murder assumed a merely technical role (Hilberg 2003, 342–43; Bauman 2000).

For those undertaking the most proximate role in the open-air shootings, alcohol offered an alternative means of negating their actions: "As one nondrinking policeman noted, 'Most of the other comrades drank so much solely because of the many shootings of Jews, for such a life was quite intolerable sober'" (Browning 2001, 82). The testimony of Battalion 101 is replete with references to open drunkenness among the perpetrators as they carried out executions, and alcohol became a routine presence across the killing units: "The mode of shooting depended a great deal on the killers' sobriety. Many of them were drunk most of the time; only the 'idealists' refrained from the use of alcohol" (Hilberg 2003, 404). Hilberg notes that drunkenness led to inefficient killing, yet it was a ubiquitous presence (Westermann 2016), encouraged among the leadership due to its desensitizing effects. Alcohol was recognized as a distancing mechanism when physical distance was no longer available: "[First Sergeant] Ostmann turned to one of his men who had hitherto avoided shooting and chided him. 'Drink up now, Pfeiffer. You're in for it this time, because the Jewesses must be shot. You've gotten yourself out of it so far, but now you must go to it'" (Browning 2001, 108). Here, one form of negation is consciously substituted for another to ensure the continuation of killing. Sometimes, physical distance and inebriation would combine: "At the site of mass execution in August 1941 at Kamenets-Podolsk . . . individual shooters who experienced reservations about shooting children were periodically excused to take a break and drink schnapps before returning to the firing line" (Westermann 2016, 7).

Other substitutable and supplementary negations were available. In many cases the most proximate act of killing was delegated to local communities or auxiliary police. Seemingly spontaneous local outbursts of violence against Jewish populations were often in fact deliberately organized by the *Einsatzgruppen* (Arad, Gutman, and Margaliot 1999, 389), both to spread the burden of the killings and to dilute the legal and psychological responsibility of the Germans (Hilberg 2003, 318; cf. Lower 2011 on genuinely spontaneous pogroms). Although such pogroms were brutally violent, in terms of numbers and organization the creation of auxiliary police was more significant and allowed German units to choose which groups they could live with killing: "As time went on, Ukrainians were used in several cities and towns for the unpleasant work of wiping out the families of Jewish men. Einsatzkommando 4a went so far as to confine itself to the shooting of adults while commanding its Ukrainian helpers to shoot children" (Hilberg 2003, 323). When these strategies failed or were unavailable, another option for negating mass murder was language. For Hilberg the extensive use of euphemisms to refer to murder among unit commanders constituted a repressive mechanism for coping with the psychological effects of the violence; his lengthy list includes such terms as "liquidated," "finished (off)," "special treatment," "major cleaning actions," "resettlement," "executive activity," and "treated appropriately" (2003, 338). He also describes the rationalizations used by commanders to justify killings as a defensive measure against "the Jewish danger," with rumors and propaganda contributing to particularly sickening acts of collective violence (2003, 339–40).

There were evidently many options for those who wished to negate their participation in the killings, strategies for (not) witnessing which were indulged and even encouraged by unit leaders, from physically evading the scene to communicating their discomfort, obscuring their perception in inebriation, deferring to authority or soliciting the assistance of others, or psychologically transforming the act itself in terminology and stories. Each was vital for the construction of a "political planet" in which the mass murder of civilians could take place (Browning 2001, 72). Yet perhaps most significant for the psychological burden of the perpetrators were those stories not told. Browning provides the following illuminating example, referring to the early Józefów massacre by Battalion 101:

When the men arrived at the barracks in Biłgoraj, they were depressed, angered, embittered, and shaken. They ate little but drank heavily. Generous quantities of alcohol were provided, and many of the policemen got quite drunk. Major Trapp made the rounds, trying to console and reassure them, and again placing the responsibility on higher authorities. But neither the drink nor Trapp's consolation could wash away the sense of shame and horror that pervaded the barracks. Trapp asked the men not to talk about it, but they needed no encouragement in that direction. Those who had not been in the forest did not want to learn more. Those who had been there likewise had no desire to speak, either then or later. By silent consensus within Reserve Police Battalion 101, the Józefów massacre was simply not discussed. (2001, 69)

The act of witnessing begins with an experience of obligation: becoming a *you* who is addressed by an occurrence, without necessarily understanding or comprehending that address (Carter-White 2012; Lyotard 1988). It is only completed, however, with the act of retelling that experience before an audience, in doing so deploying the subjective powers of language and comprehension and thus becoming an *I* who testifies (Derrida 2000). In the quotation above, the mass murderers of Battalion 101 refuse to complete the circuit of witnessing, refuse to recapitulate their sovereign subjectivity as an *I* who could own and possess the actions of a genocidal killer, instead remaining in the voided subject position of a *you*, one who sees but does not know or speak. This is one sense in which negativity was active in the mobile killing operations: negations of proximity and witnessing that would allow those perpetrators who felt uncomfortable with the task to continue its implementation. The next section examines a contrary sense of negativity, one which emerged from the experience of witnessing murder at unmitigated proximity.

Witnessing as Negation

In the previous section, the relationship between witnessing and negation was presented in the form of a problem and solution, whereby witnessing was enforced by a degree of proximity to the killing that caused psychological disturbance for the killers. This approach is limited, however, in its inability to address the prevalence of enthusiastic and sadistic violence among the mobile killing squads, performed by perpetrators for whom proximity seemingly required no negation. The change in focus from reluctant to hardened or even gleeful killers is necessary, not only because in many cases the latter constituted the trajectory of the former (Browning 2001), but also to avoid perpetuating the idea espoused by such architects of genocide as Himmler that the Holocaust was conducted by way of "clean" killing (see Stone 1999). As a corrective to the perpetrators' obfuscatory claims of calm and orderly slaughter—as if such a notion is possible—Andrew Charlesworth describes the sickening quality of Nazi depravity in the East (2003). Torture (Angrick 2008; Lower 2002), sexual violence and rape (Chalmers 2011; Hedgepeth and Saidel 2010), sadism encouraged by cheering crowds (Kühne 2010): far from the image of reluctant and distraught killers, the word that Dominick LaCapra uses to describe this dimension of the mobile killings is "carnivalesque" (1997, 269). In this section I suggest that, distinct from the negation *of* witnessing examined in the previous section, there was an additional, complementary, and in a sense "positive" relationship between witnessing and negation in the open-air killings, where witnessing functioned *as* a form of negation in the service of building a fortified perpetrator community.

Central to this analysis is Kühne's work (2010) on the relationship between violence and community in the Nazi *Weltanschauung* or "world-view" (Giaccaria and Minca 2016). Kühne asks why the German nation failed to collapse until its final military defeat, despite heterogeneous attitudes toward the Nazi regime and the trauma of war, and in doing so he identifies the role of violence in forging a sense of "intensified togetherness" (2010, 2). For Kühne, German collective identity and sociality in the Third Reich emerged not in spite of but because of the practice of genocide, and with it the "revolutionary ethos" of having abandoned conventional moral systems and entered into a homogenous community bound together by crime (5). Through mutual identification with a pariah nation ordinary Germans found a sense of belonging that the German Right had claimed was destroyed by Western liberalism and modernity (Herf 2003). Core to this sense of belonging was the "sophisticated ideology of antiuniversalistic, dichotomist ethics" (Kühne 2010, 59) developed by the Nazis:

> The perfect SS man was not the one who sacrificed his physical well-being, but the one who abandoned the moral world which asked for pity for others, for mercy, and forgiveness, and which made those who fail feel guilty. The ideal SS man did not need to feel guilty for having acted mercilessly. According to the new Nazi ethics, mercilessness to the putative enemies served Aryan survival; thus, performing mercilessly was "good." (Kühne 2010, 62)

The negation of the other was therefore integral to the Nazi political project of establishing a *Volksgemeinschaft* or "People's community" (Bartov 1998). Negation, not in the previous sense of distancing and neutralizing the troubling presence of the victims, but an explicit, acknowledged, witnessed degradation and destruction of the other, a proximate negation that would dramatize the separation of "Aryan" society from the rest of humanity in an "outburst of affect" (Stone 1999, 371). The mobile killing operations were an ideal stage for enacting this dramatization.

The dramatization of community through violent negation would often take on literal theatrical arrangement. Kühne documents how "terror in the East often served as entertainment" (2010, 77), with symbolic attacks on Jewish identity and culture threaded into escalating violence:

> Without any order or plan to kill or even round up the Jews, police officers combed the Jewish sections of [Bialystok] and plundered houses and shops. Jews who looked anything like anti-Semitic stereotypes were favored targets of humiliation. The policemen set their beards on fire, made them dance, or just shot them down. Soon, the police units had worked themselves into an orgy of blood. In the afternoon they drove more and more Jews—men, women, and children—into the main synagogue, shut the doors, and shot whoever tried to escape. Some petrol canisters were fetched and poured inside. It took only a few shells before the building went up in flames. Some seven hundred people suffered an agonizing death. (Kühne 2010, 79)

The theatrical staging of violence was completed by perpetrator audiences taking photographs and "celebrat[ing] their splendid community" (Kühne 2010, 77). The quotation above is illustrative in that the violence was spontaneous and lacking in any pretense of instrumental functionality: the destruction of Jewish cultural and physical life was simply something to be enjoyed, and in the euphoric company of others. To paraphrase Kühne, the negation of the victims' sociality enhanced the bonds of the perpetrator community (2010, 78).

To disappear as an *I* capable of making moral decisions was the ultimate aim of the ss killer (Kühne 2010, 62). However, unlike those troubled perpetrators who sought comfort in the moral absolution of becoming a *you*, a voided subject who merely receives instructions and negates responsibility and proximity, these events of celebratory, communal killing attest to a proximate violence that afforded individuals the opportunity to reinvent themselves as a *we*: the abolition of the self as a line of flight toward an absolute identification with the moral code of the group.

This distinction is again reflected in how such events of violence were witnessed by the killers themselves. Kühne gives the example of the city of Nowy Sącz, where twenty to thirty police officers killed thousands of Jews between 1941 and 1944. Among the many events of violence during this period, on April 28, 1942, a police unit engaged in a particularly chaotic and bloody massacre of three hundred Jews. In contrast to those perpetrators seeking to suspend the circuit of witnessing by refusing to recount the past before an audience, after the massacre the officers enjoyed an evening of celebration, drinking, and competitive boasting about the day's events: "such sudsy gatherings were always about boasting" (2010, 73). Having embraced the Nazi ethics of violence and criminality, the killers' joyous completion of their testimony and subsequently heightened sense of togetherness provided the stage for further violence; in the case of April 28, the evening continued with a spontaneous, drunken rampage through the Jewish ghetto, murdering at least fifty Jews in their homes (Kühne 2010, 74; see also Westermann 2016).

The cyclical dynamic of violence and witnessing was not confined to Nowy Sącz. In towns and cities across Nazi-occupied Europe, victims served as props for the perpetrators' construction of a community of violence, allowing individuals to overcome and reinvent themselves as an embodiment of Nazi ethics (Kühne 2010). Violence here was not something that required the negation of witnessing; the killers' proximate witnessing of humiliation and slaughter was precisely the means by which they negated the sociality of the victims and strengthened the grounds for their "revolutionary" political community (Herf 2003).

Up to now two archetypes of the Nazi killer, encapsulating two different relationships between witnessing and negation, have been examined: reluctant killers who sought to negate their actions by suspending their witnessing, losing the responsibility of the *I* in the *you* of voided sovereignty and subjectivity, and enthusiastic killers who ecstatically witnessed the negation of their victims, using the violence to overcome the moral framework of the *I* and reinvent themselves as part of a pariah *we*. However, the purpose of this heuristic device is not to establish a dichotomy between the two, not only because of the continuum that existed between these extreme positions, but fundamentally because these positions, and the relationships between witnessing and negation that they embodied, existed in a symbiotic, immunitary framework that enabled the mobile killing unit to operate to such a devastating degree.

Immunity and the Negation of Negation

I must emphasize that from the first days I left no doubt among my comrades that I disapproved of these measures and never volunteered for them. Thus, on one of the first searches for Jews, one of my comrades clubbed a Jewish woman in my presence, and I hit him in the face. A report was made, and in that way my attitude became known to my superiors. I was never officially punished. But anyone who knows how the system works knows that outside official punishment there is the possibility for chicanery that more than makes up for punishment. Thus I was assigned Sunday duties and special watches. (Reserve Police Battalion 101 member, quoted in Browning 2001, 129)

There is no record of any member of German groups tasked with conducting mass killing having suffered serious official punishment as a result of refusing to participate (Kühne 2010). Instead, indirect forms of punishment notwithstanding, such individuals "gained a certain immunity" (Browning 2001, 129) due to their reputation and were excluded from involvement; in Esposito's terms, they became immune in the sense of being "disencumbered, exonerated, exempted" (2015, 5). The meaning of "immunity" can be extended to further examine the complex dynamics of negativity present in the mobile killing units. Returning to Beorn and Knowles's analysis of the spatial division of labor among the *Einsatzgruppen*, the perpetrators believed that physical distance from the scene of killing equated with innocence and thus immunity from criminal prosecution, something that was therefore frequently exaggerated in postwar testimony (2014, 114). The presence of more physically proximate killers thus enabled those who kept a physical distance to negate their own role in supporting the system of killing by comparison to the more obvious violence of others within their community:

> Psychologically, the burden on the killers was much reduced. The Hiwis [foreign volunteers] . . . did most of the shooting. According to Sergeant Bentheim, his men were "overjoyed" that they were not required to shoot this time. Those spared such direct participation seem to have had little if any sense of participation in the killing. After Józefów, the roundup and guarding of Jews to be killed by someone else seemed relatively innocuous. (Browning 2001, 85)

Reluctant killers thus maintained an ambiguous relationship with their colleagues—while they may have genuinely disapproved of the killing operations, precisely that condemnation placed their own genocidal actions in a more innocuous light. It was therefore in the interests of their immunity, now articulated according to the legal sense of the word (Esposito 2015), that these perpetrators hovered on the border of the community, maintaining a connection through the negation of (a certain type of) negation.

A certain immunitary relationship was present too for those perpetrators fully engaged in the killing. From the perspective of those for whom the violent negation of their victims provided an opportunity for camaraderie amid the construction of a pariah nation, the perpetual presence of comrades who were unable or unwilling to carry out that violence provided a necessary reminder of precisely its transgressive and, according to Nazi ethics, revolutionary nature. As Kühne writes, "uniting people by collective crime works best if people are aware of their crime, thus of their separation from the rest of the world" (2010, 93), and the presence of those perpetrators who sought to negate their role in the killing provided this awareness. They were, as Kühne observes, a "built-in out group" providing self-definition to the emerging community, often explicitly framing their inability to participate as deriving not from moral judgment of the community but from their own "weakness," thus legitimating the group's ethics of "toughness" (2010, 87). The immunitary framework of negativity now takes on a biomedical meaning: if the Nazis sought to establish a radical distinction between the inside and outside of the *Volksgemeinschaft* forged in violence and criminal complicity, those members of the community who negated the bonding mechanism of proximate violence constituted an alien entity that violated these borders, albeit to a minute degree and in a controlled manner that ultimately served to strengthen the distinction between inside and outside. This, for Esposito, is the definition of actively induced immunity:

> The dialectical figure that thus emerges is that of exclusionary inclusion or exclusion by inclusion. The body defeats a poison not by expelling it outside the organism, but by making it somehow part of the body. . . . The immunitary logic is based more on a non-negation, on the negation of a negation, than on an affirmation. The negative not only survives its cure, it constitutes the condition of effectiveness. (2015, 9)

The negativity of perpetrators unable to reinvent themselves as a model of Nazi ethics was thus retained within the body of the community as a weakness to be perpetually witnessed, negated, and overcome by a group ethos of toughness and violence that was strengthened and confirmed in the process.

The opposite faces of negativity examined in this chapter, the perpetrators' negation of their own role in the violence and the perpetrators' negation of their victims through an absolute investment in violence and the ensuing mythology of community, come to overlap entirely if we return to the attempts made by the mobile killing units to manage and suppress witnessing of their crimes. In one instance, efforts to use euphemistic language, prevent the distribution of photographs, and secure the border around murder sites were intended to obstruct the witnessing of outsiders and, perhaps, to obscure and relieve the guilty consciences of the killers themselves. Yet the very necessity of such measures served to "construct . . . a cult of secrecy that radiated monstrous moral transgression" (Kühne 2010, 90). The greater the negation of the violence and complicity that bonded the "revolutionary" community of killers, the greater its inflation and affirmation. This is why, Kühne suggests, such prohibitions were barely enforced: the gesture of negation was sufficient to construct the "aura of secrecy" (2010, 90) and infamy redolent of a group that viewed itself as having irreversibly abandoned modern civilization and left any attendant moral values far behind.

Conclusion

A problem with using perpetrator testimony in the analysis of genocide is the motivation of such witnesses to retrospectively negate the extent of their involvement (Boswell 2011; Browning 2003). Rather than contest these negations, my approach in this chapter has been to take them at face value by conceptualizing negativity as itself a fundamental component of *being involved* in a genocidal project. This means trying to understand negativity not as an alibi that might lessen an individual's responsibility for violence, but rather as a means of articulating that responsibility within an overarching system of political violence. Through this analysis negativity appears both in reflexive strategies and in visceral bodily relations, and in each case it was crucial for the continuation of violence.

Negativity appears most directly as a conscious strategy in the conduct of perpetrators who sought to negate their role in the killing by negating themselves, in various ways, as witnesses. In the postwar trials these negations were indeed successful: of the 210 members of Reserve Battalion, 14 were indicted and only a handful of unit leaders received prison sentences, and even this was a "rare success" among Order Police investigations in resulting in any prosecutions at all (Browning 2001, 146). Despite the efforts of postwar prosecutors to put entire murder complexes on trial (Wittmann 2003), these initiatives were hamstrung by the requirements of German law to demonstrate personal initiative and a clear connection between motivation and action, causing a bias in prosecutions toward those guilty of distinctively base crimes or those in leadership positions responsible for planning mass murder (Pendas 2000). What was absent but necessary at the time was an understanding of seemingly negative action, when incorporated into a wider system, as having the capacity to not only support but propel and radicalize genocidal violence. The history of the mobile killing units offers an explicit demonstration of how negation can play a constitutive role in mass killing, and this is one reason why it needs to be recognized as "more than a prelude to the later industrialized killings that occurred in the death camps" (Beorn and Knowles 2014, 90).

The significance of these strategic negations should not, however, obscure the centrality of embodied and affective negations to the deadliness of the mobile killing units. Such "evasive" actions as missing an execution shot at point-blank range or fleeing into nearby forests to vomit are as likely bodily responses to (the perpetrators' own role in) the traumatic scene of violence as the product of conscious deliberation. Furthermore, the prevalence of posttraumatic stress disorder among *Einsatzgruppen* (MacNair 2002) suggests that the efficacy of negation as a reflexive strategy designed to lessen personal implication in the killing was at best limited and provisional, amid the visceral horror of the unfolding violence. I have tried to show that, in addition to and sometimes in tension with calculative negations of distance and evasion, the extraordinary violence of the open-air shootings took place in an affective political context whereby the visceral negation of the victims created a powerful emotional bond of moral transgression among participants, with the bodily repulsions of more reluctant killers serving to amplify this sense of pariah communality. Alongside a conceptualization of organized killing that can incorporate the legal culpability of self-negating perpetrators, it is necessary to investigate further how "direct," embodied relations of violence create, sustain, and undercut those structural "political planets" that geographers have established as fundamental to the phenomenon of genocide.

Notes

I am grateful to Mitch, David, and Paul for the opportunity to develop the ideas in this chapter, and for their support and insightful feedback throughout. The chapter wouldn't have got far without initial encouragement from Sheila Hones, and Marcus Doel provided invaluable comments on an early draft.

1. Although there is no mention of female German participants in the mobile killing units in the historical works discussed in this chapter, this might reflect the general lack of research on female perpetrators of the Holocaust (see Dwork 2017; Lower 2013).

References

Angrick, Andrej. 2008. "The Men of Einsatzgruppe D: An Inside View of a State-Sanctioned Killing Unit in the 'Third Reich.'" In Ordinary People as Mass Murderers: Perpetrators in Comparative Perspectives, edited by Olaf Jensen and Claus-Christian W. Szejnmann, 78–96. Hampshire UK: Palgrave Macmillan.

Arad, Yitzhak. 1999. Belzec, Sobibor, Treblinka: The Operation Reinhard Death Camps. Bloomington: Indiana University Press.

Arad, Yitzhak, Israel Gutman, and Abraham Margaliot. 1999. Documents on the Holocaust: Selected Sources on the Destruction of the Jews of Germany and Austria, Poland, and the Soviet Union. 8th ed. Lincoln: University of Nebraska Press.

Barnes, Trevor, and Claudio Minca. 2013. "Nazi Spatial Theory: The Dark Geographies of Carl Schmitt and Walter Christaller." Annals of the Association of American Geographers 103 (3): 669–87.

Bartov, Omer. 1998. "Defining Enemies, Making Victims: Germans, Jews, and the Holocaust." American Historical Review 103, no. 3 (June): 771–816.

Bauman, Zygmunt. 2000. Modernity and the Holocaust. Ithaca NY: Cornell University Press.

Beorn, Waitman W., and Anne K. Knowles. 2014. "Killing on the Ground and in the Mind: The Spatialities of Genocide in the East." In *Geographies of the Holocaust*, edited by Anne K. Knowles, Tim Cole, and Alberto Giordano, 88–118. Bloomington: Indiana University Press.

Boswell, Matthew. 2011. "Downfall: The Nazi Genocide as a Natural Disaster." *Holocaust Studies* 17 (2–3): 165–84.

Browning, Christopher. 2001. *Ordinary Men: Reserve Police Battalion 101 and the Final Solution in Poland*. London: Penguin.

——. 2003. *Collected Memories: Holocaust History and Postwar Testimony*. Madison: University of Wisconsin Press.

Burds, Jeffrey. 2013. *Holocaust in Rovno: The Massacre at Sosenski Forest, November 1941*. New York: Palgrave Macmillan.

Carter-White, Richard. 2009. "Auschwitz, Ethics and Testimony: Exposure to the Disaster." *Environment and Planning D: Society and Space* 27 (4): 682–99.

——. 2012. "Primo Levi and the Genre of Testimony." *Transactions of the Institute of British Geographers* 37 (2): 287–300.

——. 2016. "The Interruption of Witnessing: Relations of Distance and Proximity in Claude Lanzmann's *Shoah*." In *Hitler's Geographies: The Spatialities of the Third Reich*, edited by Paolo Giaccaria and Claudio Minca, 313–28. Chicago: University of Chicago Press.

Chalmers, Beverley. 2011. "Sexual Villainy in the Holocaust." In *Villains: Global Perspectives on Villains and Villainy Today*, edited by Burcu Genc and Corinna Lenhardt, 231–41. Oxford: Inter-Disciplinary.

Charlesworth, Andrew. 2003. "Hello Darkness: Envoi and Caveat." *Common Knowledge* 9, no. 3 (Fall): 508–19.

Cooper, Allan D. 2009. *The Geography of Genocide*. Lanham MD: University Press of America.

Derrida, Jacques. 2000. *Demeure: Fiction and Testimony*. Stanford CA: Stanford University Press.

Doel, Marcus. 2017. *Geographies of Violence: Killing Space, Killing Time*. London: Sage.

Dwork, Debórah. 2017. "A Critical Assessment of a Landmark Study." *Holocaust Studies* 23 (3): 385–95.

Egbert, Stephen L., Nathaniel R. Pickett, Nicole Reiz, William Price, Austen Thelen, and Vincent Artman. 2016. "Territorial Cleansing: A Geopolitical Approach to Understanding Mass Violence." *Territory, Politics, Governance* 4 (3): 297–318.

Esposito, Roberto. 2015. *Immunitas: The Protection and Negation of Life*. Cambridge UK: Polity.

Friedländer, Saul. 1998. *Nazi Germany and the Jews: Volume 1; The Years of Persecution, 1933–1939*. New York: Harper Perennial.

————. 2008. *The Years of Extermination: Nazi Germany and the Jews 1939–1945*. New York: Harper Perennial.

Fritzsche, Peter. 2009. *Life and Death in the Third Reich*. Cambridge MA: Harvard University Press.

Giaccaria, Paolo, and Claudio Minca. 2016. "For a Tentative Spatial Theory of the Third Reich." In *Hitler's Geographies: The Spatialities of the Third Reich*, edited by Paolo Giaccaria and Claudio Minca, 19–44. Chicago: University of Chicago Press.

Harrison, Paul. 2007. "'How Shall I Saw It . . . ?' Relating the Nonrelational." *Environment and Planning A* 39: 590–608.

————. 2010. "Testimony and the Truth of the Other." In *Taking-Place: Non-Representational Theories and Geography*, edited by Ben Anderson and Paul Harrison, 161–80. Surrey UK: Ashgate.

Hedgepeth, Sonja M., and Rochelle G. Saidel, eds. 2010. *Sexual Violence against Jewish Women during the Holocaust*. Hanover NH: University Press of New England.

Herf, Jeffrey. 2003. *Reactionary Modernism: Technology, Culture, and Politics in Weimar and the Third Reich*. Cambridge UK: Cambridge University Press.

Hilberg, Raul. 2003. *The Destruction of the European Jews, Vol. 1–3*. New Haven CT: Yale University Press.

Klee, Ernst, Willi Dressen, and Volker Riess, eds. 1991. *"The Good Old Days": The Holocaust as Seen by Its Perpetrators and Bystanders*. Old Saybrook CT: Konecky & Konecky.

Kühne, Thomas. 2010. *Belonging and Genocide: Hitler's Community, 1918–1945*. New Haven CT: Yale University Press.

LaCapra, Dominick. 1997. "Lanzmann's *Shoah*: 'Here There Is No Why.'" *Critical Inquiry* 23, no. 2 (Winter): 231–69.

Little, Jo. 2017. "Understanding Domestic Violence in Rural Spaces: A Research Agenda." *Progress in Human Geography* 41 (4): 472–88.

Lower, Wendy. 2002. "'Anticipatory Obedience' and the Nazi Implementation of the Holocaust in the Ukraine: A Case Study of Central and Peripheral Forces in the Generalbezirk Zhytomyr, 1941–1944." *Holocaust and Genocide Studies* 16, no. 1 (Spring): 1–22.

————. 2011. "Pogroms, Mob Violence and Genocide in Western Ukraine, Summer 1941: Varied Histories, Explanations and Comparisons." *Journal of Genocide Research* 13, no. 3 (September): 217–46.

————. 2013. *Hitler's Furies: German Women in the Nazi Killing Fields*. London: Chatto & Windus.

Lunstrum, Elizabeth. 2009. "Terror, Territory, and Deterritorialization: Landscapes of Terror and the Unmaking of State Power in the Mozambican 'Civil' War." *Annals of the Association of American Geographers* 99 (5): 884–92.

Lyotard, Jean-François. 1988. *The Differend: Phrases in Dispute*. Minneapolis: University of Minnesota Press.

MacNair, Rachel. 2002. *Perpetration-Induced Traumatic Stress: The Psychological Consequences of Killing*. Westport CT: Praeger.

Pendas, Devin O. 2000. "'I Didn't Know What Auschwitz Was': The Frankfurt Auschwitz Trial and the German Press, 1963–65." *Yale Journal of Law & the Humanities* 12, no. 2 (Summer): 397–446.

Philo, Chris. 2017. "Squeezing, Bleaching, and the Victims' Fate: Wounds, Geography, Poetry, Micrology." *GeoHumanities* 3 (1): 20–40.

Rhodes, Richard. 2003. *Masters of Death: The ss Einsatzgruppen and the Invention of the Holocaust*. New York: Vintage.

Springer, Simon, and Philippe Le Billon. 2016. "Violence and Space: An Introduction to the Geographies of Violence." *Political Geography* 52:1–3.

Stone, Dan. 1999. "Modernity and Violence: Theoretical Reflections on the Einsatzgruppen." *Journal of Genocide Research* 1 (3): 367–78.

Tyner, James. 2009. *War, Violence, and Population: Making the Body Count*. New York: Guildford.

———. 2012. *Genocide and the Geographical Imagination: Life and Death in Germany, China, and Cambodia*. Lanham MD: Rowman & Littlefield.

Tyner, James, and Joshua Inwood. 2014. "Violence as Fetish: Geography, Marxism, and Dialectics." *Progress in Human Geography* 38 (6): 771–84.

Westermann, Edward B. 2016 "Stone-Cold Killers or Drunk with Murder? Alcohol and Atrocity during the Holocaust." *Holocaust and Genocide Studies* 30, no. 1 (Spring): 1–19.

Wittmann, Rebecca E. 2003. "Indicting Auschwitz? The Paradox of the Frankfurt Auschwitz Trial." *German History* 21, no. 4 (October): 505–32.

11 Tragic Democracy
The Politics of Submitting to Others

Mitch Rose

Suppose that what motivates religion is . . . a response not
to the powers and uncertainties of nature but to the powers
and uncertainties of others not wholly unlike oneself.

—Stanley Cavell

It is as if substance of the I is made of saintliness. It is
perhaps in this sense that Montesquieu rested democracy
on virtue.

—Emmanuel Levinas

Introduction

In February 2000 the philosopher Jacques Derrida delivered a series of
lectures in Cairo entitled "Egyptian References: Origin, Orientalism and
Theory of Deconstruction." Although my apartment was only a few blocks
away, the Supreme Council of Culture kept the invite list closed, so I had to
content myself with coverage in the local papers. *Al-Ahram Weekly* provided
a lucid synopsis of Derrida's main presentation and a detailed description
of questions. Amina Rashid (a literary critic at Cairo University) asked
whether deconstruction perpetuates intellectual dependency and sustains
a colonial relationship. Ahmed al-Barquwy (professor of philosophy at
Damascus University) stated that the end of philosophy had only reached
its end in Europe. The veteran Egyptian journalist Mohamed Sid-Ahmed
asked whether deconstruction is an intellectual luxury that can only be

enjoyed by the West. While *Al-Ahram* did not detail Derrida's precise responses to these questions, it made an impressive summary: "aside from further explaining his thought," it stated "[Derrida] simply proceeded to deconstruct his opponents' positions, pointing out that he is neither an agent of globalisation nor a utopian dreamer, but simply a professeur struggling to extend the scope of possible democracy" (Al-Ahram 2000)

What I remember when I read the coverage of Derrida's visit so many years ago was wondering whether this statement, this sentiment, of Derrida's was perhaps less innocent than it sounded—"simply a professeur struggling to extend the scope of possible democracy." I have no idea if these are Derrida's words. Frankly, I doubt it because there is very little about this project that Derrida would view as simple. Indeed, the resistance to deconstruction showed by the audience that night was precisely the resistance to the question of *possible* democracy. This was not a resistance to the idea of democracy—as in questions about specific institutions and forms of governance—or whether democracy is possible. Democracy thought in such terms was something that I know many in that room wished for. But I wondered whether it was a resistance to the possibilities of democracy—about the *scope* for democracy—and the extent to which that scope could be extended.

Another story I remember that connects to Derrida's talk involved the Sherpa at my local grocery store, Ahmed. I knew Ahmed because he carried my (usually one bag) of groceries home for me each week (thus are the expectations of noblesse oblige for the foreign in Egypt). During these walks Ahmed would often ask me about America, and I would try to correct or at least complicate the various impressions he had from Hollywood films. One time he was quizzing me intensely about the notion of freedom: "Does freedom mean you can do whatever you want?" he asked me. "No," I replied. "There are laws that limit what we can do. But laws in the U.S. are difficult to create." "This is the problem with America," he stated. "In America you have too much freedom. People there act like they can do anything and it will be okay." At the time, I remember being surprised by the intensity of the remark. Didn't Ahmed want more freedom and, if so, at what point would he determine that he had had enough? What did it mean to have too much freedom? The question in Ahmed's mind did not concern democracy per se. He liked the idea of democracy or at least the idea of having a choice over the mode of government in Egypt. But he clearly worried about the scope of democracy and the degree to which it could be extended, that is, the degree to which it could give rise to a world where one could do anything.

While I have written elsewhere about the January revolutions in Tahrir and the forms of hope and hesitancy they elicited in Egypt and the United States (Rose 2019), this chapter focuses on the revolution's demise. When Muhammad Morsi was elected on June 24, 2012, he promised to represent all Egyptians, not simply the Muslim Brotherhood but the liberal wing of the revolution who fought side by side with the Islamicists in Tahrir Square. Morsi only won 52 percent of the vote and that was running against Ahmed Shafiq, Mubarak's former prime minister and representative of the Egyptian generals, and by extension, the former regime (Shenker 2012). While many liberals did not trust Morsi, they trusted Shafiq even less and hoped that Morsi would see beyond his party to build an inclusive government. By autumn, however, the debate over the new constitution unwound the country's faith in Morsi. Touting the notion of his "electoral legitimacy," Morsi allowed for the insertion of an Iran-style separation of powers that would give the sheikhs of Al-Azhar the right to modify and/or veto democratic legislation. Liberal hopes for greater civil liberties were also dashed as Morsi began relying on the military to dampen dissent. When the new constitution was blocked by the Supreme Constitutional Court (predominantly staffed by Mubarak-era judges), Morsi upped the ante by declaring his powers to be above the court. The move prompted what commentators called the second revolution. Liberals and other activists returned to Tahrir to demand the resignation of the president and his power grab. In response, the Brotherhood organized counter demonstrations. The civil war that the Mubarak regime warned would be the result of democracy looked like it was coming to pass. And the consequence was one most Egyptians saw coming: on July 3 (less than three weeks after the elections), Abdelfattah al-Sisi, head of the Supreme Council of Armed Forces (SCAF), staged a coup that once again put the military in charge of the state.

The January revolution is one that can only be described as tragic. Given how much the revolution had achieved in Tahrir Square: the concord between the liberals and the Islamicists, the fall of Mubarak and his family, the challenge to military rule, all these remarkable successes measured a generosity between factions that no one in Egypt (much less the world) foresaw. And yet, the eventual acrimony fell directly into the former regime's hands, ushering in a government even more uncompromising than the one the revolution ousted. This tragedy of democracy was tragic in the Aristotelian sense, predicated on the fatal flaws and errors of judgment of the key players involved. But this tragedy was indicative of a more existential tragedy; a tragedy intrinsic to the ambition of democracy itself and its appeal to measure and extend its scope. The aim of this chapter is to think about how the tragedy of the January revolutions reveals something not simply about Egypt but about democracy itself and its intimate relationship with tragedy.

Like much of my previous work, the chapter is divided into two predominant sections. The first section tells the story of the revolution through the tragic story of a single individual, Muhammad al-Beltagy, a moderate member of the Muslim Brotherhood who sought to unify the disparate elements of Egyptian society—Muslim, Christian, conservative, liberal, secular—into a coherent political coalition during the events of Tahrir. Al-Beltagy was instrumental in the revolution, and his personal rise and fall tracks the course of the revolution more broadly. The discussion is sourced primarily from the *New York Times*, the *Guardian*, the *Washington Post*, and other broadsheet newspapers. It also relies on *New York Times* correspondent Robert Worth's text *Rage for Order*, a brilliant and well-evidenced analysis of the revolutions in Egypt, Tunisia, Syria, Libya, and Yemen (2016). The second section draws upon the American skeptic Stanley Cavell (1999) and the political theorist Chantal Mouffe (2000, 2013) to argue that it is the utter unknowability of others, the inability to understand another's interest, desires, and needs (not to mention our incapacity to meet them), that makes democracy necessarily tragic. For Cavell (1999), other people resist, fundamentally and utterly, our ability to bring them into the light of comprehension. For Mouffe (2000) the political implications of this are *not* that we should fight against it, but rather that we should acknowledge and accept it as a limit. The tragedy of democracy is the tragedy of having to submit to (and be responsible for) other people's otherness. The question of politics, therefore, is not a question about whether democracy is tragic but how to accept democracy's tragedy: How do we come to terms with our submission to the otherness of others? How do we reckon with submitting to those who will misunderstand us, mis-know us, and inevitably fail us? To be democratic means to acknowledge this fate and the forms of hope and tragedy that lie within it.

In making this argument, this chapter builds upon several interventions I have made about democracy and the role of government (Rose 2014, 2019). In contrast to work by Iveson (2007), Mitchell (2003), Staeheli (2010), and Purcell (2013), I do not see institutional democracy as an impediment to freedom. On the contrary, I have argued that institutional democracy is a spatial-temporal solution to a philosophical problem, that is, the problem of living with other people: people that are not simply not like you but who are utterly mysterious; with needs you cannot satisfy and demands you cannot fulfill. In the past I framed this problem as the problem of the bad neighbor: the neighbor that is not simply confounding but offensive, advocating beliefs you cannot acknowledge and practices you cannot countenance (Rose 2019). In this chapter, the emphasis is on the tragedy inherent to democracy itself; the tragedy intrinsic to submitting one's own otherness to others and asking others to submit to yours. Unlike Purcell (2013), I do not see this tragedy as something that must be surmounted in order to discover our *own* power or our *own* freedom. On the contrary, I understand democracy as something that must be submitted to. Democracy, as I will argue here, is submission. This is its tragic and necessary truth.

Part 1: The Tragedy of Other Politics

Before the demonstrations began in Tahrir, Dr. Muhammad al-Beltagy was already a well-known political figure. He was an MP for Shubra al-Khema (one of Cairo's poorest neighborhoods), and he ran a free medical clinic in his district. He was also known for being part of a new generation of Muslim Brotherhood leaders who were attracted to its well-organized outreach programs and grassroots organization but not its unyielding ideology. Unlike many in the Brotherhood, he was well acquainted with other oppositional movements and had a long history of working with socialists, liberals, and Christians on various issues. Born and educated in Alexandria, he joined al-Azhar School of Medicine in 1982 on a full scholarship and was active in various student causes. Following graduation, he was denied a faculty position due to his political activities, which eventually led him to run for parliament.

When mass demonstrations began in Tahrir in January 2011, the Brotherhood were initially reluctant to be involved. Suffering from intensified harassment over the last five years, the leadership's response was tepid and cautious (Trager 2016). Al-Beltagy was a key voice in turning the Brotherhood's views around. Working closely with his allies in the People's Popular Parliament (a multiparty opposition committee that emerged during the demonstrations), al-Beltagy rejected the Brotherhood's message that members should recuse themselves and defiantly worked to build a united revolutionary council between Islamic and liberal camps. When the regime fell on February 11, al-Beltagy's reputation rose as one of the few leaders capable of forging a united alliance between Egypt's factions. While he had the street credibility of the Brotherhood, he was not saddled with their reputation for myopia. When he was interviewed on Egyptian state television about what he stood for, he spoke of "a social and political compromise: a government with mildly Islamicist social policies and a free-market economy" (Worth 2016, 128). While this was an idea that was appealing to many Egyptians, it was not clear who could lead the country to such a vision. The signs, however, were hopeful. The Muslim Brotherhood agreed not to run in the presidential elections—a maneuver that put the secularists, military, and international community at ease—and the scaf had appointed a Council of Fifty, representing the array of Egypt's opposition parties, to negotiate a new interim constitution.

And yet, it was not long before cracks began to appear. While both the military and the Brotherhood were keen for elections to take place as soon as possible, liberal and secular groups worried that the lack of time gave an advantage to the Brotherhood, who already had an organizational advantage. Even if the Brotherhood were not fielding their own candidate, they would no doubt use their muscle to support candidates that represented their vision (Bassiouni 2017). The Brotherhood were also sounding arrogant, predicting a turning tide in the region toward Islamic rule (Trager 2016). It would not take much to reopen the distrust between liberals and Islamicists that was papered over in Tahrir. Both groups suspected the other of secret deals with the military and/or remnants of the Mubarak regime. A couple months before the presidential elections, these suspicions were given credence when a leaked recording implicated Khaled Meshal, the leader of Hamas, and Khairat Shater, the Brotherhood's chief strategist, discussing the latter's relationship with Egyptian intelligence services (Worth 2016). At the center of their conversation was al-Beltagy and his outspoken pressure to create constitutional reform before the elections. The Brotherhood, it seemed, sought to secure political power first and reform second. Liberals of course feared that the former would not lead to the latter. When the Brotherhood changed its mind and decided to field its own candidate, these suspicions intensified. Al-Beltagy, and many of the organization's rank and file, protested the decision. They knew it would sow the seeds of distrust and destroy the Tahrir coalition.

The first round of presidential elections whittled twelve candidates, representing a broad range of political positions, down to two: Mohammad Morsi, a midranking but obedient member of the Brotherhood, and Ahmed Shafiq, former prime minister and candle-holder for the old regime. This left Egyptians with a stark choice. Al-Beltagy was unhappy, but it was unclear if his displeasure was with Morsi per se or with his fear that the election would be rigged in Shafiq's favor. The response of the Brotherhood leadership to this concern was to reach out to remnants of the old regime, hoping to win their support. Al-Beltagy, however, reached out to liberals and old political allies requesting that they support the Brotherhood's candidate in exchange for Morsi's agreement to govern from the center. It was an astute maneuver. If al-Beltagy could bolster Morsi's centrist support, it could potentially give him more room to alienate Islamicist hard-liners (like the Salafists), deepening Morsi's coalition and lessening his reliance on the fringe. Al-Beltagy was relatively successful in this bid, getting big-name figures from the revolution (the Google worker Wael Ghoneim and journalist/novelist Alaa Aswany) to attend a press conference pledging their support to Morsi if he agreed to usher in reform.

The unity, however, did not hold. Morsi and the Brotherhood were over-confident about their position. While they won the election, their majority was slim and their opponent was one of the most disliked characters of the old regime (Emam 2011). They also lacked an understanding of the vul-nerability of their position and the need to build a broad coalition. Morsi had none of al-Beltagy's skills for bridge-building and putting oppositional factions at ease. Winning the election for the Brotherhood meant power, and they looked to the traditional levers of state to secure it. The reforms that al-Beltagy (and many in Egypt) were looking for were becoming increasingly remote. Morsi was not attempting to build a consensus, but an institutional power base centered on the military and security services. As Worth (2016) suggests, what the Brotherhood "didn't understand was that the generals . . . didn't want his cooperation; they wanted his head" (144); and Morsi's cracking of consensus was providing the perfect opportunity.

The constitutional crisis was the event that finally destroyed Morsi and the Brotherhood's credibility. It not only worried liberals but most ordi-nary Egyptians who hoped the elections would lead to an extension of civil rights, not further curtailment. The consequence of Morsi's ham-fistedness was not simply political but existential. Egyptians handed Morsi and the Brotherhood the opportunity to speak for them. And Morsi and the Brotherhood did not see this as a position of responsibility. Once the liberals came to understand that the Brotherhood would not represent their interests, they went back to Tahrir, but this time with a different agenda. In the initial demonstrations, protestors went with something they could all agree on—to topple a corrupt regime. Now the demonstrators went to disrupt consensus, to articulate their difference from those that ruled. In this sense, the demonstrations were not simply about naming themselves as x. It was also about naming the Brotherhood as y. And in the gulf being forced open between x and y, it became very difficult for most Egyptians to know where they stood. Many people, like al-Beltagy, were Muslim *and* liberal, Muslim *and* secular, religious *and* socialist, for justice *and* for Islam. Yet such positions were becoming increasingly untenable among the emerging political narratives. Even al-Beltagy was confounded on how to find middle ground. Riots began breaking out around Brotherhood offices, some of which were perpetrated by liberal groups but others (most likely) aided by the military. On state television, al-Beltagy softly criticized Morsi's style but was harsher on the liberals for exacerbating division. Didn't they see that protesting the Brotherhood played right into the hands of the old regime? When one of al-Beltagy's long-time associates and friends from the socialist party, Khaled Abdulhamid, asked him to stop Brotherhood members from confronting antigovernment protestors at the presidential palace, he balked:

Khaled: if the Brotherhood come there will be blood. It would be blood between the people, between one social group and another, not just police brutality. This is the beginning of the end.

Beltagy: we're the biggest political party in the country and you've already taken over Tahrir. We cannot even go there now. Where should we demonstrate? In a bathroom? (Worth 2016, 146)

Khaled's words were prescient. The divisions were no longer between the people and the government but between people and people, one social group and another. A month after the presidential palace riot Khaled had his first child, and al-Beltagy called to offer his blessings. Khaled did not answer, and the two never spoke again (146).

In the coming months a consolidated movement against the Brotherhood had taken shape, and while al-Beltagy had made numerous overtures to various centrist leaders, his efforts were too little too late (Trager 2016). The "second revolution" demonstrations in Tahrir were in full swing and the turnout was as big, if not bigger, than they had been the previous January. The Islamicists, meanwhile, had set up their own demonstrations at Rabaa al-Adawiya square. The military responded by issuing a statement that if the demands of the people were not met by the government, they would intervene. The liberals cheered this announcement, believing the military was on their side. When the coup happened on July 3, thousands of Brotherhood followers flocked to Rabaa to support the government. A sit-in camp was created, barricades were set up, and the army surrounded the square calling for the arrest of al-Beltagy and other Brotherhood leaders. Many of al-Beltagy's old friends visited him and encouraged him to take up the mantle of compromise, but he became defiant. Compromise at this point was deference to the old regime. He did not understand it as compromising with those frightened of the new government.

The military invasion of Rabaa commenced on August 14, 2013. The sit-in had gone on for six weeks and positions had hardened. The Brotherhood no longer spoke of a united Egypt but of the "true way" of Islam and the hypocrisy of democracy. While it is unclear how many people were killed on that day (estimates range from 623 to 2,600), it was without question a massacre. Among the dead was Asmaa al-Beltagy, Muhammed's seventeen-year-old daughter and close confidant (Sherlock and Samaan 2013). She was assassinated by a sniper while working in a makeshift clinic. While one would think such events would revitalize protest against the military, many liberal and secular Egyptians welcomed the invasion, justifying its necessity and downplaying the numbers dead. In the subsequent months, al-Beltagy, along with the rest of the Brotherhood leadership, were arrested and jailed, and soon after the military began shutting down human rights NGOs, outlawing oppositional parties, and arresting prodemocracy activists and journalists (Fisher 2015).

The funeral for Asmaa al-Beltagy was attended by thousands of Egyptians and sparked protests against the coup worldwide. Tayyip Erdoğan, the prime minister of Turkey, wept on state television as he read aloud a letter Muhammad al-Beltagy wrote to his dead daughter from jail. Printed versions of the letter hung along with pictures of Asmaa in homes and windows across the Muslim world (Daloglu 2013). In Worth's interviews with al-Beltagy before the massacre at Rabaa, he discusses his daughter as his confidante: the one to whom he confesses his doubts and fears and the one who always pushed him toward compromise and solutions. Like many involved in the protests at Rabaa, Asmaa hoped a compromise could be reached. She was not there to protest liberals or secularists or socialists but to defend a legitimately elected government; a government she, like her father, had doubts about, but that nonetheless deserved the right to rule. After her death, her father paints her as a martyr: "You have lived with your head held high, rebellious against tyranny and shackles and loving freedom. You have lived as a silent seeker of new horizons to rebuild this nation to assume its place among civilizations . . . when they told me you were murdered on Wednesday afternoon . . . I knew God had accepted your soul as a martyr. You strengthened my belief that we are on the truth and our enemy is on falsehood" (al-Beltagy 2014). Before Asmaa's death she was a smart teenage girl working in a clinic, supporting her father, hoping the conflict would end. She was not just a kid, not just a rebel, not just a daughter but something in between. Now her person was something else. Her image and her father's letter spoke to something bigger but also narrower; no longer a force of compromise but the bearer of a message. Asmaa's voice spoken by others; a voice for justice, for the revolution, for freedom, for Islam; a voice, perhaps, for all of Egypt—but no longer for herself.

Part 2: The Tragedy of Other People

The distance between Rabaa al-Adawiya and Tahrir square is twelve kilometers—a fifteen-minute taxi ride in normal traffic. But between those spaces lay the whole of Egypt, a mass of infinite differences, needs, and desires whose ambitions were tragically reduced to political polarities that destroyed the seeds of democracy. The aim of part 2 of this chapter is to think through the implications of this tragedy more carefully by exploring the touchpoints between Stanley Cavell's and Chantal Mouffe's thoughts on democracy and difference. Specifically, it develops Cavell's ideas, if not into a full-fledged theory of democracy, then at least into a line of argument that has bearing and resonance on current forms of democratic theory. Part 2 is divided into three sections and a conclusion. The first section examines the work of Stanley Cavell, focusing specifically on his conception of alterity and its relation to tragedy; the second section explores the work of Chantal Mouffe and draws some correspondences between her thoughts on democracy and Cavell's thoughts on alterity; and the third section illustrates how Cavell enhances Mouffe's conception of democracy by attending to its necessary tragedy. Part 2 concludes by arguing that acknowledgment of the other in politics means acknowledging the tragedy of politics. It means recognizing that our relations with others in politics is always a relation with something unknowable, unpredictable, and ultimately unaccommodatable. And yet it is something to which we must (at some level) submit. Understanding submission to alterity as the condition of democracy helps us see how democracy is necessarily tragic and that attempts to expand the scope of democracy are inherently fraught.

TO KNOW AND ACKNOWLEDGE

Cavell is an American philosopher working primarily in the analytic tradition. While he has written prolifically on literature, drama, aesthetics, and film, I am focusing on his most well-known work, *The Claim of Reason* (1999): a text that attempts to redefine the terms of skepticism as a problem in philosophy. The central issue of the text is what he calls "the problem of other minds": how do we know that the appearance of other people is indicative of the existence of other minds—that is, of inner lives that are more or less like our own? Much of the text engages with the question of pain and suffering discussed by Wittgenstein. How do we know that the appearance of pain and suffering in another person is indicative or expressive of a true internal state or experience (a state or experience of being in pain)? Through an exhaustive exploration of the various kinds of objective criteria that could be established to judge how the outward appearances of pain (the body screaming, wincing, sweating, etc.) are indicative of internal states, Cavell concludes that all such criteria must fail. They fail not because they are poorly thought out or ill-conceived, but because as criteria they cannot—in and of themselves—establish the existence of whatever they are criteria of. In other words, criteria are devised to overcome a division between an internal and external world. But in doing so they preestablish the former as something *knowable*. Thus, rather than simply being a means to know, criteria situate the minds of others as things that *can be known*. Regardless of how refined one's criteria for distinguishing a man's scream for joy versus his scream from pain, you still cannot know:

> How are you so sure that that isn't simply the way he clears his throat, or calls his hamsters, or sings Schubert? What justifies your sharp distinction between knowing what the criteria of something are and knowing whether their object exists? The sharp distinction is between his outer behaviour and his inner experience, and no mere description of his behaviour as being "in or from or with pain" will alter that. (1999, 165–66)

For Cavell, there are no criteria that can traverse that which separates the one from the other—no line of logic or objective thought that can bring the philosopher to a place where she can know (conclusively) what this scream represents, expresses, or says about another being.

For Cavell this problem shines a light upon the problem with skepticism more broadly. As Cavell sees it, philosophy presents the problem of skepticism as one that needs to be *solved*. Thus, the search for criteria is the search for a means to ground our hope, desire, or faith that other people are knowable and thus open to investigation and understanding. In response, Cavell approaches skepticism not as something to be solved but something to be lived with: "I do not . . . confine the term [scepticism] to philosophers who wind up denying that we can ever know; I apply it to any view which takes the existence of the world to be a problem of knowledge" (104). Skepticism does not mean attempting to surmount the limits of what we can know but living with them: "my ignorance of the existence of others is not the fate of my natural condition as a human knower, but my way of inhabiting that condition" (432). It means "taking the very raising of the question of knowledge in a certain form, or spirit, to constitute scepticism"

(432). In many ways Cavell's entire philosophical project can be thought of as a contemplation of what it means to live with skepticism, that is, with the condition of not knowing. In this sense, I want to look more closely at two specific implications.

The first implication concerns Cavell's conception of other people. As Critchley (2005) identifies, there is a strong correspondence between the position of Cavell and that of Levinas (1969) in their conceptualization of the otherness of others. In short, both authors conceptualize the other person as a being who infinitely withdraws from knowledge. There is "something about the other person" Critchley states, "a dimension of separateness, interiority, secrecy or what Levinas calls 'alterity' that escapes my comprehension" (2005, 26). For both Cavell and Levinas, it is precisely this dimension of separateness—this aspect of the other that remains (that must remain) mysterious—which ensures that the other remains an other, that is, that prevents the other from collapsing into sameness. For once the other becomes penetrable to my knowledge, they cease to be a wholly unique being. For alterity to exist in the world it must retain a difference that resides outside my knowing, impenetrable to me, protected from what I can bring into comprehension and thus sublimation. For Cavell this dimension not only guarantees the separateness of the other but also the distinctive character of the self: it ensures "that I am not exhausted by all the definitions or descriptions the world gives of me to me" (1999, 390).

The second implication is it allows Cavell to make an interesting distinction between knowing and what he terms *acknowledgment*. While the former is a form of violence, a way of erasing or eradicating the other's distinctiveness, of subsuming the other into our own modalities of understanding and sense-making, the latter is a means of living with not-knowing. Acknowledgment, in short, is a recognition of the other's difference. It is a recognition of the unbridgeable divide that separates the "I" from the "you." It is an attempt to acknowledge the other's distinctive humanity without attempting to name or describe it (Sparti 2000). To be clear, Cavell does not see acknowledgment as an abridged form of knowing or a compromised knowing. On the contrary, acknowledgment is analogous to skepticism more broadly in that it situates *a limit as a condition*. In other words, acknowledgment is a spirit of living with limits; a position that does not attempt to transcend limitation but uses it to undermine the violence of knowing.

Such a position helps us see how tragedy inheres in all relations. Because there is no criteria for understanding others, for bringing other people into our orbit of comprehension, everything we say runs a risk (Macarthur 2014). There is a fundamental blindness and deafness to the interiority of others, an impenetrable silence that compels us to fill the void with the echoes of our own thoughts (our own projected ideas, hopes, and ambitions), and claim they originate from the other. Cavell's famous example is Othello's incapacity to recognize what he did not know of Desdemona. Caught between his own jealousy and Iago's insidious intrigue, Othello hears and sees in Desdemona a character of his own making—a character that by the end of the play he claims he knows. Without the capacity to measure Desdemona's actions and words against some external criteria, Othello must fall upon his own projections to measure her love. Instead of acknowledging her distance, he closes the gap with his forms of knowing, losing both her and himself in the process. "It is the failure to acknowledge the other's separateness from me that can be the source of tragedy," Critchley states. "What does the moral of this tragedy consist? One might say that it simply consists in the fact that we cannot ultimately know everything about the other person, even and perhaps especially when it comes to the people we love. . . . we have to learn to acknowledge what we cannot know and that the failure to do this was Othello's tragic flaw" (2005, 26).

The point here is not—to be clear—that our relations with others are fated toward division, violence, and death. This would be a woefully paltry and cynical view of social life (not to mention love). But it is to suggest that tragedy inheres as a condition of our relations with others. As Cavell notes, distance does not beget silence. On the contrary, the inclination to recognize and name ourself as an "I" is founded in responding to the silence that settles (that must settle) between us: "*I (have to) respond to it*," Cavell states, "it calls upon me; it calls me out. I have to acknowledge it" (1999, 161 my emphasis; also see Ward 2011). The tragedy of our relations with others resides in the empty space between us and the demand it makes to fill it: empty voices longing for each other in a horizonless sea. This is not to say that love and fulfillment cannot happen. Only that those felt connections and correspondences cannot be predicated on a relation of knowing. Indeed, this is why Cavell falls back so often on literature, film, and drama (rather than philosophy) to illustrate his ideas; a tradition that is far more capable of exploring relations (and their possibility) in conditions of not knowing. In sum, tragedy inheres as a condition of our relations. It is always already there, sitting between us, defining the inaccuracy, insufficiency, and failure that is the nature of our being-with others.

POLITICS AND THE POLITICAL

Thus far I have discussed Cavell's conception of skepticism and the tragic dynamic it establishes for our relations with others. The aim of this section is to illustrate how these ideas bear on political theory. This means illustrating how Cavell's ideas correspond to those of Chantal Mouffe (2000, 2013). While Mouffe never explicitly draws upon Cavell (her inspirations are more continental), there is much in her writing that resonates with Cavell's ideas, and they thus provide an effective vehicle for exploring Cavell's political potential. The areas of correspondence I focus on are twofold: First, Mouffe does not approach difference as something that can be transcended. In opposition to the long-term aim in political theory of finding a rational basis for political unity, Mouffe does not seek a consensual political ideal. On the contrary, she accepts the distance between political subjects as a condition of politics. Second, Mouffe understands the acknowledgment of difference as a significant political moment. While acknowledgment for Mouffe operates in a slightly different register than it does in Cavell, there is a similar emphasis on reconciling not with others per se but the difference of others, that is, with the irreconcilable distance between us. In many ways Mouffe's work can be characterized as an exploration of how the difference of others can be accommodated—without being mitigated— within a theory of democracy.

A good starting point for understanding Mouffe's conception of difference is an essay she wrote in the late nineties critiquing the Universalist ideal of liberal democracy. Drawing upon the work of Carl Schmitt, Mouffe agrees with his founding premise that there is a distinction to be made between democracy and liberalism. While the former is represented by a set of institutional structures and cultural expectations, the latter is represented by a Universalist conception of rights and law—notions that transcend any particular political system, democratic or otherwise. She goes on to argue that not only is there no necessary relation between liberalism and democracy, but that they are in a fundamental tension. Liberalism has a Universalist outlook; its ideological logic extends to humankind. Democracy, however, is a form of representational government and as such it represents those that elect it. While liberalism endeavors to transcend community, democracy defines it. Democracy governs via a coalition of interests established via criteria of belonging that are (by definition) exclusive. Seen in such terms, Mouffe argues that liberalism constitutes a danger for democracy. In liberalism's incapacity to conceptualize a community—a distinction between "us" and "them"—it nullifies the political content of democratic practice. Equality for all, Mouffe (2000) argues, is a "practically meaningless, indifferent [conception of] equality" (40). Indeed, without a political community (what Mouffe calls a *demos*) the rights that liberalism seeks to promote have no substance. They do not cling to any particular subject but float in abstracted idealized terms. Thus, for the ideals of liberalism to matter, they must be instantiated within a concrete political community, that is, through the articulated wants of an "us" against the wants of a "them."

To be clear, Schmitt conceptualizes the boundaries that establish this community in ethnolinguistic terms, and it is precisely his crude conception of difference that leads him to conclude that liberal democracy is impossible. Mouffe, however, seeks to elaborate a different conception of community: a conception that seeks unity in purpose rather than unity in ethnicity or race. This is a difference capable of establishing forms of political hegemony—modalities of consensus around specific political interests—to pursue goals to which the subjects themselves cannot be reduced. As Mouffe suggests, "what Schmitt fears most is the loss of common premises and consequent destruction of . . . political unity" (55). And Mouffe agrees with Schmitt as far as she thinks the loss of political unity is a danger. But her aim is to define the community in distinctly provisional terms: a temporary alignment of interests that does not transcend the context in which they were born, that is, a unity based upon political convenience. Thus, like Schmitt, Mouffe's (55) first question is "how to envisage a form of commonality strong enough to institute a 'demos,'" a political community working together to have their common interests heard. But her second question is how to make sure that demos is "compatible with certain forms of pluralism: religious, moral and cultural pluralism, as well as a pluralism of political parties" (55).

Mouffe's commitment thus involves an inevitable turning away from Schmitt in order to develop a distinctive conception of difference; a concept not dissimilar to that of Cavell. We can see this in two areas. First, like Cavell, Mouffe argues that other people defy knowability: the other is a being whose identity is undecidable and indecipherable both to others and to the self. Second, both Mouffe and Cavell put forward a conception of acknowledgment. For Cavell acknowledgment means acknowledging not only the distance between us but the failure of trying to bridge it. For Mouffe acknowledgment is less about the unbridgeable space itself and more about the antagonism it situates. Indeed, for Mouffe, the question is not about comprehension but about politics. While Cavell explores how the space between us forces us to speak (and represent each other falsely), Mouffe explores how it forces us to struggle. Tragedy and antagonism are two sides of the same coin. And they both emerge from acknowledging difference.

In sum, Mouffe presents us with a political theory that proceeds from the presumption that difference cannot be mitigated, negotiated, or surmounted. Antagonism, like tragedy, is a condition of social relations. Unlike democratic rationalists, like Habermas (1987) and Rawls (1993), who view antagonism as something to be transcended through rational debate, Mouffe takes the distance between the "I" and the "other" (and the antagonistic struggle that that distance begets) to be a founding condition for any political theory. Thus, we can hear within Mouffe's debate with democratic rationalists arguments not dissimilar to those Cavell has with skeptics. In both cases not knowing the other—of letting the other be other and acknowledging the other's infinite otherness—is taken as a basic principle rather than as something to be transcended. Living with antagonism is like living with skepticism. It is an acknowledgment of the alterity inherent to all human relations.

THE CLAIM TO COMMUNITY

The aim of part 2 of this chapter thus far has been to explain Stanley Cavell's conception of the other and illuminate the touchpoints it shares with Mouffe's theory of democracy. The final section drills down into the work of these two theorists to illustrate that while they have similar theoretical positions, they have somewhat different political orientations. While Mouffe seeks to emphasize the political potential inherent to unconditional alterity, Cavell emphasizes its tragedy. The point of this distinction is not to undermine Mouffe's sense of optimism or temper her faith in democracy, but to suggest that if we want our democratic politics to be less pathological (less dismissive of the other and the other's difference) then we need to acknowledge its inherent tragedy.

As already discussed, Mouffe understands the demos as a provisional political community constituted through relations of struggle and exclusion. It is not surprising therefore that she would understand the process of establishing a demos as a modality of political hegemony. If we understand hegemony in the Gramscian sense, that is, as a formation of power that operates through *consent*, then we can see what Mouffe is getting at. For Gramsci (1995), consent is a form of ideological mystification constituted via structural and/or discursive means. Consent, in Gramsci, is thus an erasure of difference. It is the mechanism by which society is normalized into agreement. For Mouffe, however, consent is understood as a form of *lending one's voice*. It is consenting to the fabrication of a "we" in order to be politically effective. Understanding hegemony in such terms is, for

Mouffe, a pragmatic—rather than ideological—solution to the problem of alterity. Lending one's voice is a temporary agreement to submit to a demos. It means allowing one's voice to be provisionally subjugated in the name of certain desired futures without foreclosing other hegemonic formations that may be pursued in other contexts. Hegemony, in Mouffe, is thus a mode of submission rather than subjugation. It is not a matter of losing one's soul but lending one's voice.

One can potentially find hope in such a conception of hegemony. First, it changes the way we conceive the consenting subject. While Gramsci's subjects are seduced into exploitative power relations, Mouffe's are never fully integrated into the hegemonic formations that give them a voice. Second, it changes the way we view the hegemon. Rather than examining the hegemon as a singular entity that has manufactured our consent, Mouffe presents it as a provisional political event whose capacity to cultivate submission is precarious and situational. Finally, and most significantly, it changes the way we view struggle. In approaching hegemony as a strategic construction, our opponents appear not as enemies that must be destroyed but as adversaries that must be democratically defeated. For Mouffe, such an approach makes politics less pathological since the aim is not to destroy the other, but to combat their ideas and the futures they put forward. This vision of the good politics is thus one that allows hegemonic formations to thrive and be opposed in a manner that acknowledges the difference between and within the demos. In doing so we recognize the provisional stage upon which our political battles are waged and open ourselves to the possibility of other political formations. In stark opposition to theorists such as Hardt and Negri (2006) and Ranciere (1999), Mouffe's conception of hegemony establishes a faith in democratic politics as it provides a pragmatic means of acknowledging the other. For Mouffe, democracy is the means by which the event of submission is formalized, that is, the means by which the difference of the other is both distilled into and protected from the politics of the "we": "liberal democracy is precisely the recognition of this constitutive gap between the people and its various identifications. Hence the importance of leaving this space of contestation forever open" (Mouffe 2000, 56).

And yet, Mouffe does not recognize how this situation, while certainly hopeful, is also tragic. Recall for Cavell that the origin of all relations—and thus the origin of any demos—resides in the condition of becoming knowable. Thus, submitting to the demos is not simply about submitting to a set of common interests or a notion of the common good. It is submitting to criteria—criteria by which we become an object of someone else's knowledge. It is only when we see submission in such terms that we can understand why submission to the demos is both necessary and tragic. It is necessary because without submission one would not have a political voice. As Owen (2012) suggests, having a political voice does not mean having a platform where one's own passions can be heard. On the contrary, it means assenting to the condition whereby you speak for others and others speak for you. Similarly, Cavell states, "to speak for oneself politically is to speak for the others with whom you consent to association, and it is to consent to be spoken for by them . . . who these others are, for whom you speak and by whom you are spoken for is not known a priori" (27). It is precisely the condition of not knowing "for whom you speak and by whom you are spoken for" that is tragic. While our alterity no doubt transcends the demos, in submitting to it we become known. Like Othello we come to speak for the other because the other is silent. Like Desdemona we come to be spoken for because we cannot express our own mystery. And yet we have no choice but to speak and be spoken for. To be political is to speak for and be spoken for by other people; other people we do not know and cannot be known by, but in whose language and politics we become knowable. It is only when we see submission in such terms that we can understand why democracy is necessarily tragic. Tragedy is not simply a potential in politics, it is its nature. The tragedy of submission is democracy's fate.

Conclusions

With tanks surrounding Rabaa square and the military preparing for their eventual intervention, the generals released a number of statements to the media preparing them for the eventual outcome. The statements ostensibly spoke for the Egyptian people. They spoke about the excesses of fanatical

Islam, how the government stole power from the people, and the erosion of the democratic process. The square, however, spoke a different story. Worth describes signs around Rabaa proclaiming "Actors for Morsi," "Christians for Morsi," "Liberals for Morsi," and a number of secular and socialist leaders stood with the Brotherhood at Rabaa making common cause, submitting to a government not because they agreed or liked its policies but because it was elected. In the meantime, many of al-Beltagy's allies were still visiting him, hoping to find some accommodation between Egypt's factions. Unfortunately al-Beltagy had become increasingly uncompromising. His suspicion of the military was no doubt understandable as was his disappointment with liberal parties for encouraging them to intervene, but his belief that the Egyptian people would join with the protestors at Rabaa, and that he was at the vanguard of a movement that would inspire all of Egypt to submit, was both fantastical and pathological. Al-Beltagy and the protestors at Rabaa were blind to what was coming.

But is this not the way of tragedy? In the stories of Aeschylus, Sophocles, and Shakespeare the drama often begins with the foretelling of a character's destiny, the ending that will undoubtedly happen. But what determines this fate is not the inevitability of its conclusion but the decisions and choices that lead to it. The tragedy of Oedipus is not that he kills his father and sleeps with his mother. Those events have been foretold. The tragedy of the tragedy is Oedipus's blindness; the fact that he commits those acts willfully, arrogantly believing that he has escaped a destiny he brazenly fulfills. The tragedy brewing at Rabaa was one that many people in Egypt and the world saw coming. As observers in *Al-Ahram*, the *New York Times*, the American State Department, and the Muslim Brotherhood itself looked for a way to find compromise, the main protagonists blindly carried on.

While I have argued that democracy is inherently and necessarily tragic, this is not to suggest that it is hopeless or futile—far from it. To understand this, we need to recognize that there are two tragedies at work in democracy. The first is the tragedy of other people. The tragedy of being among others who are utterly strange, not just ethnically and culturally diverse but cognitively, emotionally, and psychologically different. This is the tragedy Cavell illuminates so well and provides the conceptual fulcrum for this chapter. The second tragedy is the tragedy of democracy. A tragedy that is less existential but equally intractable. As I have argued, there is more to democracy than lending one's voice. We must also submit. The tragedy of democracy is the tragedy of this submission. It is the tragedy of being *beholden* to others whose interests we do not know, whose desires we cannot understand, and whose actions we cannot predict. To see what is hopeful about this situation, we need to turn back to the question of acknowledgment. While Cavell emphasizes the need to acknowledge the otherness of others and Mouffe emphasizes the need to acknowledge the antagonisms of this situation, I would add a third form of acknowledgment. Democracy means acknowledging the responsibility immanent to submission. It means recognizing the precarity of putting oneself in the hands of others and the frailty of asking others to put themselves in your hands. It means submitting to others you do not like (e.g., the actors, liberals, and Christians for Morsi) not because you are invested in their politics, but because you will need them to submit to you when their demos is defeated. To not acknowledge this responsibility is to be blind to the tragedy at the heart of democracy. It is to be blind to fate. And it is to invite the inevitable consequences that such blindness invites.

A few days before the massacre at Rabaa, Worth (2016) interviewed Ali Mashad, a doctor and former member of the Brotherhood whose *Democracy Now!* YouTube videos from Tahrir went viral. Like many in Egypt, Mashad could see the tragedy at Rabaa unfolding and lamented what it foretold: "My heart is with the ordinary people there who will be killed," he states. "The people went out to protest on June 30 because they lost their beliefs in democracy. The people at Rabaa have lost their belief too. Where are we going? Oligarchy? Theocracy? I am confused" (158). For Mashad the revolution in Egypt was over. Its demise was not due to the military, the massacre, the arrests, or the closures. All of these things were still to come. Rather, it was over because he could not find a direction. "I never before wanted to leave Egypt," he states, "now I am thinking I have no place here" (158). Mashad looked for somewhere to lend his voice, a community to which he could submit. He sought to extend the scope of democracy. But (tragically) he had no place.

Notes

Earlier drafts of this chapter were presented at the AAG annual meeting in Washington DC and at Edge Hill University.

References

Al-Ahram Weekly. 2000. "Derrida Perhaps." *Al-Ahram Weekly*, February 17–23, 2000, 469.

Bassiouni, M. Cherif. 2017. *Chronicles of the Egyptian Revolution and Its Aftermath: 2011–16*. Cambridge UK: Cambridge University Press.

Beltagy, Muhammad al-. 2014. "Letter from Dr Mohamed Beltagy to His Martyred Daughter." *Middle East Monitor*, February 7, 2014.

Cavell, Stanley. 1999. *The Claim of Reason: Wittgenstein, Skepticism, Morality, and Tragedy*. Oxford: Oxford University Press.

Critchley, Simon. 2005. "Cavell's 'Romanticism' and Cavell's Romanticism." In *Contending with Stanley Cavell*, edited by Stanley Cavell and Russell B. Goodman, 37–54. Oxford: Oxford University Press.

Daloglu, Tulin. 2013. "Erdogan Shows His Softer Side." *Al-Monitor*, August 23, 2013.

Emam, Amr. 2011. "Elections in Egypt by the Fall." *New York Times*, March 31, 2011, A11.

Fisher, Max. 2015. "An Activist Once Called the Last True Liberal in Egypt Was Arrested by the Military on Sunday." *Vox*, November 9, 2015.

Gramsci, Antonio. 1995. *Selections from the Prison Notebooks*. New York: International.

Habermas, Jürgen. 1987. *The Philosophical Discourse of Modernity: Studies in Contemporary German Social Thought*. Cambridge MA: MIT Press.

Hardt, Michael, and Antonio Negri. 2006. *Multitude: War and Democracy in the Age of Empire*. London: Penguin.

Iveson, Kurt. 2007. *Publics and the City*. Oxford: Blackwell.

Levinas, Emmanuel. 1969. *Totality and Infinity*. Pittsburgh PA: Duquesne University Press.

Macarthur, David. 2014. "Cavell on Skepticism and the Importance of Not-Knowing." *Conversations: The Journal of Cavellian Studies* 2 (July–August): 2–23.

Mitchell, Don. 2003. *The Right to the City: Social Justice and the Fight for Public Space*. New York: Guilford.

Mouffe, Chantal. 2000. *The Democratic Paradox*. London: Verso.

———. 2013. *Agonistics: Thinking the World Politically*. London: Verso.

Owen, David. 2012. "Democracy, Perfectionism and 'Undetermined Messianic Hope': Cavell, Derrida and the Ethos of Democracy-to-Come." In *The Legacy of Wittgenstein: Pragmatism or Deconstruction*, edited by Ludwig Nagl and Chantal Mouffe, 139–56. Frankfurt: Peter Lang.

Purcell, Mark Hamilton. 2013. *The Down-Deep Delight of Democracy*. Chichester: Wiley.

Ranciere, Jacques. 1999. *Dis-agreement: Politics and Philosophy*. Minneapolis: University of Minnesota Press.

Rawls, John. 1993. *Political Liberalism*. New York: Columbia University Press.

Rose, M. 2014. "Negative Governance: Vulnerability, Biopolitics and the Origin of Government." *Transactions of the Institute of British Geographers* 39 (2): 209–23.

——. 2019. "Hesitant Democracy: Equality, Inequality and the Time of Politics." *Political Geography* 68:101–9.

Shenker, Jake. 2012. "Egypt Elections: Shafiq V Morsi." *Guardian* (blog). June 18, 2012.

Sherlock, Ruth, and Magdy Samaan. 2013. "Egypt: Grief of Muslim Brotherhood Leader's Family at Death of Teenage Daughter." *Telegraph*, August 15, 2013.

Sparti, David. 2000. "Responsiveness as Responsibility: Cavell's Reading of Wittgenstein and King Lear as a Source for an Ethics of Interpersonal Relationships." *Philosophy and Social Criticism* 26 (5): 81–107.

Staeheli, Lynn A. 2010. "Political Geography: Democracy and the Disorderly Public." *Progress in Human Geography* 34 (1): 67–78.

Trager, Eric. 2016. *Arab Fall: How the Muslim Brotherhood Won and Lost Egypt in 891 Days*. Washington DC: Georgetown University Press.

Ward, Graham. 2011. "Philosophy as Tragedy or What Words Won't Give." *Modern Theology* 27 (3): 478–96.

Worth, Robert Forsyth. 2016. *A Rage for Order: The Middle East in Turmoil, from Tahrir Square to ISIS*. London: Picador.

Afterword

We opened this book with an articulation of how we arrived at the negative in this project. Extending a hand for orientation, we outlined how our distinctive take on the negative is defined by a preoccupation with irresolvable limits, and we explained how this differs from other iterations of the negative posed by thinkers that have sought to focus on its operative, transpositional work. The main body of the collection has necessarily been devoted to our contributors who artfully refract our opening wager in their own unique ways, drawing upon a range of theorists, concepts, methods, and empirical lures. While they share a common denominator around the politics of limits, there are multiple renderings of the negative circling around this collection. As we have witnessed, situations of rupture, exhaustion, interruption, hesitancy, and loss induce different limits construed by the circumstances of diverse figures. The negative pierces each chapter in distinctive ways, bringing specific aspects to the fore, from a hesitant impasse (Zhang) to a gap between action and responsibility (Carter-White); and from a jarring temporal interruption from outside (Dubow) to a target of weaponized governance (Joronen). Rather than stymie the conversation by snapping the negative into a singular conception, we hope that this diversity of iterations of the negative provides sufficient latitude for geographers to appreciate something useful and applicable to their own individual work.

So what might this collection offer? Conceptually each author presents a series of distinctive grammars and vocabularies that one might use to approach the question of the negative, from insufficiencies (Harrison) and interruptions (Dubow), to impasses (Zhang) and unknowabilities (Rose). Accordingly we hope that such grammars and vocabularies, which stress nonexchangeable relations of nonrelation, challenge geographers to approach the question of relations in a more circumspect way. Methodologically the chapters provide different insights into how the negative might be reckoned with, whether through reflective autobiography (Zhang) or engaging archival sources (Carter-White). Taken together we hope that these techniques, and the careful ways that they are developed here, might compel geographers to avoid erasing the negative from accounts that have tended to prioritize positive presences. Pragmatically the chapters provide different stances on the relationship between irresolvable limits and transformative action. Some offer reparative readings where limits catalyze modes of transformative action (Maddrell, Bissell), whereas for others these limits close down such possibilities (Wylie, Harrison). For others still, we witness oscillations of construction and destruction (Philo). We hope that diversity might provide geographers with a means to consider how knowing one's capacities and powers must be intimately tethered to an acknowledgment of one's incapacities and vulnerabilities.

Notwithstanding the diversity of stances and agendas showcased here, what unites each contribution is how the negative features as an ineliminable aspect of corporeal experience. For each author, it is a problem that incessantly returns, in spite of attempts to move on, to remedy, to transcend. As we argued in the introduction, the dominant figure of the negative is the circle, speaking to situations that return to the same problem, in different forms. In that spirit, our aim in bringing this collection to a close is to circle back to some of our initial concerns; not to reiterate them, but to bring them back in a manner that allows us to see them in a new light: the same problem again (and again) but hopefully this time more approachable, such that aspects can be taken forward.

First, let's return to the problem of defining the negative by what it is not. The negative is not an ontology. It does not make claims about what the world *is* or provide new objects to describe its various constituent components. On the contrary, our conception of the negative introduces a certain skepticism of ontology, of what is. The negative is what precedes ontology and thus emerges as the problem to which all ontologies respond.

The aim of this collection, therefore, is not to introduce a new theoretical framework (like new cultural geography or nonrepresentational theory) that can be imbibed and applied to various case studies. It is to illuminate a perspective that lends itself to a distinctive style of analysis even if it does not require a specific suite of concepts, terminologies, or positions (as the chapters amply demonstrate). To say that one is interested in the negative is not the same as saying one is interested in affect, neoliberalism, or even the unconscious, all of which demand certain ontological positions. To speak of the negative is to speak about that which comes before ontology and thus leaves the question of ontology at once open and simultaneously denuded of its conceptual power.

Second, let's return to the problem of politics. If we accept that ontology is limited, then we are freed from being saddled with its various political demands. Ontologies of life demand that we affirm life; ontologies of the world demand that we affirm the world. The negative, however, frees us from such affirmations. While the negative has political implications, those implications are more about subtracting than provisioning. We anticipate that some readers will see this as unhelpful. What could possibly be beneficial about taking away our political compass and the various resources it provides? In response, while engaging the negative *does* undermine faith in our (human) power, it does so by insisting on a permanent sense of responsibility. To be responsible means to not rely on ontology to direct us toward the good, the just, and the proper. On the contrary, responsibility directs us toward a certain vigilance: a necessity to return (again and again) to the question of responsibility, to the question of how to be responsible. While the purpose of ontology is to answer this question for us, by telling us what the world is like and how to properly take care of it, responsibility is a more open-ended proposition. To be responsible means to act knowing that no action will be sufficient. It means recognizing that every action burdens us with further obligation.

Finally, let's return to our current political moment. We opened the conversation with a discussion of negative times. To be crystal clear, our preoccupation with the politics of irresolvable limits does not position us against the kinds of reparative actions that are needed to address the wicked problems that blight the world, from disgraceful inequality to destabilizing climate change. Admitting how the negative is a component of our political inclinations and engagements is not the same as throwing in the towel or waving a flag of surrender. There are urgent problems that demand our attention and do require new knowledge. But unless we admit the negative—unless we reckon with how we are positioned in nonexchangeable relation to that over which we have no power—we forget how these problems both arise from and implicate ineliminable conditions of our corporeal experience that cannot be willed away. Admitting the negative therefore provides a more benevolent view on the constitution of worldly problems that geographers are committed to engaging. Flying in the face of fantasies of (and demands for) adaptation and resilience, bodies fail, they get stuck in impasses, they hesitate; they are utterly exposed to the radically unassimilable other that has total bearing over them. Rather than beating ourselves up for falling short again, we must accept how politics—both big and small, revolutionary and empathetic—is always a precarious, faltering response to this primary incapacity. Of course our knowledge of the good, the just, and the right matter. But such ontological commitments matter less than the summons to be responsible and our willing acceptance of this obligation.

Contributors

David Bissell is associate professor in the School of Geography, Earth and Atmospheric Sciences at the University of Melbourne, Australia. His research explores the social, political, and ethical consequences of mobile lives through projects on commuting, labor mobility, technological automation, and the on-demand economy. His work is informed by theories of passivity, vulnerability, and exposure.

Richard Carter-White is lecturer in human geography at Macquarie University, Australia, and previously held lectureship positions at the University of Tokyo. His research interests include geographies of disaster, trauma and testimony, theories of community and biopolitics, and camp geographies. He is currently engaged in projects investigating the spatialities of Nazi Germany and the Holocaust, and postdisaster communities and landscapes in Tōhoku, Japan.

Jessica Dubow is reader in cultural geography at the University of Sheffield, United Kingdom. She works at the intersection of cultural geography, philosophy, and critical and aesthetic theory. She has also published in various interdisciplinary journals including *Critical Inquiry*, *New German Critique*, *Art History*, *Journal of Visual Culture*, *Comparative Literature*, and *Parallax*. Her latest book is *In Exile: Geography, Philosophy and Judaic Thought* (Bloomsbury, 2020).

Paul Harrison is an assistant professor in the Department of Geography at Durham University, United Kingdom. His research interests are in cultural geography, philosophy, and cultural theory, predominantly exploring phenomenology and deconstruction. His work focuses on the themes of witnessing, passivity, and vulnerability, and has recently been concerned with critical accounts of life and the ethics of affirmation.

Mikko Joronen is a Finnish Academy research fellow at the Tampere University, Finland. His research focuses on the politics of vulnerability in the occupied Palestinian territories, space and political ontology, and geographical theory. His recent publications deal with questions of waiting, vulnerability, wounding, and everyday resistance in Palestine, and the relationships between ontology, space, and politics.

Avril Maddrell is professor of social and cultural geography at the University of Reading. She is a feminist geographer whose research focuses on inclusive spaces, landscapes, and practices of death, mourning, and remembrance, and sacred mobilities and gender. She is an editor of *Social & Cultural Geography*, former editor of *Gender, Place and Culture*, and author, coauthor, or coeditor of numerous books, including *Complex Locations* (Wiley, 2009), *Deathscapes: Spaces for Death, Dying, Mourning and Remembrance* (Ashgate, 2010), *Consolationscapes . . .* (Routledge, 2019), *Memory, Mourning, Landscape* (Rodopi, 2010), *Sacred Mobilities* (Ashgate, 2015), *Christian Pilgrimage, Landscape and Heritage* (Routledge, 2015), and *Contemporary Encounters in Gender and Religion* (Palgrave, 2017).

Chris Philo researches and teaches at the University of Glasgow, Scotland. His work concentrates on the geographies of spaces occupied by people with mental health problems, the subject of his 2004 monograph on the geographical history of "asylums" in England and Wales, subtitled *The Space Reserved for Insanity*. Recent work, with Ebba Högström, has engaged with the "spatial stories" of an old asylum in Glasgow that is now an expansive, modern, mental-health campus. He is obsessively interested in the history and theory of geographical inquiry, as well as with subfields such as rural geography, animal geography, children's geographies, and more.

Mitch Rose is senior lecturer in the Department of Geography and Earth Sciences and a reader in the graduate school at Aberystwyth University,

United Kingdom. His research interests revolve around cultural and political theory, material culture and landscape, and geohumanities. He also writes about the history, politics, and culture of Egypt and the Middle East, where he has lived and researched.

John Wylie is professor of cultural geography at the University of Exeter, United Kingdom, and one of the editors of the journal *cultural geographies* (Sage). He first became interested in questions of landscape and experience as a PhD student and has pursued this ever since, through studies of walking, haunting, and drawing, among other topics. In recent years he has written on the politics and ethics of landscape belonging and has tried to explore the intersections of landscape and creative expression through collaborations with visual artists, performers, and other creative practitioners.

Vickie Zhang is a postdoctoral scholar in the School of Geography, Earth and Atmospheric Sciences at the University of Melbourne, Australia. She explores changing working-class life through qualitative methods and post-phenomenological theories of embodiment, with a focus on contemporary China. Her research tracks life after loss for workers affected by coal mine closures in regional Australia and China.

Index

In the Cultural Geographies + Rewriting the Earth series

Topoi/Graphein: Mapping the Middle in Spatial Thought
Christian Abrahamsson
Foreword by Gunnar Olsson

Negative Geographies: Exploring the Politics of Limits
Edited by David Bissell, Mitch Rose, and Paul Harrison

Animated Lands: Studies in Territoriology
Andrea Mubi Brighenti and Mattias Kärrholm

Mapping Beyond Measure: Art, Cartography, and the Space of Global Modernity
Simon Ferdinand

Psychoanalysis and the GlObal
Edited and with an introduction by Ilan Kapoor

A Place More Void
Edited by Paul Kingsbury and Anna J. Secor

Arkography: A Grand Tour through the Taken-for-Granted
Gunnar Olsson

To order or obtain more information on these or other University of Nebraska Press titles, visit nebraskapress.unl.edu.